DATE DUE FOR RETURN

- 4 MAY 20

THE IMPORTANCE OF THE DON QUIXOTE MYTH
IN THE WORKS OF ANTONIO BUERO VALLEJO

Carmen Caro Dugo

Mellen University Press
Lewiston/Queenston/Lampeter

Library of Congress Cataloging-in-Publication Data

Caro Dugo, Carmen, 1963-
  The importance of the Don Quixote myth in the works of Antonio
Buero Vallejo / Carmen Caro Dugo.
     p.   cm.
  English and Spanish.
  Includes bibliographical references (p.   ) and index.
  ISBN 0-7734-9015-9
  1. Buero Vallejo, Antonio, 1916-   --Sources. 2. Cervantes
Saavedra, Miguel de, 1547-1616--Influence. 3. Cervantes Saavedra,
Miguel de, 1547-1616. Don Quixote. 4. Mental illness in
literature. 5. Dreams in literature. I. Title.
PQ6603.U4Z57 1995
862'.64--dc20   94-48926
                                                                      CIP

A CIP catalog record for this book is available from the British Library.

Copyright © 1995 The Edwin Mellen Press

The Edwin Mellen Press   The Edwin Mellen Press
       Box 450   Box 67
  Lewiston, New York   Queenston, Ontario
   USA 14092-0450   ·   CANADA L0S 1L0

                 The Edwin Mellen Press, Ltd.
                   Lampeter, Dyfed, Wales
                 UNITED KINGDOM SA48 7DY

            Printed in the United States of America

To my Father and Mother

Table of Contents

Preface   vii

Acknowledgements   xi

Buero Vallejo's drawings of Don Quixote and Sancho   xii

Introduction   1

Chapter I   MADNESS: *The paradoxical nature of quixotic lunacy*   15

Chapter II   DREAMS: *The inspiring power of the world created by the imagination*   61

Chapter III   ISOLATION: *The quixotic alienation of the individual*   95

Chapter IV   FAITH: *The power of attraction and transformation of quixotic confidence*   135

Chapter V   ETHICS: *The virtues of the quixotic spirit*   163

Chapter VI   FALSE QUIXOTES: *The simulated quixotism of the "activos"*   197

Conclusion   235

Appendix   *Entrevista a Antonio Buero Vallejo*   243

Bibliography   257

Index   267

Preface

For little short of fifty years the plays of Antonio Buero Vallejo have dominated the theatrical scene in Spain. They mirror a history he has lived and helped to shape. Born at Guadajara, near Madrid, in the middle of World War I, he took an early, eclectic interest in both literature and drama, but a precocious pictorial talent suggested a career in art. In 1934, accordingly, he entered the famous Escuela de Bellas Artes de San Fernando. Less than two years later, however, this first vocation was frustrated by the outbreak of the Civil War, the central and most traumatic event in his nation's life this century. Buero's father, a professional soldier, was one of its early victims, and he himself served as an officer on the Republican side. Franco's victory, the beginning of 36 years of right-wing dictatorship, saw Buero arrested - for some months under sentence of death - and imprisoned in jail after jail until his release in 1946. In the difficult years that followed, however, he wrote his first few plays, and in 1949 the first to be performed, *Historia de una escalera*, astonished both critics and public, not least by the maturity of its dramatic technique. Seven years and eight premières later, *Hoy es fiesta* confirmed his status as his country's outstanding playwright.

By now he was living, as he has ever since, in a modest apartment building in the north-east of central Madrid. Before or after the Civil War, many other left-wing intellectuals had abandoned their native land; Buero stayed and became its conscience, was said to have 'put it on trial'. His dissenting voice, to be sure, was muffled by the censors, but no-one today can doubt that he won in 1960 a debate with Alfonso Sastre in defence of *posibilismo* - expressing in public a protest as clear and uncompromising as one could get away with.

The nine plays he wrote between 1958 and Franco's death in 1975 were set in remote historical periods, under other despotic rulers, or in carefully unidentified south-European countries, but all were transparently critical of the state of contemporary Spain. One indeed, about police, was first performed in English at Chester in 1968, and could not be produced in his homeland until 1976. The following year saw the first performance of his last historical play, *La detonación* (edited and translated as *The Shot* by David Johnston in 1993); a dramatic biography of the liberal journalist Mariano José de Larra, from the perspective of the last five minutes before his suicide in 1837, it is also a convincing apologia for its author's approach to writing under Franco.

His plays since then, by contrast, have been set in the Spain of today, and deal more directly with the new democracy's problems, both political and social. Throughout his career, in fact, his plays have engaged with such problems; but despite (or in part because of) that fact, their import in universal. All also address broader human issues, existential and metaphysical. All are deeply thoughtful tragedies; but as such (their author maintains) all confront the eternal conflict of necessity and freedom, between bleak despair and inextinguishable hope. All replace resignation or complacency with a cautious faith in the future. All attempt to 'open eyes' and pose fundamental questions. To these, however, Buero offers no doctrinaire solutions, but rather a visionary belief that mankind will succeed in transcending - some day - its present limitations.

At the same time, Buero has always been a meticulous practical playwright. Though always ready to consider changes at the rehearsals he attends, he envisages with a painterly eye and unfashionably prescribes the minutest production details; he regards it as his duty as a dramatist to provide 'performance texts'. Above all, he always experiments. His incessant innovations, though they may seem to come in waves (the use of naturalistic monologues, of 'oracles', narrators and *raisonneurs*, and above all of 'immersion effects', including dreams and hallucinations) have always sought to effect a balance between emotional involvement and intellectual detachment. Even in plays in which, as he puts it, the Dionysiac element might seem to exclude the Apollonian, the latter is always present, as Mary Rice has argued in a recent volume: *Distancia e inmersión en el teatro de Buero Vallejo* (New York, 1992).

He excels, moreover, as creator of characters, most obviously in the case of his protagonists. Many clearly mirror himself and are the bearers of his inspirational message, though many bear too the burden of his own uneasy conscience. Many indeed, as Jean Cross Newman has shown in another recent book, *Conocimiento, culpa y trauma en el teatro de Antonio Buero Vallejo* (Valencia, 1992), are acute psychological studies. A large proportion are afflicted by handicaps both genuine and symbolic (that the spectator in made to suffer), but endowed by a familiar paradox with compensatory experiences and insights (that the spectator also shares). His deaf characters can 'hear'; those disabled by different kinds of blindness have also 'second sight'. Above all, at least nine of those who suffer - in plays of the 60s and 70s especially - from some species of mental disorder are in other respects illuminatingly 'sane'.

It is hardly surprising that a Spanish writer so single-mindedly committed to moral regeneration, so concerned with the role in society of the visionary individual, and so fascinated by the interplay between subjective perception and so-called objective reality has been influenced throughout his life by the quintessentially Spanish but universal myth of the mad-wise Knight of La Mancha, especially as it is widely interpreted since the Romantic period. That influence has often been recognised, above all by Buero himself, though in the interview included as an appendix to this volume he has provided much fuller detail of its impact on his life and work. To what extent it pervades his thought, his writing and especially his characterization has never till now, however, been fully studied and proven. Dr Caro has documented its appearance and assessed its importance throughout the dramatist's *oeuvre*, of which she shows both detailed and comprehensive knowledge, as well as adducing and subjecting to critical re-assessment the relevant though mostly piecemeal observations of previous scholars. She deals with its different aspects in balanced, self-contained chapters, in each of which the corpus of Buero's plays is reviewed (with justifiable exceptions) in systematically chronological order.

In short, her book achieves its purpose admirably. As her External Examiner wrote of the thesis on which it is based, it not only establishes beyond all doubt that the presence of Cervantes in the theatre of Buero Vallejo is seminal to his work, but has much to say about that theatre that is genuinely new.

Professor Victor Dixon
Trinity College,
Dublin

Acknowledgements

I would like to acknowledge the assistance of Professor Victor Dixon, Trinity College, Dublin, who encouraged me to undertake this study and guided me throughout my work. I would also like to thank my family and friends for their constant support. I am especially indebted to Antonio Buero Vallejo, for giving me personal insights into his work, and for allowing me to reproduce his own drawings of Don Quixote and Sancho in this book.

Introduction

Antonio Buero Vallejo, born in 1916, is indisputably the outstanding Spanish dramatist of our day. His life and works, and especially his twenty seven plays, whose composition, performance and publication have been fully documented, have in consequence been the object of innumerable studies, some of which have focussed on those features of his technique which are specifically theatrical. Too few, however, have attempted to address in any systematic and comprehensive way his depiction of character, and the use therein of underlying myths, although the creation of these, as we shall see, is for Buero of supreme importance. One such myth, that of Don Quixote, is therefore the subject of the present study; for while others have been detected in his work, it is in my belief by far the most significant. Its presence can be felt in one way or another, as Buero has acknowledged and I shall demonstrate, throughout most of his plays.

Buero has never been reluctant to admit the influence of some other writers on his works, or to acknowledge that he cannot escape the strong influence of Spanish and universal literary tradition. He has said that he is grateful when people point out the influence of certain writers on his work, and he readily accepts critics' various theories.[1] In his 'Discurso' on receiving the Cervantes Literary Prize, however, he acknowledged that, before all those writers, came Cervantes:

> Debo reconocer asimismo con toda humildad el alto magisterio cervantino. Cuantas veces se ha advertido cómo, detrás de tal o cual obra mía se hallaban ciertos

> escritores cuya influencia en mi teatro agradezco y yo
> mismo he señalado, me he dicho: sí. Pero detrás de todos
> estuvo previamente, para algunos de ellos y para mí,
> Cervantes.[2]

In the speech quoted above, Buero points out that it would be hard to
reduce the eternal life of the quixotic myth to mere literary formulae:
"¿Cabría reducir a fórmulas literarias -si así pudieran llamarse- las
causas de la vida inacabable del libro y el mito cervantinos?" (p.26).
With his novel Cervantes has plumbed the depths of humanity, has
touched universal, mythical aspects of man: "Pero Cervantes acertó a
tocar resortes humanos tan hondos en su gran novela, que ninguna otra
de las nuestras ha podido alcanzar, ni su boga española, ni su dilatada
difusión internacional. Resortes, pues, universales además de
hispánicos" (p.25).

Buero was quite familiar with the quixotic myth from very early in his
life. He thinks his first readings of the great novel happened when he
was approximately ten or eleven years old.[3] In spite of this familiarity,
he does not find it easy to identify the exact causes of the powerful
attraction that the novel exerts on him. On the one hand, he finds it
obvious; on the other hand, it is enigmatic.

> Me atrae enormemente el hallazgo "ético" -con sus
> limitaciones- que representa el hidalgo manchego y que
> linda con la locura, pues de otro modo sería imposible; y me
> atrae el formidable hallazgo estético de la obra, suma de
> espejos reflectantes en que realidad y fantasía se
> construyen mutuamente. (Personal letter, 27 April 1989)

This combination of reality and fantasy attracts Buero enormously.
According to him, this openness to a fantastical world, the world of
dreams, is proper to good literature of all times. "Esa apertura,
unificación de conceptos contrapuestos, es otra de las genialidades del
Quijote y es uno de los aspectos que resaltan más en la mejor literatura
de casi cualquier tiempo, incluido el nuestro" (Personal interview with
Buero Vallejo, 21 December 1989). Américo Castro said that "Don

Quijote es el mayor portador del tema de la realidad oscilante. ...
Cervantes se sirvió literalmente, una y otra vez, del hecho de ser
interpretables en forma distinta las cosas que contemplamos."[4] Buero
firmly believes in this oscillation, in the instability of reality itself:

> En la realidad, tanto las cosas que están a nuestro
> alrededor como nosotros mismos, son objetos cambiantes, o
> sujetos cambiantes en el caso humano. Y son cambiantes,
> no solamente en el tiempo, porque cambian realmente tanto
> física como psíquicamente en el tiempo, sino que son
> cambiantes en la apreciación de los demás. (Interview)

He also applies this changing viewpoint to the critical approach to the
novel itself. There have been multiple interpretations of the great
novel, and this, according to Buero, is not only legitimate, but perfectly
normal, because we, the readers, "no somos ahora, a nuestra propia
apreciación, lo que éramos hace dos minutos."[5]

The knight's incursions into the fantastical world are indeed very
productive. Buero does not disregard them or consider them useless;
they are precisely what makes the work of art possible, and what
enriches any literary creation.[6] "Ensoñación", Buero believes, is not
only productive, but indispensable. The fantastical world which
Cervantes succeeded in fusing so admirably with reality, not only should
not be rejected, but should be explored. "He intuido, creo, que, si la
verdad de los molinos debe sustituir a la ensoñación de los gigantes,
también hay que rastrear incansablemente los fantásticos brillantes que
aquéllos esconden".[7] This is what, I believe, Buero tries to do in many
of his plays. The incursions into unreality in his works are often based
on a deeper understanding of reality itself, and this, he admits, is
directly connected with Don Quixote's experience: "...desviaciones
hacia la imaginación, hacia la irrealidad, que pueden, sin embargo,
sustentarse en un sentimiento más profundo de lo que la realidad misma
puede ser, y que también en ese sentido coinciden más o menos con las
lucubraciones de don Quijote en su aventura vital" (Interview). Buero

is one of those readers who take Don Quixote seriously, without denying his madness.

Having spoken of the "hallazgo ético" and "hallazgo estético", he refers to the "hallazgo mítico" which Don Quixote provides. Again, in his speech on receiving the Cervantes Prize, Buero refers to Don Quixote as "nuestro mayor hallazgo mítico" (p.26), and to the influence that it has had on many other writers. He gives the example of H.G. Wells, whom he says he admires unconditionally. The reason why he admires him, and is not ashamed of admitting Wells' influence on his own work, is precisely that he considers him "uno de los supremos creadores de mitos de la literatura de nuestros días" (Interview).[8] Buero is interested in myths, and in myth-makers. Cervantes has much to contribute to universal literature because he supplies an essential myth. Without the quixotic myth, he says, "las letras universales padecerían grave manquedad y, por consiguiente, lo sufriría asimismo la incierta aventura de los hombres en la Tierra" ('Discurso', p.25).

Buero is interested in the individual, but also in what he has in common with mankind, what is universal in him. That is why he is fascinated by myths. As Bill Moyers has said, "what human beings have in common is revealed in myths. Myths are stories of our search through the ages for truth, for meaning, for significance. We need for life to signify, to touch the eternal, to understand the mysterious, to find out who we are." Joseph Campbell confirms that "myths are clues to the spiritual potentialities of the human life".[9] This touching the eternal is what Buero admires in *Don Quixote*, and what he tries to do himself. Buero explores the mysterious, the world of dreams, of madness, because he is also searching for truth, for meaning. "Through the dream the presence of myth in human consciousness receives its due form of inverted commas".[10] "The myth is the public dream and the dream is the private myth".[11] In the world of the imagination, man finds the true meaning of his existence, of his reality.

Buero's version of *Don Quixote* is called simply *Mito*, suggesting the universality of the quixotic myth, which can throw light on man's interpretation of reality at all times.[12] In this play we see the confrontation between the dreamer and his society, which Cervantes managed to describe admirably, and which to Buero is much more than the reaction of ordinary people to a madman.

> Si la lectura superficial del libro ofrece la constante burla y descrédito de toda fantasía como locura y disparate, ello no invalida el hecho formidable de ser las imaginaciones del conmovedor caballero las que caracterizan la obra de principio a fin, y sin ellas no habría sido la cumbre literaria que es. Tales lucubraciones son la lanza con que el esforzado Alonso Quijano pelea contra la "depravada edad" -así la califica- que las suscita. ('Discurso', p.26)

He refers to Cervantes' "recurso técnico...consistente en disponer acontecimientos ilógicos y quiméricos sobre el suelo de la más evidente realidad inmediata". In *Mito*, Buero catches the essence of the quixotic myth and applies it to Eloy's time and circumstances, to our time, to our reality; he does this without changing what is eternal, universal, in the quixotic myth. At the same time, by applying the universal myth to a very specific reality, exploring the world of fantasy and imagination, he is trying to address concrete evils of a very specific society, time and circumstances. This is what great writers have been able to do, and this is what Buero admires in Cervantes:

> Si tornamos la vista a nuestros mayores maestros, en ellos volveremos a advertir cómo supieron sumergirse en las vivas aguas de la imaginación creadora sin dar la espalda a los conflictos que nos atenazan y de los que también debemos ser resonadores. ('Discurso', p.27)

The position of the dreamer in his society is thus similar to that of the writer. Buero can see that Cervantes was a writer who "deleitó" but also "inquietó" ('Discurso', p.27). He would like to do the same himself.

> Desde el momento en que uno intenta hacer una obra que no solamente sea gustosa para el lector o el espectador, sino además problemática e inquietadora, por enfocar en ella

> problemas que nos atañen a muchos o a todos... entiendo
> que mi teatro, hablando en general, ha podido ser y seguir
> siendo un teatro inquietante para aquél que tenga -y Dios
> se la conserve- capacidad de inquietarse. (Interview)

Like Cervantes, writers live in a dangerous world. In *La detonación*
Buero deals with the problems to which a sincere and honest writer
exposes himself. He is aware of the risks he has to run if he wants to
write. "Los escritores están en una pugna con su sociedad que, aunque
puede derivar en situaciones más o menos armónicas, de hecho es una
pugna y, por lo tanto, representa un riesgo" (Interview).[13] The
confrontation of the dreamer with his society is not unlike that of the
writer with his. And the position of Cervantes in his world is like
Buero's just as the quixotic myth reappears in the shape of flying
saucers.

Ricardo Doménech has studied what he calls "el trasfondo mítico" in
Buero's theatre.[14] This "trasfondo mítico" constitutes the unifying
element in Buero's plays. According to Doménech, one cannot really talk
about a distinction between "social" plays and those which are not really
concerned with Spanish society, because the same mythical background
runs through all. "Este trasfondo mítico aparece como una mediación
entre el teatro de Buero y la sociedad española."[15] The presence of
these myths in Buero's plays and the fact that they have been accepted
by his contemporaries also prove that those myths are permanently
valid. By using them, Buero is not seeking refuge in the world of the
imagination, but striving to find a valid interpretation for the society of
today.[16]

The "trasfondo mítico" often appears on the surface in the text of his
plays. Buero has made it clear that he is concerned with quixotism for
various reasons, and there is ample evidence for this. Apart from the
obvious references to *Don Quixote* in *Mito*, other direct allusions to the
knight, to quixotism or to passages of the novel, are found in *En la
ardiente oscuridad*[17], *Madrugada*[18], *Irene o el tesoro*[19], *Hoy es
fiesta*[20], *Un soñador para un pueblo*[21], *El tragaluz*[22], *Jueces en*

la noche[23]. In both *El concierto de San Ovidio* and *Caimán*, there are multiple references to the search for the impossible, for the ideal woman, etc, which also bear an unmistakably quixotic imprint[24]. In most of the other plays mentioned, quixotism is referred to in a negative fashion by those characters who do not incarnate any of the quixotic values, or participate in the quixotic spirit. However, as I will try to show, quixotic values are present at a deeper level, and Buero explores the world of the imagination, as did Cervantes.

I have divided my study of quixotism in Buero into six chapters. The first two deal with the world of the imagination as explored by Cervantes and Buero. Chapters Three and Four attempt to show how the quixotic heroes, who are not afraid of plunging into the world of dreams and madness, end up isolated from the other members of society, because, as Martha Halsey states, "those around Don Quijote and those around Buero's many characters in whom Don Quijote appears, are blind to the spiritual reality represented by their visions."[25] But at the same time they inspire great faith in those who get to know them, and pass on their ideals to those who take them seriously. Chapter Five tries to deal with the essence of quixotic ethics. The final chapter considers the "activos", those characters who preach and practise a false quixotism, false because it lacks the essential element of contemplation.

Buero has not denied the influence on himself and his work of the Generation of 1898.[26] As I think this study will show, Buero's quixotism is not far from Unamuno's or Azorín's. Like Unamuno, Azorín, or Galdós, Buero does not laugh at Don Quixote.[27] He takes quixotism seriously, as a way of daring to recognize the dangers in a particular society, and inciting its members to think and therefore act accordingly, promoting and practising an ethics of peace, love, justice and truth, without the fear of being laughed at or of being called "madmen".

NOTES TO INTRODUCTION

1. See *Teatro español actual* (Madrid: Cátedra, 1977), pp.69-81.

2. See 'Discurso de Antonio Buero Vallejo en la entrega del Premio Cervantes 1986', *Anthropos* (Dic. 1987), nº 79, 25-27 (p.27). Also see Ricardo Doménech, *El teatro de Buero Vallejo* (Madrid: Ed. Gredos, S.A., 1973), p.244, footnote 6.
A useful discussion of Buero's quixotism is to be found in chapter six of D.W. Johnston's doctoral thesis on the influence of Miguel de Unamuno on the work on Buero Vallejo (The Queens's University, Belfast, October 1982), in which Johnston suggests that both Buero and Unamuno have revivified and recast the figure of Don Quixote. According to him, Buero's theatre has consistently concerned itself with quixotism. Unamuno's quixotism has for Buero the supreme value of non-conformism. This form of quixotic rebellion is incorporated by Buero into many of his characters. For both Unamuno and Buero, quixotism is a form which gives body to what they view as man's need to salvage the authenticity of his existence through a heroic struggle against the impossible. Quixotism becomes an invitation to live and create, is pervaded by a spiritual intensity and constitutes a firm ethical drive pushing constantly towards goodness. Quixotism reasserts the value of imagination, gives form to the desired resolution of the action-contemplation dichotomy. Finally, quixotism is, above all else, the ethic of love; it becomes the basis for all love, for all ethics. And on that basis, argue both authors, man may find his only certain salvation.

Few critics have failed to recognize Buero's quixotism. José Ramón Cortina even finds an echo of *Don Quixote* in the plot of *La señal que se espera*:

> En el argumento de *La señal que se espera* puede verse la sombra de Cervantes, autor que, según ha reconocido Buero en carta personal, ha influido en la concepción de sus obras. Los sucesos de la tragedia guardan cierta similitud con *El curioso impertinente*, novela intercalada en la primera parte del *Quijote*. (J.R. Cortina, *El arte dramático de Antonio Buero Vallejo* (Madrid: Ed. Gredos, 1969), p.39)

The connection, however, between *El curioso impertinente* and Buero's play seems to be quite far-fetched.

3. "Creo que mis primeras lecturas, incompletas, del *Quijote* debieron de realizarse a mis nueve o diez años, aunque, por supuesto, el mito de sus dos personajes centrales me era familiar, como a casi todo español, desde mucho antes. Supongo que hacia mis once años leí la novela del todo y, desde entonces, la habré releído varias otras veces, además de

releer con frecuencia pasajes espigados, aquí o allá, de la obra" (Personal letter from Antonio Buero Vallejo, 27 April 1989).

4. Américo Castro, *El pensamiento de Cervantes* (Barcelona: Ed. Noguer, 1972), pp.83 & 84.

5. According to Buero, it is legitimate to approach the novel from numerous angles. Cervantes' genius made this possible:

> Yo creo que la confrontación de don Quijote con la realidad inmisericorde, y su concepción del mundo como un lugar donde la caballería andante sigue vigente, son dos concepciones opuestas, ... pero estas concepciones opuestas no son incompatibles. La obra misma lo demuestra. Para la consideración de la novela quijotesca, inclinarse más hacia uno de los dos aspectos no es incompatible con inclinarse hacia el otro. Y se puede uno inclinar más hacia un lado o hacia el otro, según incluso la etapa vital que se esté viviendo, según la concepción concreta de una obra que uno quiera escribir. (Interview)

6. "El contraste entre lo que llamamos real y lo que tildamos de fantástico fortalece nuestras creaciones y es ejemplar en la novela del ingenioso hidalgo" ('Discurso en la entrega del Premio Cervantes', p.26).

7. 'Brillante', published in *Diario 16* (8 marzo 1987), quoted in *Antonio Buero Vallejo, Premio Miguel de Cervantes 1986* (Biblioteca Nacional, Abril-Junio 1987), p.29.

8. In *Teatro español actual*, p.74, he calls Wells "el más formidable creador de mitos, después de Kafka, que ha habido en la literatura de nuestro tiempo".

9. Bill Moyers makes the first remark while interviewing Joseph Campbell, in Joseph Campbell, *The Power of Myth* (New York: Doubleday, 1988), p.5.

10. William Righter, *Myth and Literature* (London and Boston: Routledge & Kegan Paul Ltd., 1975), p.4.

11. Campbell, *The Power of Myth*, p.40.

12. In his doctoral thesis mentioned in note 2, Johnston says that "in this opera we find a similar synchronic view of quixotism, that is, as an embodiment of timeless human truths." "Myth in general," - he adds - "and in the work of Buero and Unamuno in particular, is the embodiment in an appropriate imaginative form of man's intuition of his present state and of his aspirations towards a new future."

Eloy's quixotism, as well as the Father's and Mario's madness in *El tragaluz*, and David's connection with Don Quixote, have also been explored by Martha Halsey in *Antonio Buero Vallejo* (New York: Twayne Publishers, Inc., 1973). She concludes:

> **Quixotism**, Buero believes, may be efficacious and lead to sane and dynamic social action. (...) The ideals of Don Quijote, he believes, have particular relevance for contemporary times. "Bueroism" has been spoken of as a search for love, faith, justice, and, in short, peace. Or, if one prefers, for truth, and as a way of understanding the problems of our time, as a way of fighting for a better world where injustice is impossible and where man advances, confident and secure, in search of widespread perfection. (p.134)

She quotes Buero's words from a lecture on the importance of Unamuno: "Therefore great geniuses become quixotized, they assume a sort of lucid madness and evolve toward action that is seemingly - but only seemingly - sterile... The madness of Don Quijote, Buero adds, is also the madness of Larra and Unamuno. For Buero, quixotism is not sterile because it is synonymous with individual integrity and responsibility" (p.136).

13. According to Buero, the dangers to which Cervantes was exposed, and those which contemporary writers have to face, differ, but their situation is very similar:

> Todos los escritores escribimos en un mundo peligroso. Y todo ser humano actúa en un mundo peligroso. Y esos peligros, en determinados casos concretos, se acentúan, se concretan en alarmas muy determinadas. Y en el Siglo de Oro esa alarma determinada se llamaba ascendencia conversa, Inquisición,... Ahora, de forma más sinuosa o más indirecta, las coerciones y agresiones que el escritor puede recibir de la sociedad son muy alarmantes, o muy negativas, hasta el extremo de poder llegar a anularlo. (Interview)

The writer's confrontation with his society is thus quixotic, but Buero is ready to wage the battle: "...estoy intentando, tal vez quijotescamente, enfrentarme con mis Instituciones, con mis Fundaciones, que son también las de todos los presentes" (*Teatro español actual*, p.81).

14. "Nosotros creemos encontrar en el teatro de Buero un trasfondo mítico que tiene, como núcleo esencial, magnético, la fusión de tres mitos fundamentales: Edipo (no sólo en *Llegada de los dioses*), Don Quijote (no sólo en *Mito*) y Caín y Abel (no sólo, por ejemplo, en *El tragaluz*)" (Doménech, *El teatro de Buero Vallejo*, p.242).

15. Doménech, *El teatro de Buero Vallejo*, p.282.

16. Magda Ruggeri Marchetti stresses Buero's application of universal myths to specific situations: "Sappiamo che molti miti costituiscono il substrato dell'opera di Buero. Già altri critici hanno segnalato nel suo teatro la presenza di Edipo (*Llegada de los dioses*), di Caino (*El tragaluz*), del Quijote (in quasi tutte le opere) di Sigismundo e della sua antitesi tra sogno e realtà (*La fundación*), della Caverna platonica *El tragaluz*); ma queste tre opere sono vere ricostruzioni. È nota la tendenza di Buero ad intuire, analizzare ciò che può nascondere la versione abituale della leggenda; non per distruggerla, ma per approfondirla. A parte questo interesse, senza dubbio, come sempre, vi sono stati motivi di reazione al contesto sociale che lo hanno spinto a determinata scelte. L'autoritarismo di Ulisse in un paese impoverito da una guerra spaventosa, il contrasto tra la verità di Riquet e gli inganni della corte, la morale di comprensione e verità di Gesù in una società alienata, erano chiaramente forme di critica alla situazione spagnola" (*Il teatro di Antonio Buero Vallejo o il processo verso la verità* (Roma: Bulzoni Editore, 1981), p.112).

A few years earlier, Manuel Alvar made similar observations with regard to *La tejedora de sueños*: "Buero Vallejo ha elaborado -un eslabón más- motivos odiseicos que no se han secado en el espíritu del hombre, los conozca o los ignore, pero su originalidad ha estado no sólo en la creación de un código para transmitirnos su mensaje, sino también en dar virtualidad al mito con una serie de intuiciones que están vivas para los hombres a los que se habla; me refiero ahora, no a la universalidad de sentimientos, sino a la circunstancia tradicional que les hizo cobrar sentido en la España de 1952. Ha entendido lo que fue la creación homérica, la ha hecho renacer con nueva vida y, además, le ha dado validez para quienes -en su lengua- pudieran oírla o leerla" ('Presencia del mito: *La tejedora de sueños*', in *Estudios sobre Buero Vallejo*, edited by Mariano de Paco, *Los Trabajos de la Cátedra de Teatro* (Murcia: Universidad, 1984), p.312).

17. Antonio Buero Vallejo, *En la ardiente oscuridad. Un soñador para un pueblo* (Madrid: Espasa-Calpe, S.A., 1988), p.28.
(See Chapter Six, p.203.)

18. Antonio Buero Vallejo, *Madrugada* (Madrid: Ediciones Alfil, 1960), p.24.
(See Chapter Six, p.208.)

19. Antonio Buero Vallejo, *Irene o el tesoro*, in *Teatro* (Buenos Aires: Ed. Losada, S.A.), 1962, p.163.
(See Chapter Two, p.66.)

20. Antonio Buero Vallejo, *Hoy es fiesta*. *Aventura en lo gris* (Madrid: Ed. Magisterio Español, S.A., 1974), pp.107 & 110. (See Chapter Five, p.182.)

21. *Un soñador para un pueblo*, pp.115-6. (See Chapter Two, p.67.)

22. Antonio Buero Vallejo, *El tragaluz*. *El sueño de la razón* (Madrid: Espasa-Calpe, S.A., 1988), pp.83 & 85. (See Chapter Six, p.218.)

23. Antonio Buero Vallejo, *Jueces en la noche*. *Hoy es fiesta* (Madrid: Espasa-Calpe, S.A., 1981), p.48. (See Chapter Six, p.220)

24. See, for example, *El concierto de San Ovidio*. *La Fundación* (Madrid: Espasa-Calpe, S.A., 1986), pp.49, 92, etc., and, *Caimán*. *Las cartas boca abajo* (Madrid: Espasa-Calpe, S.A., 1981), pp.21, 55, 57, 93.

25. Halsey, *Antonio Buero Vallejo*, p.130.

26. "Yo mismo he dicho, y también otros estudiosos lo han dicho, que en mi obra había influencias innegables, a veces muy acentuadas, de Unamuno, por ejemplo, o de Galdós, o del 98 en general" (*Teatro español actual*, p.70).

27. For the writers of the Generation, Don Quixote provides an example of personal quest for new ideals and beliefs which will be the beginning of a spiritual renewal. Azorín, for example, makes the point that Cervantes did not condemn idealism, but sterile enthusiasm, "la fantasía loca, irrazonada e impetuosa que rompe de pronto la inacción para caer otro vez estérilmente en el marasmo... Y ésta es la exaltación loca y baldía que Cervantes condenó en el Quijote; no aquel amor al ideal, no aquella ilusión, no aquella ingenuidad, no aquella audacia, no aquella confianza en nosotros mismos,..." (José Martínez Ruiz, *La ruta de Don Quijote*, edited by H. Ramsden (Manchester University Press, 1966), p.68).

   Buero has also mentioned Benito Pérez Galdós. As Galdós' biographer wrote, "it was commonly believed that he knew by heart sizable portions of *Don Quijote*" when he was still a schoolboy; and that, when he was already very old, "in the absence of newspapers on Mondays, he had selections from the *Quijote* read to him. Possibly under the influence of the knight of La Mancha, Galdós seemed determined to demonstrate the superiority of mind over matter" (H. Chonon Berkowitz, *Pérez Galdós, Spanish Liberal Crusader* (Madison: University of Wisconsin Press, 1948), pp.33 & 444).

Galdós' quixotic "caballero encantado" goes through a pilgrimage of self-purification and devotes his energies to the arduous task of regenerating - or rather transforming, Spain: "Campesino primero, obrero después, Tarsis, transformado en Gil, es llevado por las tierras castellanas en peregrinación purificadora, en pos de la verdadera España intrahistórica y trabajadora -explotada, hambreada, reprimida- y de su amante, la maestra Cintia-Pascuala. Terminada la peregrinación, unida ya la pareja y con un niño, Héspero, símbolo de un futuro mejor, los héroes se incorporan a la lucha por desencantar y regenerar España entera" (Julio Rodríguez-Puértolas, ed., Benito Pérez Galdós, *El caballero encantado* (Madrid: Cátedra, S.A., 1977), p.42).

Chapter I
MADNESS
The paradoxical nature of quixotic lunacy

Don Quixote's madness has been viewed from many different angles. To establish what was Cervantes' own notion of his hero's madness is certainly not an easy task. We will have to try to come to grips with the concept of quixotic madness before we are ready to judge to what extent Buero's heroes suffer from the same sort of insanity. The view different critics take of Don Quixote's insanity is in keeping with their general approach to the work. Much depends on what they think is the nature of the great novel. In his *Teoría del Quijote* Fernando Rielo refers to the varied approaches to the knight's insanity. Those different opinions could be plotted on a curve. At one end of that curve he would place those who explain Don Quixote's madness from a merely medical angle; at the opposite extreme would be opinions like that of Avalle-Arce. He describes Avalle-Arce's view of Don Quixote's madness, which is related to its interpretation by Plato as "liberación divina de los módulos ordinarios de los hombres". "Don Quijote", he continues, "posee esa 'locura divina de la que habló Platón', cuya sublimidad se explica por la 'potencia de amar' que manifiesta a lo largo de todas sus acciones." Fernando Rielo himself adds to that divine aspect an element of beauty: "...una locura metafórica o literaria que, en armonía con la esencia mística del Quijote, se resuelve en la hermosura divina descrita en función de una justicia humana." Thus, Fernando Rielo talks about a "supuesta locura", and relates madness to mysticism.[1]

It will prove useful to look at Unamuno's interpretation of Don
Quixote's insanity: "Hizo en aras   Llenósele la fantasía de hermosos
desatinos, y creyó ser verdad lo que sólo era hermosura ... Perdió
Alonso Quijano el juicio, para ganarlo en don Quijote: un juicio
glorificado".[2] The knight sacrificed his mind for his people's sake. A
very similar view is taken by Rielo, referring in this case not to Don
Quixote's but to Cervantes' madness: "El valor de Cervantes es, en mi
humilde opinión, el de un alma grande y tierna que pone su razón al
servicio de una locura: la justicia en el mundo. ¡Y menuda locura!"[3]
Cervantes and his hero suffer, that is to say, from the same insanity.

For Unamuno, if Don Quixote has made himself mad for the sake of
his people, he, on the other hand, recovers his mind "glorified",
elevated. It attains a superior quality; it becomes a brighter mind which
penetrates reality, which sees with greater lucidity. Unamuno would
also call mad "todo el que se toma en serio el mundo. ...   ¿Y no
deberíamos ser locos todos?",[4] he wonders.

Madariaga does not deny that Don Quixote is a real lunatic, but he
also refers to Cervantes' singular achievement of "making wisdom glow
out of the deeds of a lunatic".[5] Madness for Madariaga is a source of
wisdom which borders on the divine. It is indeed a privilege of which
only certain people, amongst them Don Quixote, are worthy. Insanity
is not seen as a disease, but as a raised state of the mind which yields
knowledge.   It is his earnestness and good faith that make Alonso
Quijano worthy of that privilege:

> Thus putting two and two together we find what sort of a
> man is Alonso Quijano - a fine type of Spanish gentleman,
> a friend to solitude, given to swift pacing, nay galloping,
> over the fields of imagination and worthy in his earnestness
> and good faith to overstep the borderline of sanity on the
> side which touches the divine.[6]

Anthony Close also talks about a madman who is partly mad and
partly wise, about two different compartments in Don Quixote's brain.
"However," - he says -, "it seems nearer the truth to say that the hero's

madness and wisdom interwine, while still being distinguishable from each other."[7]

In his *El ingenio de Cervantes y la locura de Don Quijote*, Mauro Olmeda affirms that in Cervantes' conception of his hero there is implicit the idea that madness has a trascendental meaning, and that delirium is only a creative idea which has been perverted.[8] He also talks about a "locura simulada". According to Olmeda, Cervantes never meant to say that Don Quixote, the greatest character of all times, was mad at all. His was only a literary madness. "Cervantes no dijo seriamente jamás que el más excelso de los personajes de su creación fuese un loco" (p.244).

Olmeda also refers to the influence of Juan Huarte on Cervantes in his creation of the madman. He has to admit that he contradicts himself, by first saying that no madness is involved, and then making use of Huarte's theories to explain Don Quixote's insanity in medical terms. Olmeda recognizes the paradox. "¿Será posible", he wonders, "explicar esta antinomia del gran entendimiento de un loco?" (p.253). In an attempt to explain it he turns to Huarte again: "Otra tercera forma de ingenio se halla... con la cual dicen los que la alcanzan cosas tan delicadas, tan verdaderas y prodigiosas, que jamás se vieron, ni oyeron, ni escribieron, ni para siempre vinieron en consideración de los hombres. Llámalo Platón 'ingenio superior, acompañado de demencia': con ésta hablan los poetas dichos y sentencias tan levantados, que si no es por divina revelación no es posible alcanzar." Don Quixote could then suffer from the so-called "poetic insanity", also suffered by "Demócrito Abderita, un loco imaginativo atacado de demencia poética, y, como es el caso de don Quijote, los desvaríos de la fantasía del Abderita le hacían aparecer alternativamente ante las gentes como personalidad de entendimiento poderoso y como loco rematado" (pp.253-4). Olmeda, thus, uses Huarte's arguments to support his own idea of the madness-wisdom paradox.

Rafael Salillas had already discussed the source of Cervantes' inspiration in his *Un gran inspirador de Cervantes. El doctor Juan*

Huarte y su "Examen de ingenios". Olmeda himself refers in his 'Apéndice' to a further study on the matter by Otis Green; in this study Green affirms that "well-read contemporaries of Cervantes would have followed the course of Alonso Quijano's transition from a country gentleman of 'choleric temper' to an 'imaginative' and 'visionary' monomaniac, and would have interpreted this transformation, as Cervantes had conceived it, in the light of their knowledge of Greek-Arabic physiological and psychological theories regarding the balance and imbalance of the bodily humours."[9] Huarte's theories would explain Don Quixote's evolution in the novel: "Alonso Quijano is a man primarily 'colérico'; ...his natural condition is exacerbated by a 'passion' and by 'lack of sleep', which produce a hypertrophy of his 'imaginative faculty'; ...his madness follows a natural trajectory away from, and back to, normality. ... Don Quijote's adventures could have happened only to a 'colérico', a man by nature 'caliente y seco', and... such a man was, according to Renaissance psychology, of necessity 'ingenioso'."[10]

In his edition of Huarte's *Examen de ingenios para las ciencias*, Esteban Torre considers that Salillas somewhat exaggerated the connection between that work and *El ingenioso hidalgo don Quijote de la Mancha*. But he himself admits later: "Realmente, existen coincidencias que no pueden ser pasadas por alto."[11]

Olmeda subscribes to the views of Salillas and Green because he believes that quixotic insanity cannot be analysed by reference to modern psychopathological concepts. "Sería improcedente acudir a los dominios de la psicopatología de nuestra época" (p.246). At the same time, however, he establishes that Cervantes is undoubtedly a precursor of modern psychopathology. He mentions Carlos Gutiérrez Noriega's 'La contribución de Miguel de Cervantes a la psiquiatría.' According to this doctor, Cervantes looks at madness in a remarkably unprejudiced and deeply humane fashion:

Al leer sus novelas -verdaderas historias clínicas- no cabe la menor duda de que Cervantes formuló de la locura una concepción completamente diferente y superior a sus contemporáneos, sin excluir a los más ilustres, anticipándose en esto a Pinel, el fundador de la clínica psiquiátrica y de la higiene mental, por lo mismo, en dos siglos. ... Cervantes es el primero en advertir con el criterio de un verdadero clínico moderno, que junto a la locura, y aún antes que ella está el tipo psicológico.[12]

Rielo says, as we have seen, that those who want to seek a medical explanation for the knight's madness are at the opposite end of the curve from those who consider insanity to be divinely inspired or a source of wisdom. It now seems, though, that those extremes are not so far apart. At least Huarte does not seem to have thought that they were incompatible. Olmeda emphasizes that one of the conclusions of Huarte's application of the theory of the humours to the study of insanity is that "todos, absolutamente todos, estamos enfermos ... Porque la sanidad de los hombres no consiste en un punto indivisible, sino que tiene anchura y latitud" (p.250). These views are indeed not unlike those of the recent revolutionary R.D. Laing. There does not seem to be a defining line which limits the boundaries of madness. "Sanity or psychosis is tested by the degree of conjunction or disjunction between two persons where the one is sane by common consent",[13] he says in *The Divided Self*. Laing talks about madness as not a breakdown but potentially a breakthrough and liberation. The schizophrenic, according to Laing, is in a privileged position to let in light, and can often be in possession of a truth to which the so-called sane do not have access. Psychosis, thus, becomes a higher form of sanity.[14] "Ezequiel, in Jaspers's opinion, was a schizophrenic", Laing says. Huarte himself discovered the power of prophecy in some disturbed minds together with other mental qualities with which the sane are not endowed: "Y es que si el hombre cae en alguna enfermedad por la cual el celebro de repente mude su temperatura -como es la manía, melancolía y frenesía- en un momento acontece perder, si es prudente, cuanto sabe, y dice mil disparates; y si es necio, adquiere más ingenio y habilidad que antes tenía."[15] He gives the example of a peasant, who, having lost his wits, spoke in a refined and polished language in such a way that his eloquence could be compared to Cicero's.[16] And he also tells the story of someone who could speak in verse, though when he was sane he was incapable of composing poetry.[17] Another young man, a page, became bright, witty and wise when he lost his mind. Everyone came to listen to him and to seek advice from him, and his own master prayed to God that he would not be cured. Neither the patient himself nor his master appreciated his cure or thanked the doctor because, they said, he who was wise when mad became foolish when cured.[18] Huarte also knows of cases of mad people who were able to foresee future events. He speaks of a woman who told everyone the truth about their virtues and defects, and on one occasion foresaw that the barber who was bleeding her was going to die and that his wife would marry someone she knew. She told the barber, and the prophecy was fulfilled less than half a year later.[19] Huarte quotes Aristotle on this point: "...confiesa claramente Aristóteles que, por calentarse demasiadamente el celebro, vienen muchos hombres a conocer lo que está por venir, como son las Sibilas."[20] This is not unlike Laing's schizophrenics who let in light because their mind is open.

In his witty *Praise of Folly*, Erasmus of Rotterdam maintains that "most men are foolish and everyone is foolish in many ways."[21] He also relates madness to the divine, and uses Plato's theories and the Scriptures to support his arguments. Folly is a source of happiness: "Is there anyone happier than that class of people who are commonly called morons, fools, nitwits, and simpletons...?" Fools also have the virtue of truthfulness: "They alone are candid and truthful. What is more praiseworthy than truth?" (p.125).

Not every madness, according to Erasmus, is a pitiable one, "not every madness is a calamity. Otherwise, Horace would not have said: 'A pleasant madness inspires me'. Nor would Plato have placed the frenzy of poets and seers among the chief blessings of life; and the oracle would not have called the labours of Aeneas insane." He considers it essential to distinguish between the two types of madness, because one is sent from hell by the Furies and makes people lustful, thirsty for war, insatiably greedy. The second type of madness, however, "is far different from this and should be desired above all things. It arises whenever a cheerful error of the mind frees the spirit from care and at the same time anoints it with manifold delight." Like Huarte, Erasmus is aware of the advantages of certain delusions:

> The Greek in Horace's *Epistle* had the right idea. He was so mad that he, all alone, would sit for days on end in a theater, laughing, applauding, and enjoying himself because he thought a play was going on when really there was no one on stage. In all other things he was sane enough, joyful with his friends, kind to his wife, and able to put up with his servants, who could even open up a bottle without his getting angry. When the care of family and physician had freed him from his sickness and he was himself again, he protested to his friends saying, "Why, you have killed, not cured me, my friends, since you have taken from me such great pleasure and destroyed my enjoyable delusions." He was right; for they were the mad ones and needed the medicine more than he, since they thought that such an enjoyable delusion was some sort of evil and should be cured by medicine. (p.127)

There is thus an enjoyable and innocent sort of madness which does not necessarily need to be cured; it is a harmless source of pleasure and delight, which does not render the individual incapable of attending to his duties.

God himself had opted to take on foolishness, to appear as a madman. Erasmus quotes St Paul at length, trying to prove that "the whole of Christian religion seems to have a certain relationship with some kind of folly but fails to agree at all with wisdom" (p.169). Christ chose the foolishness of the Cross to heal, and he recommended foolishness to his apostles, who were not wise men. The apostles appeared drunk, Paul seemed mad; but, before them, Christ himself had been called mad by his fellow-villagers: "When word came to them who were nearest him, they went out to restrain him; they said, he must be mad" (Mark 3. 21). "Christ did not merely choose to be surrounded by lunatics" - says Michel Foucault; "he himself chose to pass in their eyes for a madman,... Madness thus became the ultimate form, the final degree of God in man's image, before the fulfilment and deliverance of the Cross."[22]

Erasmus thinks that those who identify with Christ's teaching fully, who try to put it into practice, are often seen as insane. "Those whom the ardor of religion has totally consumed... throw away their wealth, they neglect injuries, permit themselves to be deceived, fail to discriminate between friend and foe, shrink from pleasure, and cram themselves with hunger, vigils, tears, labors, contumelies. They prefer death to life and, in short, seem to have grown impervious to sensation and live as if their souls no longer dwelt in their bodies. What is this other than insanity?" (p.169).

This living "as if their souls no longer dwelt in their bodies" agrees in many ways with Plato's view that the soul is tied down with earthly chains. When the soul attempts to attain its freedom, it is called insane. "Yet we see people so afflicted predict the future, understand foreign languages hitherto unknown, and give every evidence of some divine quality. There can be no doubt that now that the mind is somewhat liberated from the contagion of the body it begins to exercise its native abilities" (p.170). This liberation of the mind is of course akin to mystical ecstasy, "where the spirit rises above the things of sense and man is utterly beside himself, not knowing whether he is in the body or out of the body."[23] This is only a foretaste of what the soul will experience in heaven, when the body will be absorbed by the spirit. "Then the spirit will be in a marvellous manner absorbed by the Highest Mind,... In this way the entire man will be outside of himself, and his happiness will be due to no other than that, so placed, he will share in the Highest Good which draws all to Itself" (p.172). This is why those who go through mystical experiences while on earth suffer from something very akin to madness.

It is clear then that the madness-wisdom paradox had been common long before Cervantes conceived his Don Quixote. The knight is not Cervantes' only mad character. In *El licenciado Vidriera*, for instance, we have the example of a man whose wisdom everyone admired and whose

advice everyone sought, so long as he was mad. Alban K. Forcione
points out that the Licenciate's madness is clearly connected with
superior insight.[24] Cervantes presents a student who "atendía más
a sus libros que a otros pasatiempos".[25] Just before he went mad,
Tomás was in bed for six months, "en los cuales se secó y se puso, como
suele decirse, en los huesos, y mostraba tener turbados todos los
sentidos" (p.36). The Licenciate himself is convinced that it is precisely
his "ser de vidrio" that increases his understanding and wisdom: "Decía
que le hablasen desde lejos, y le preguntasen lo que quisiesen, porque
a todo les respondería con más entendimiento, por ser hombre de vidrio
y no de carne." As happened with the page Huarte mentioned, everyone
came to ask him difficult questions and he answered them wisely while he
was mad: "Le preguntaron muchas y difíciles cosas, a las cuales
respondió espontáneamente con grandísima agudeza de ingenio; cosa que
causó admiración a los más letrados de la Universidad y a los profesores
de la Medicina y Filosofía, viendo que en un sujeto donde se contenía tan
extraordinaria locura como era el pensar que fuese de vidrio, se
encerrase tan grande entendimiento" (p.37). But once he recovered
from his disease, he sadly had to bear people's indifference; no one came
any more to ask him questions and he had to leave Spain.

One should not, on the other hand, forget Anselmo's "manifiesta
locura" (*Quixote*, I,33) in wanting to put to the test his own wife in his
obsession for "honra". Or Felipo de Carrizales's pathological obsession
with jealousy, a madness which, far from helping anyone, brings about
pain and suffering. It is not the product of a brighter or enlightened
mind, but of a mind closed to light. Cervantes censures this obsessive
mind, and he later shows its cure. In his prologue to Part II of *Don
Quixote* Cervantes writes of two madmen, one from Seville and another
one from Córdoba. He then refers to Don Quixote's "discretas locuras".
He certainly did not apply the same adjective to the madness of
Carrizales or Anselmo. Theirs is not "discreta" and therefore is not of
benefit to anyone.

Don Quixote and the Glass Licenciate are not isolated examples of a paradoxical madness. Insanity has consistently been connected to superior insight. Don Quixote's contemporary, King Lear, is also called a fool. He will only be wise when he loses his mind. Both Lear and his Fool realize that wisdom and madness go together. Only when Lear is ready to become a good fool, does he understand the truth, which makes him mad, and wise. Other characters wonder at the strange mixture of wisdom and madness. On hearing the king speak, Edgar exclaims: "O! matter and impertinency mix'd; reason in madness."[26]

Shakespeare's Lady Macbeth is also aware that, if she and her husband were to think seriously of the consequences of their actions, they would lose their mind. When she is eventually fully aware of her grave guilt, she becomes insane. Lady Macbeth had been oblivious enough to justify her own deeds when she craved for power, but once she understands the true nature of her actions, she goes mad. Again, full understanding of the truth, as in Lear's case, brings about insanity, madness, but also a deeper knowledge of the truth.

This paradoxical insanity is by no means new. As early as the fifth century B.C., Cassandra, Priam's daughter, who could also foresee the future, could know the depth of the souls of people around her, had been called "wild creature", "lying prophet", "gipsy", "tale-spinner".[27] "Why, she is mad, hears only her own frenzied thoughts", Clymnestra says in Aeschylus' *Agamemnon* (p.79). The chorus tries to prevent her from speaking, calling her insane. "She is insane, poor girl, or god-possessed", and insist that her words are "void of meaning" (p.82). They urge her to decode her mysterious words but when she prophesies the truth they refuse to believe her. Her superior knowledge, and gift of prophecy, is associated with madness.

To use a more recent Spanish example, in *La casa de Bernarda Alba* we have another madwoman: María Josefa, Bernarda's mother, the only character who is able to tell the truth. Unlike most of the other women in the play, she says what she thinks openly, and also foresees what is going to happen. In spite of her age, she openly confesses that she wants to get married, as she clearly sees that none of the other women in the house will. María Josefa feels asphyxiated by the suffocating atmosphere of a closed house. "Pepe el Romano es un gigante. Todas lo queréis. Pero él os va a devorar, porque vosotras sois granos de trigo. No, granos de trigo, no. ¡Ranas sin lengua!"[28] In her madness, she understands better than any of the others that their hidden passion will end up devouring them.

Dostoyevski's quixotic *Idiot* is a good example of the same paradox. "I have always been an invalid"[29], the prince repeats over and over again thoughout the novel. Yet he seems to have an extraordinary gift for getting to know people, for making others love him, especially children. They become attached to him as soon as they meet him, and they know at first sight that they can trust him.[30] People who get to know him are surprised that he is called an idiot, for he seems to have a clear understanding of everything that is going on around him. Aglaya also considers it unfair for people to call him simple: "And if anybody says that your mind is - is sometimes affected, you know - it is unfair. ...even if your surface mind be a little affected ..., yet your real mind is far better than all theirs put together. Such a mind as they have never dreamed of; because really, there are two minds - the kind that matters, and the kind that doesn't matter" (p.418).

They call the prince "the poor knight", after Cervantes' knight. "A month ago you were turning over the pages of your *Don Quixote*, and suddenly called out 'There is nothing better than the poor knight', Colia says (p.236). Aglaya put a letter she received from the prince "into a large book... She laughed when,..., she happened to notice the name of the book, and saw that it was *Don Quixote*, but it would be difficult to say exactly why" (p.178).

The man whom they call the idiot is precisely the one who gets to the depth of the others' souls. "Here you are, as simple and innocent as a knight of the golden age, and yet... yet... you read a man's soul like a psychologist!" (p.297). After only a short conversation with Regojin he is able to foresee: "He would marry her [Nastasia] tomorrow! - marry her tomorrow and murder her in a week!" (p.30).

The quixotic prince is aware himself of the paradoxical nature of his disease:

> He remembered that during his epileptic fits, or rather immediately preceding them, he had always experienced a moment or two when his whole heart, and mind, and body seemed to wake up to vigour and light; when he became filled with joy and hope, and all his anxieties seemed to be swept away for ever; these moments were but presentiments, as it were, of the one final second (...) in which the fit came upon him. ... when the attack was over, and the prince reflected on his symptoms, he used to say to himself: "These moments, short as they are, when I feel such extreme consciousness of myself, and consequently more of life than at other times, are due only to the disease - to the sudden rupture of normal conditions. Therefore they are not really a higher kind of life, but a lower." This reasoning, however, seemed to end in a paradox, and lead to the further consideration: "What matter though it be only disease, an abnormal tension of the brain, if when I recall and analyze the moment, it seems to have been one of harmony and beauty in the highest degree - an instant of deepest sensation, overflowing with unbounded joy and rapture, ecstatic devotion, and completest life?"
> (pp.215-6)

His disease is thus the cause of a greater intensity of life, of more self-consciousness, beauty and light. Dostoyevski's idiot, inspired by Don Quixote, suffers from, and is aware of, his paradoxical disease. And everyone who meets him notices this dual aspect of his nature: simplicity and wisdom; deep understanding of others and poor opinion of himself; insanity and exceptional refinement of soul. Dostoyevski creates his quixotic hero with a paradoxical nature, thus showing his view that Don Quixote's madness is not just a laughable one.[31]

This is the context within which, I believe, we must look at Don Quixote's madness. Cervantists who maintain that Don Quixote's words are full of wisdom, and that the hero should not be laughed at, are certainly not going against tradition.

Undoubtedly, Don Quixote's intelligence surpasses in brightness that of many of those who call him mad. In Part I, Chapter 37, Cervantes tells us:

> De tal manera y por tan buenos términos iba prosiguiendo en su plática don Quijote, que obligó a que, por entonces, ninguno de los que escuchándole estaban le tuviese por loco; antes, como todos los más eran caballeros, a quienes son anejas las armas, le escuchaban de muy buena gana.

Many characters in the novel are surprised at the knight's reasoning. In Part II, Chapter 16, for example, we read: "Admirado quedó el del Verde Gabán del razonamiento de don Quijote, y tanto, que fue perdiendo la opinión que con él tenía de ser mentecato". In that chapter Don Quixote refers to his own madness in these words:

> ¿Quién duda, señor don Diego de Miranda, que vuestra merced no me tenga en su opinión por un hombre disparatado y loco? No sería mucho que así fuere, porque mis obras no pueden dar testimonio de otra cosa. Pues, con todo esto, quiero que vuestra merced advierta que no soy tan loco ni tan menguado como debo de haberle parecido.

According to Sancho, not even a village priest, who for the squire is the acme of all wisdom, can be compared to his master in wit, courage or eloquence:

> ¿Es posible que haya en el mundo personas que se atrevan a decir y a jurar que este mi señor es loco? Digan vuestras mercedes, señores pastores: ¿Hay cura de aldea, por discreto y por estudiante que sea, que pueda decir lo que mi amo ha dicho, ni hay caballero andante, por más fama que tenga de valiente, que pueda ofrecer lo que mi amo aquí ha ofrecido? (II,58)

The wisdom-madness paradox is undoubtedly an obvious feature of the knight. Olmeda admits that many characters who meet Don Quixote take him for a madman: the inn-keeper who knighted him (I,3), Vivaldo and his companions (I,13), the merchants from Toledo (I,4), the wenches in

Maritornes's inn (I,27), etc. Some other characters, however, do not dare to say that Don Quixote is merely mad. Don Diego de Miranda describes him as follows: "No sé que te diga, hijo... Sólo te sabré decir que lo he visto hacer cosas del mayor loco del mundo, y decir razones tan discretas que borran y deshacen sus hechos" (II,18). "Es un loco bizarro", Don Lorenzo says himself in the same chapter. Roque Guinart writes a letter to his friend in Barcelona and tells him about Don Quixote: "Era el más gracioso y el más entendido hombre del mundo" (II,60). And the priest from Don Quixote's village also notices that "como no le toquen en sus caballerías, no habrá nadie que lo juzgue sino de muy buen entendimiento" (I,30).[32]

As was pointed out in the Introduction, Buero has admitted that he was considerably influenced by his reading of H.G. Wells, and in particular that when writing *El tragaluz* he recalled *Christina Alberta's Father*.[33] This is particularly interesting in respect of madness. *Christina Alberta's Father* deals with a middle-aged Englishman deluded into believing he is the reincarnation of an ancient Sumerian king. After too much reading, Albert Edward Preemby gets the fantastical idea that he really is Sargon, a Mesopotamian monarch who has been sent back to the world with an important mission. After he goes mad, his daughter refers to his madness in very similar terms to those of Sancho, mentioning his rational and coherent speech: "He is perfectly logical and coherent. He talks I think rather better and more clearly than usual... He is not a bit crazy. He is just possessed by this one grand impossible idea."[34] Later on Bobby states: "It's a little dear of a lunatic ... If it's lunatic at all ... He is quite tidy in his person and he hangs together - mentally he hangs together" (p.187). Dr Devizes expresses his view that "Having an exceptional mind isn't insanity... or else we should put all our poets and artists in asylums" (p.269).

Through Preemby, who believes himself to be Sargon King of Kings, Wells develops his view that madmen have sacrificed themselves for the sake of others: "... there is a real and important purpose in madness. It is a sort of simplification, removal of checks and controls, and a sort of natural experiment. The secret things of the mind are laid bare. But then if poor souls are to suffer that sort of thing to yield knowledge for others, they ought to be treated properly" (pp.369-70). Preemby, or Sargon, wonders what is inside madness: "I cannot understand this madness"; "I cannot understand this riddle that has been set me. Why does the Power, why does God, permit men to be mad? When they are mad they are beyond good and evil. What are they? Men still? What becomes of justice, what becomes of righteousness - when men go mad?" (p.316). "I do not understand why there is madness. It puzzles and distresses me" (p.369).

Undoubtedly, madness is a mystery; it can become a riddle in that it does not seem to have a purpose. Even if madness could be explained scientifically in all its manifestations, in such a way that one could tell with reasonable accuracy where there is or there is not madness, the question "Why does madness exist on this earth?" is certainly most difficult, if not impossible, to answer.

Buero too is attracted by what he calls the mystery of madness. He acknowledges the difficulty of explaining what madness really consists of: "¿Qué hay dentro de la locura? Habría que estar loco para saberlo. La locura es una situación anímica que miramos desde fuera cuando creemos no estar locos. La miramos desde fuera pero, de hecho, como casi cualquier otro aspecto de la autenticidad humana, es un misterio" (Interview). He is well aware that this interest in madness is one he shares with Cervantes. "Cervantes procedió sirviéndose de su penetrante observación... por intuiciones y adivinaciones propias de su genio, y llevado de la singular atracción que le producían los locos."[35] His own interest appears to have become particularly intense in the sixties and seventies. Though *Irene* was written earlier (1953-54), and *Caimán* later (1980), *Las Meninas* (1960), *La doble historia del Doctor Valmy* (1964), *El tragaluz* (1966), *Mito* (1967), *El sueño de la razón* (1969), *Llegada de los dioses* (1971), *La Fundación* (1972-73), and *La detonación* (1975-77), all have mad-sane characters. Madness, however, is only one more limitation among the many which men suffer. Pedro Laín Entralgo speaks of

> la "deficiencia física": la carencia de alguna capacidad que por naturaleza debe poseer el hombre. La ceguera de todos en *En la ardiente oscuridad*, la de David y sus compañeros en *El concierto de San Ovidio*, la de Julio en *Llegada de los dioses*, la de Euriclea en *La tejedora de sueños*, la de Pedro Briones en *Las Meninas*. La sordera de Goya en *El sueño de la razón*, la de Pilar en *Hoy es fiesta*, la de la madre de Daniel en *La doble historia del doctor Valmy*. El daltonismo del protagonista de *Diálogo secreto*. La mudez de Anita en *Las cartas boca abajo*. La locura ocasional de Goya en *El sueño de la razón* y la permanente de El Padre en *El tragaluz*, la de Tomás en *La Fundación*.[36]

In spite of these deficiencies, or precisely because of them, these characters are often morally superior, or are gifted with other talents which those who are considered normal do not possess. "El sordo y el ciego vienen a ser, en consecuencia, tribunal moral de quienes con ellos convivimos, bien porque con su mirada nos remiten a nosotros mismos, a nuestro fondo insobornable, bien porque con su ceguera ven más que nosotros."[37] Madmen are thus mysteriously gifted with a deeper knowledge of things and people. The topos recurs very frequently in Buero's works, and the consideration of quixotic lunacy will prove helpful in order to understand in what sense some of his characters are called "locos".

In Buero's plays some characters use the term "loco" or "locura" improperly to refer to others who behave in what they would deem an extraordinary way, or who, as Unamuno said, exhibit the madness of taking their life and their neighbours' lives seriously. This is true for instance of David, Silvano, Esquilache,... But, since such characters are merely labelled mad because of their ideals, they will be dealt with in the next chapter. On the other hand, one also finds "videntes", seers who are accused of being insane because of what the other characters consider incoherence; they, however, have knowledge even of future events and are therefore able to prophesy. In the first act of *El terror inmóvil*, for example, we find Tío Blas, a miserable old man who talks unceasingly and whom nobody believes; nevertheless, he speaks the truth. In that act he warns Álvaro: "Todos cocinamos en este sucio mundo. Cocinamos nuestro yantar, cocinamos nuestras alegrías y desgracias. Cocinar y siempre cocinar."[38] In a few moments he penetrates Álvaro's soul: "Desde que entré a verte vi tu miedo. ... Tienes miedo. Por eso te ríes a veces" (p.36). After guessing that Álvaro does not love his son and foreseeing a misfortune, Tío Blas admits his madness: "Y si no te gustó mi historia... no hagas caso. Son cosas que salen de esta cabeza trastornada" (p.37). Out of that "cabeza trastornada", however, comes the truth that initiates the audience into the nature of the tragedy and anticipates the development of the whole play. In fact, Álvaro will end up "cooking" his own misfortune, his wife's and his son's. The crazy and "marrullero" old man, as Camila calls him, guesses, nobody knows how, that Álvaro is a miserable, frightened-to-death being. Camila and Álvaro call tío Blas "el que sueña". Part of his madness is that he cannot stop telling what comes to his mind, even if he does not understand or believe it himself:

> Álvaro.-No creo en tus dichos.
> T. Blas.-Yo tampoco, pero son ciertos. Se me ponen en la mollera y tengo que decirlos... Después, todos nos reímos.
> (...)
> Álvaro.-¡Cállate!
> T. Blas.-¡No puedo! ¡De verdad que no puedo! (pp.35 & 36)

Like Lear's fool, he cannot lie. After announcing "Viene un torbellino como el del polvo de los caminos... y en el centro estás tú con tu hijo" (p.37), Tío Blas disappears in this first act only to reappear again in the penultimate "cuadro", foreseeing the end of Álvaro's tragedy: "Ahora te miro a los ojos y me vienen unas palabras... tontas... que no entiendo. El tiempo ha terminado" (p.83). His prophecy turns out to be accurate; even though Tío Blas himself does not seem to know why he is talking to Álvaro in such a way, his words are actually borne out by the tragic end.

Oriana is also called "loca" and "cabeza trastornada" in *Casi un cuento de hadas*. She is again, paradoxically, the one who foretells with certainty and accuracy what is going to happen to some of the other characters. She knows Leticia and Laura much better than their own parents, the king and queen. She sees in Laura her own image, and therefore foresees that she will end up in the tower, will have to resign herself to remaining unmarried, because the life of the ugly Laura must be a repetition of old Oriana's.

In the first act of the play, when the queen suggests that they consult Oriana on the question of her Highness's marriage, the chancellor Darío calls Oriana a "vulgar charlatana", and the king adds: "¡Peor! ¡Es una loca!"[39] However, we see how she foresees the future with admirable precision. To Leticia's question "¿Cuándo me casaré?" she answers without hesitation: "Dentro de medio año." Leticia, the simple princess, believes Oriana to be a fairy: "¿Eres tú un hada? (*Oriana sonríe sin contestar*) ¡Lo eres! ¡Yo sé que lo eres!" (p.64).

The future that she foretells for Laura ("...todos serán hijos tuyos; muñecos vivos a quienes cuidar..."; "La torre", Laura understands), does not please the elder princess. She resists becoming Oriana's successor, refuses to accept for herself a future which does not coincide with her own plans. Laura, therefore, does not consider Oriana a wise woman, but calls her a liar: "Mentirosa bruja... ¡Cállate! ¡Todo lo que dices son mentiras! ¡Locuras de tu cabeza trastornada! ... ¿La torre? ¡Óyelo bien: nunca la pisaré!" (p.92) Regardless of that firm decision, at the end of the play Laura takes her doll and says goodbye with an "¡Adiós!" that sounds very definitive. It may well be that she is heading for the tower, that Oriana's prophecy is becoming a reality. Once again, the words of a "cabeza trastornada" come true.

Gaspar, in *Diálogo secreto*, is another old man who, like Tío Blas, does not seem to be coherent. His answers to questions make no sense to the other characters unless they are ready to admit certain things. Once they have admitted their responsibility or are ready to examine their behaviour more deeply, Gaspar's words begin to make sense; and the audience will also understand the implication of his scattered remarks. Fabio accepts Gaspar but does not take his presumed wisdom seriously. "A mí él... incluso me divierte. (Ríe) Cuántas veces nos habrá dicho mi padre: ¡'Si le conocierais'! Estos viejos tienen una idea de sí mismos demasiado elevada. Pero están todos guillados."[40]

The memory of Gaspar had also been present in the happy days that Fabio recalls on occasions:

> Fabio.-Cosas de tu abuelo. Según él, Gaspar lo sabía todo. (...)
> Aurorín.-Y ese Gaspar, ¿lo sabía todo?
> Fabio.-(Burlón) Ya lo creo. Lo mirabas y, ¡paf!, te decías: éste lo sabe todo.
> Braulio.-(Grave) Nadie lo sabe todo. Pero él... comprendía. Un chaval extraordinario. (p.57)

Gaspar seems to be incoherent when he hears that Aurora's drug-addicted boyfriend has committed suicide. He mutters words which refer to unemployment and women. They insist on his explaining what his words mean but he is not ready to explain yet. "Cuando bebe es cuando más se le despeja el cacumen", Braulio says. As he has not drunk for two hours ("Como el último vasejo fue hace ya dos horas...", p.63), he remarks on Samuel Cosme's suicide and Fabio's responsibility with apparent incoherence:

> Gaspar.-(Habla para sí, pero se le oye) Natural... Hay tanto paro... (Todos lo miran, sorprendidos.)

And a few seconds later:

> Gaspar.-(Mirando al suelo) Las mujeres son lo más grande del mundo. Ya quisiéramos nosotros... (Fabio menea la cabeza, lamentando su incoherencia.) (p.66)

He is then asked by Aurora whether he has understood what they are talking about, and Braulio insists that he give his opinion, all he says is "Son lo más grande del mundo... Sí... Ya lo creo" (p.67).

When asked about his past by Fabio, his speech becomes more coherent. Fabio wants to find out why the idea of unemployment came to his mind, but he is not ready to answer this time either:

> Fabio.-Oye, Gaspar. ¿Era otra incoherencia lo del paro también llevaba su intríngulis?
> Gaspar.-¿Lo del paro? (*Sonríe*) ¡Ah, sí! ...
> Fabio.-¿Qué querías decir?
> Gaspar.-¡Qué importa! Ni me acuerdo.
> Braulio.-A mí también me ha intrigado lo del paro. No seas zorro, Gaspar, y acláranos lo que querías decir.
> Gaspar.-¡Si no me acuerdo! (p.69)

Nevertheless, allusions to both unemployment and women recur when Aurora is mentioned:

> Gaspar.-Me alegro. Mañana estará mas tranquila. (*Va hacia la izquierda con su leche. Se pasa la mano por el cabello.*) ¡Qué cosas! Y es que... hay tanto paro...
> Fabio.-¿Otra vez con el paro? (*Se levanta*).
> Gaspar.-¿Eh?... Es el miedo... a perder el trabajo (*Ríe*) que yo ya no tengo. Más parado no puedo estar.
> Teresa.-Por fortuna, en esta casa no hay paro.
> Gaspar.-Pero el miedo, Teresa, el miedo...
> (...)
> Gaspar.-Si no fuera por las mujeres... ¡Ah! Sois de abrigo... Fuertes como panteras. (pp.71-2)

In the first part of the play, then, we learn that, on the one hand, Gaspar is supposed to know everything, to have had insight into things and a particularly alert mind. Teresa and Fabio remember Braulio saying: "Pero aquel muchacho era... todo un carácter. ¡Y una lumbrera! Analizaba lo que pasaba en el mundo mejor que muchos políticos veteranos, nos aconsejaba en los momentos difíciles, nos animaba..." (p.50). We also learn that he seems to be particularly bright after he drinks, though other times he is thought to suffer from incoherence. Braulio's trust in his old friend is complete and, as will be seen, Aurora does not seem to think that Gaspar's words are meaningless.

At the beginning of the second part we learn that she has been chatting to him. "En estos días los he sorprendido dos o tres veces charlando en voz baja", Teresa tells her husband. What Teresa still calls "incoherencia" begins to make sense and constitutes eventually the explanation of Fabio's miserable situation, the result of a fatal error.

> Teresa.-Ya sabes lo incoherente que es... cuando no bebe.
> Que las mujeres somos listas como diablos... Que Aurorita
> es más lista que un diablo... Y que no son cosas suyas.
> (p.91)

But Gaspar begins to make full sense. His admiration for both Aurora and Teresa is justified. He is right in calling Aurorita "lista": she guessed that her father was colour-blind ("Daltonismo es lo que a ti te pasa", he tells Fabio, *"terminante"* on p.103), that he had cheated his readers and had tried to deceive even his wife. Teresa is also admired by the old man as he confesses:

> Teresa, tengo setenta años y no puedo echar a mala parte
> mis palabras. Ojalá hubiese encontrado a tiempo... una
> mujer como tú. Pero veinticuatro años de cárcel no dan
> muchas oportunidades. (p.114)

Braulio said that women are "fuertes como panteras". He knows that Teresa was always aware of her husband's weakness, but has chosen to remain by him, to look after him, to save him.

With regard to his comments on unemployment, Gaspar himself explains their meaning: they were directly related to Fabio's fear of losing his position:

> Gaspar.-... todo eso es una solemnísima porquería. Pero
> es general. Se trata de sobresalir, de evitar el paro.
> Fabio.-¿El paro otra vez?

> Gaspar.-Naturalmente, porque a nadie le garantizan las judías aunque las leyes digan que tienes derecho a trabajar y a comer... Hasta los ricachones temen al paro: el que les vendría encima si se quedasen sin dinero... Y tú te mueres de miedo de que descubran tu trapisonda... Un caso vulgar. (p.118)

Fabio was not ready to believe that Gaspar was exceptional but, at the critical moment, he ends up seeking Gaspar's advice. Like Oriana and Tío Blas, Gaspar seems to possess a special capacity to understand reality, or at least has a quicker insight into it. Their expression of this perception of reality can be seen as mere incoherence by other characters who are not as quick to interpret facts and therefore are tempted to call them "mad".

I will now look at certain characters who, without having lost their wits fully or being wrapped in an air of mystery, or at least without being generally classified as madmen, suffer from some sort of hallucination, a state of mind which occasionally leads them to behave in a way which those surrounding them would consider unusual, and which is only the consequence of their deeper understanding of reality.

In *La doble historia del doctor Valmy* Buero makes a psychiatrist present the cases of two couples who were his patients: Mary and Daniel Barnes, and a "Señor" and "Señora". Mary had already been treated by the doctor before she married Daniel. "Yo la había tratado, cuando aún era soltera, de algunos trastornos nerviosos que cedieron fácilmente a los fármacos... y al matrimonio"[41], the doctor dictates to his secretary. Though she had improved, the doctor says later that "en el fondo seguía siendo una persona nerviosa" (p.41). Mary herself tells her ex-pupil Lucila that she has experienced a great deal of suffering: "Yo he sufrido durante muchos años" (p.71). Though Daniel, her husband, appears to need medical treatment, Mary is the one who loses her mind precisely when he thinks that he is about to recover. The deep awareness of the suffering that her husband inflicts on others terrifies her, and makes her so mad that she kills her own husband.

Daniel had initially refused to seek medical help but ends up visiting the doctor. From the beginning, the audience clearly realizes that Daniel has an exhausting and demanding job: "Siempre anda tan ocupado" (p.41); "No tengo tiempo de nada" (p.47); "Estoy siempre atrozmente ocupado" (p.52). He tells the doctor that he works long hours (p.55). His sickness is also due to the nature of his job. "¡Está enfermo porque no lo resiste!", Mary tells the grandmother (p.101). Though at first reluctant to believe the doctor's opinion about the reason for his disease, he eventually acknowledges that he is punishing himself for what he did to Aníbal Marty. As it turns out, the other members of the Security Police have also been affected by their cruel job: "Por la noche grita y se despierta", Mary has heard about Pozner from his wife (p.77); "A Dalton le duele la cabeza"; "Volski padece del estómago y siempre está de mal humor. Marsan es un vicioso" (p.119). Daniel was mad to get used to torturing, to constant physical violence, to grow insensitive to human suffering. He wants to change, but this also is considered madness by others.

Paulus, his boss, calls Daniel "loco" when the latter tells him that he prefers not to be involved with torture any more. In order to gather the courage to speak the truth, one needs to be nearly mad. "Hijo mío, te has vuelto loco", Paulus tells him when Daniel dares to admit his reservations about the institution for which he is working and many of its methods (p.120). Daniel's eyes have been opened to a new aspect of that reality with which he was familiar, and, encouraged by his wife, he speaks. This is considered madness. Doctor Valmy concludes his story by referring to his other patients' madness. At the beginning of the play they came to warn the audience that the story of Daniel and Mary "es falsa ... o por lo menos muy exagerada" (p.37). They advise the spectators to enjoy the story but not to believe it. "Y sobre todo conserven la sonrisa", they recommend (p.38). They reappear just before the resolution of the plot (the action is frozen), to remind us "que la historia es falsa". "¡No pierdan la sonrisa!", they insist (p.127). At this point the doctor says to us that, as he was about to tell the end of the story to a group of patients, this couple prevented him from doing so. He affirms that they suffer from another sort of insanity: the madness of not wanting to accept reality. The story which was told to a group of patients in an asylum is the same as the one we have just heard, and so the audience at that lecture are compared to the audience in the theatre. Thus, in describing the reaction of those two patients, Buero is also describing what could be the reaction of any spectator in the audience. There is a clear implication that we are all mad and, on the other hand, the doctor makes it clear that those spectators who refuse to believe the story suffer from the same insanity as the two patients treated by him. After saying that the couple have been discharged, the doctor explains:

> Sí; pues, en definitiva, ¿podría diagnosticárseles un desequilibrio mental porque ninguno de los dos admitiese la realidad de los sucesos que acabo de relatar? En nuestro extrañísimo mundo todavía no se puede calificar a esa incredulidad de locura. Y hay millones como ellos. Millones de personas que deciden ignorar el mundo en que viven. Pero nadie les llama locos. (p.128)

"Locos", the secretary repeats, obviously calling "locos" all those who decide to ignore the world in which they live. An expert psychiatrist refers to that sort of madness as a disease very common among ordinary people who are not generally considered ill. Madness is relative and depends on the point of view. As we will see, Irene (mad) is not treated as a sick person, whereas Dimas ("sane") ends up in hospital. In *La doble historia*, a psychiatrist calls two of his patients "locos" and then lets them go, perhaps because they are no madder than most of us.

In his *Madness and Civilization*, Michel Foucault discusses madness in the time of Goya. He calls that time the "classical period", which, - he says -, "from Willis to Pinel, from the frenzies of Racine's Oreste to Sade's *Juliette* and the Quinta del Sordo, covers precisely that epoch in which the exchange between madness and reason modifies its language, and in a radical manner" (p.XII). He states that the Goya of the *Disparates* and the Quinta del Sordo addresses himself to the madness of man cast into darkness; "it is indeed a question of that *Sleep of Reason* which Goya, in 1797, had already made the first image of the 'universal idiom'; it is a question of a night which is doubtless that of classical unreason, that triple night into which Orestes sank. But in that night, man communicates with what is deepest in himself, and with what is most solitary" (p.280). He also establishes that it is precisely through madness that a work of art, Goya's work of art, makes the world feel guilty, question itself. It shows the inadequacy of that world. Goya, like his art, was surrounded by darkness, and his work becomes the expression of his own madness. "Through madness, a work that seems to drown in the world, to reveal there its non-sense, and to transfigure itself with the features of pathology alone, actually engages within itself the world's time, masters it, and leads it; by the madness which interrupts it, a work of art opens a void, a moment of silence, a question without answer, provokes a breach without reconciliation where the world is forced to question itself. ...through the mediation of madness, it is the world that becomes culpable (for the first time in the Western world) in relation to the work of art" (p.288).[42]

In *El sueño de la razón* other characters relate Goya's madness to his courage. Calomarde is the first to refer to the painter as insane: "¡Un enfermo sin juicio, señor, como toda la cobarde caterva de poetas y pintores! Reparad en cuántos de ellos han escapado a Francia." "Él no", the king replies. "Ese baturro no tiembla tan fácilmente. Y siempre fue un soberbio."[43] They call his courage madness and pride.

Leocadia calls the painter a "viejo demente" (p.124), even though later on she will have to admit that what she calls madness is just a lack of fear: "¡La locura de Francho es justamente ésa! ¡Que se niega a un cambio de aires! ¡Que no tiene miedo." "¡Hay que estar loco para no temblar! Y yo estoy muy cuerda, y tengo miedo" (pp.127 & 128). Referring to Erasmus' *Praise of Folly*, Roland H. Bainton comments that "Folly is spontaneity, a certain recklessness, an uncalculating readiness to take risks. She overrides prudence, yet is the highest prudence. For she delivers men alike from fear and shame and thus frees them to embark on great enterprises. Without her, what cities, what empires would ever have been built?"[44]

Don Quixote's madness has also been related to his daring. Ramón de Garciasol points out: "A partir de la aventura del rebuzno el libro impar camina ladera abajo de la melancolía. Don Quijote huye ante el pueblo armado para vengar un agravio real o supuesto. ... Aquí hace crisis la locura quijotesca. Luego, a capítulo seguido, renuncia a libertar a las personas que padecen o pueden padecer fuerza en el castillo que resultó aceña. ¿Cobarde? ¿O es que empieza la aurora de la cordura? ¿Es que para ser valiente hace falta estar loco? ¿La cordura da cobardía?"[45] That seems to be Leocadia's belief, so she tries to persuade Goya "que se humille, que se humille" (p.159).

When the painter insists on his decision not to leave Spain, Duaso asks him: "¿Está loco?" Goya answers: "No estoy loco" (p.164). However, he will end up admitting: "Estoy delirando. ¡Pero lo sé!" (p.174). He is another of those madmen who refer to their own madness, like Don Quixote.

Goya's sickness is similar to Eloy's in that he has learned to judge the world surrounding him, has discovered that he lives in "un país al borde del sepulcro... cuya razón sueña" (p.211). It is the country that is crazy: it is sleeping and refuses to wake up. The painter is fully awake; perhaps, as Arrieta suggests, his madness constitutes also his strength ("su fuerza"), his ability to paint those absurdities that horrify the sane. To try to cure that great madman of his madness would be as much as wanting "que un gigante se vuelva un pigmeo porque yo soy un pigmeo" (p.191), depriving him of his courage, of his readiness to portray his profound and accurate perception of Spain.

When the knight from La Mancha wanted to show his courage, others took that nerve for madness. In Part II, Chapter 17, we see him ready to face two lions. Sancho fears his master's death. He has nevertheless already learned at this stage the difference between madness and courage. He expresses it in clear terms that Leocadia could very well envy. The Gentleman in Green asks Sancho: "Pues, ¿tan loco es vuestro amo que teméis y creéis que se ha de tomar con tan fieros animales?" Sancho replies: "No es loco, sino atrevido". The knight himself boasts of being courageous ("¿Hay encantos que valgan contra la verdadera valentía?"). He tries to make the Gentleman in Green understand: "... menos mal será que el que es valiente toque y suba al punto de temerario que no que baje y toque en el punto de cobarde." If not even rashness is to be compared to madness, much less can real courage be taken for insanity. But the brave man has to take the risk of being accused of madness, as we have also seen with don Francisco de Goya.

Julio, in *Llegada de los dioses*, is again one of those characters who stand out from their environment precisely because of their acute perception of reality. He is himself afraid of going mad ("A menudo son tan verdaderos que... temo." "¿Por tu cordura?").[46] Like Eloy, Julio cannot fail to refer with terror to the terrible disaster that seems to threaten our world. His almost voluntary blindness contributes to that chilling, crude and clear perception which makes him talk. Nuria screams, terrified: "¡Estás delirando! ¡No pasa nada! ¡Y si pasase lo sabríamos y escaparíamos!" (p.259). Hers is the voice of sanity, or of naïvety, which exclaims: "No pasa nada". Felipe also shouts at him: "¿Estás loco? ¡Nuria es mi ahijada!" (p.265). He was living a constant lie. His son has learned the truth, but he knows that, when he is brave enough to proclaim it, he will be accused of madness. That is the only way in which they will find an excuse to close their eyes in order not to see a truth that hurts: "Locuras mías, dirían todos. Y tú no los desmentirías. Todos se pondrían, y tú el primero, gafas oscuras y algodón en los oídos..." (p.318). His father's reaction at once proves what Julio has been trying to explain. He at first refuses to accept his son's explanation, so he pretends not to understand: "¿Ves como deliras, Julito? Sólo tú llevas aquí gafas oscuras." Julio is not as strong as Goya; he doubts, vacillates, is even frightened by his own visions. Verónica will make him see that what he considers his madness will become his strength, his mystery ("¡Son mi locura!" "Serán tu fuerza y tu misterio", p.342). In fact, his pictures have already shown his power to reveal the truth, in the same way as Goya's madness was his brilliant, overflowing and enviable creative force.

Juan Luis, in *Jueces en la noche*, apprehends the truth little by little. When mistakes and failures of his past come back to his conscience, he is eager to make up for them, mainly for his wife's sake. It is then that he is accused of madness by those who had contributed to his corruption in the past. When he dares to call Ginés "asesino", Ginés responds calling him "loco":

> Juan Luis.-Porque tú ya no ejecutas. Tú organizas. Ginés.-¿Estás loco? (...) ... porque en tu delirio...[47]

Juan Luis imagines the characters of his past coming back to him, accompanying him constantly, reproaching him for his mistakes. With reference to this, don Jorge says to him: "Imaginar un insistente acompañante no es demencia. Sólo sobreexcitación... Es advertir lo que pocos notan: cuánto se parece la cordura a la locura" (p.132). Through this imaginary don Jorge, Juan Luis is trying to find an explanation of his state of mind. His real madness was in fact that of living a continuous lie, trying to make happy a woman he had managed to marry only though a dirty trick. He rids himself of that "sanity" only when the images of his past remind him of his mistakes; his mind is disturbed by doubts and remorse. It is only now that he is recovering his sanity, he is beginning to face up to his own responsibility.

The characters who most resemble Don Quixote are those who lose their mind fully. Again, behind their insanity there lies a different sort of wisdom that yields truth for the others. This is the case of Irene, el Padre, Eloy, Tomás and Rosa. Buero admits to the quixotic nature of *Irene o el tesoro*: "Alguna obra... evidentemente quijotesca puede ser *Irene o el tesoro*, en la cual hay una enloquecida que ve cosas" (Interview). Irene also refers to her own madness: "Loca. Estoy loca".[48] The interpretation that Daniel gives of her madness is quite enlightening: "¿Qué vale la razón? Esta engañosa razón de tejas para abajo puede ser quizá una gran locura" (p.175). In actual fact, the logic of Dimas and his family is very close to insanity, because it is obsessive. Méndez explains:

> **Todos** estamos **locos** sin darnos cuenta. Ella enloquece por el niño que no tuvo; él por el dinero que desea a todas horas; Aurelia es capaz de enloquecer por un profesor sin cátedra o por un serial de radio... Otras mujeres enloquecen por minucias... Por ir al cine, por presumir ante las vecinas, por comprarse medias caras o pañuelos de seda... Y hay quien enloquece por vengarse. Por vengarse de quien la engañó; aunque haga muchos años; ¡por devolver engaño por engaño, desgracia por desgracia! (p.186)

Justina truly proves to be mad with ambition and malice. She had emphatically stated: "¡Pero es ella la loca, no él!" In spite of this she makes up her mind to put her own husband into the mental asylum, justifying her action with an opposite argument: "Era necesario. Porque él era el loco, él. Loco por el ahorro. Loco de tacañería" (p.190). Dimas had really lost his mind by his meanness, and had driven his daughter and wife mad as well. He seems to suffer from the type of madness to which Erasmus referred, which was sent from hell by the Furies and made people insatiably greedy. But that is not the sort of insanity Daniel is talking about when he explains to Irene: "Cuando estudiaba comprendí a Santa Teresa y a San Juan de la Cruz. También ellos vivían en un mundo donde les pasaban cosas maravillosas... locos les decían. Y es que eran santos" (p.176). Maybe this is the kind of madness Unamuno had in mind when he addressed Don Quixote in these terms: " 'He aquí el hombre', dijeron en burla a Cristo nuestro Señor; 'he aquí el loco', dirán de ti, mi señor Quijote, y serás el loco, el único, el Loco"[49]; or when he almost prays to him: "¡Oh, Don Quijote, mi San Quijote!"[50] Both heroes and saints can often fall into the same category; they are called mad by those who are contented with mediocrity, those who would not be ready to change. Eugene Ionesco's comments on mediocrity are very telling:

Les gens pensent aujourd'hui à peu près à égale distance
entre le bien et le mal, dans ce mi-chemin entre le faux et
le vrai, mais ils se tiennent plus ou moins tranquilles dans
leur médiocrité. La non-médiocrité est l'héroisme et la
sainteté.[51]

That is why also St Teresa and St John of the Cross would have been
called mad. T.S. Eliot compares saints and madmen in that they are both
exceptional. In his *The Cocktail Party* Edward and Lavinia go to the
psychiatrist to seek advice. The doctor suggests that they "make the
best of a bad job." "The best of a bad job is all any of us make of it -
except of course, the saints - such as those who go to the
sanatorium."[52]

H.G. Wells also seems to think that the sort of knowledge his mad
hero Preemby had is almost mystical: "... he knew his knowledge of it
[Atlantis] was of a different order from common knowledge, more
intuitive, mystical, profound" (p.71). There is something mystical in
Irene's madness too. She discovers that there is something marvellous
in reality, which is worth exploring and enjoying. Her wisdom is more
profound, like Mr Preemby's. La Voz in *Irene* states: "La sabiduría de
los hombres es locura y su locura puede ser sabiduría" (p.192). The
mystics' wisdom was in fact called madness. Wisdom comprises all sides
of reality, not only a part of it. Irene and Daniel share in their
knowledge of the marvellous. Dimas, Justina and Amelia, by contrast,
have a narrow, partial view of reality. La Voz explains this mystery to
Juanito, who even doubted his own existence: "Para la loca sabiduría
de los hombres tú y yo somos un engaño. Pero el mundo tiene dos
caras... y desde la nuestra, que engloba a la otra, ¡ésta es la realidad!
¡ésta es la verdadera realidad!"

Don Quixote also regards as ignorant those who have never heard of
knight-errants, because they ignore that aspect of reality. In Part I,
Chapter 45, he exclaims:

¡Ah, gente infame, digna por vuestro bajo y vil
entendimiento que el cielo no os comunique el valor que se

encierra en la caballería andante, no os dé a entender el pecado e ignorancia en que estáis, en no reverenciar la sombra, cuando más la asistencia, de cualquier caballero andante!

That side of reality which constitutes the knight's life, the reason for his existence, is actually unknown to many. They should realize, according to Don Quixote, that this is their great limitation. Those who have not discovered yet that something marvellous surrounds them, are the real madmen. That is why Dimas, not Irene, turns out to be the madman to be confined in the mental asylum. Buero emphasizes the relativity of madness by leaving the ending open, and providing two interpretations for Irene's departure. As we will see, he also does this in *Caimán*. The spectator is not told where real madness lies but is left free to decide which madness he prefers.

The Father in *El tragaluz* is the only Buero character, apart from Dimas, who actually ends up in an asylum. In him we find another strange, mysterious character, who says very little but knows and judges. As Martha Halsey puts it, "Ambiguous and mysterious, he is both a pitiable man and all-knowing judge."[53] He is the one who goes furthest in his desire to know, to apprehend reality in all its depth; he is concerned with every particular individual. On examining his postcards and magazines, he intends to find out the identity of each person who features in them. He is irritated by those who are contented with a superficial knowledge of reality:

> El Padre. La señorita ya está lista. Pero no sé quién es.
> La Madre. Pues una linda señorita. ¿No te basta?
> El Padre. ¡No, no basta! (p.26)

He again shouts at Vicente when he refers to one of the figures on the postcard as "uno cualquiera". "¡No!", the Father replies emphatically (p.29). And, on examining the postcard through his magnifying glass, he says: "No está muerto. Y esta mujer que cruza ¿quién es? Claro.

Vosotros no lo sabéis. Yo, sí." "Se cree Dios", Vicente remarks, stifling his laughter (p.30).

In front of his eldest son the Father says that his own house is a restaurant: "¡es un restaurante!" (p.31). Even though one might think that this makes no sense, it is true that the house is for Vicente a place where he goes to pay, and where his "ensaimadas" are always ready. The basement is not home for Vicente. But he does not want to understand. That is why he tries to find the explanation for his father's "disparates" in his disease: "¡Es una esclerosis senil! ... Es como un niño que dice bobadas" (pp.34-5), he says, even though he should be the one to make sense of his father's words.

The mother refuses to admit to the origin of her husband's madness. She prefers to believe that he "no se acuerda de nada"; "Palabras que le vienen de pronto... Pero no se acuerda de nada", she repeats (p.52). Mario is the only one who dares to acknowledge that his father is not just "un pobre demente". And he tries to explain: "Un hombre capaz de preguntar lo que él pregunta... tiene que ser mucho más que un viejo imbécil" (p.56). Mario has obviously understood the profound meaning of "la pregunta tremenda". That is why Vicente compares him to their father: "Está loco"; "... usted no entiende... El otro loco, mi hermano..." (p.103).

The Father went mad as a consequence of the family tragedy after the war; Mario is trying to clarify the causes for his insanity, and also wants the guilty one to admit his responsibility. When Vicente does so, the Father is the one who executes the sentence. Vicente pays with his life for Elvirita's death and for all his other crimes. The Father, once confined in the asylum, continues to ask the great question but "está tranquilo" (p.106). Mario, the second madman according to Vicente, asks the great question too: "¿Y nosotros? ¿Somos alguien?" (p.107). Once again, the madness of a character is due to his deep knowledge of reality. The mother had preferred to live a feigned happiness rather than go mad herself. When one understands reality in all its depth, above all when that reality happens to be terrible, one can lose one's mind if one is not endowed with great fortitude. The mother has seen it happening to her husband. That is why she pretends not to know, not to understand.

On their part, the Investigadores help the audience to realize the relevance of the Father's madness. To them, it is quite clear that the Father lost his mind because he was one of the few who dared to ask the "pregunta tremenda". Only a lucid mind like the Father's can recover the infinite value of an insignificant action:

> ELLA.-La acción más oculta o insignificante puede ser descubierta un día. (...) El misterioso espacio todo lo preserva.
> ÉL.-Cada suceso puede ser percibido desde algún lugar.
> ELLA.-Y a veces, sin aparatos, desde alguna mente lúcida.
> (p.43)

From a distant future, the Investigadores tell us of "la importancia infinita del caso singular"; after centuries, they have been able to recognize the value of the "pregunta tremenda" ("¿Quién es ése?"). Buero makes us look at ourselves again. The minds which we now call "locos" may well be the "mentes lúcidas" which we fail to recognize. Those lucid minds who dared to ask the great question were at the same time obscure individuals to whom no one would have listened because they were considered insane.[54] "Las personas que guardaban ya en su corazón la gran pregunta. Pero debieron de ser hombres oscuros, habitantes más o menos alucinados de semisótanos o de otros lugares parecidos" (p.88). "Él" and "Ella" want to share in that hallucination. The purpose of their own experiment is to ask the great question, and to look for an answer. They are ready to try to accomplish the task which an insane old man had started in a dark basement. It remains an insane task; but one of which they are proud:

> ELLA.-Reasumir el pasado vuelve más lento nuestro avance, pero también más firme.
> ÉL.-Compadecer, uno por uno, a cuantos vivieron, es una tarea imposible, loca. Pero esa locura es nuestro orgullo.
> (p.87)

It is worthwhile looking for an answer to their question, although it may be a difficult, even maddening, task: "Siempre es mejor saber, aunque sea doloroso", "Él" tells us.

The madman in *Mito*, of course, is Eloy. As Martha Halsey says, "many of Buero's protagonists are dreamers or visionaries who bear the indelible stamp of don Quixote. Upon none, however, is the Cervantine influence so strong as upon Eloy, the old actor in *Myth*... who is considered mad by his fellow-players because he believes in flying-saucers and Martians."[55]

The electrician calls him elliptically "[loco] de remate" (p.186). The same opinion is held by Figura 1ª ("¡Porque tú estás loco!", p.199), and the chorus of "Hombres" ("¡Estás loco! ¡De remate!"). Eloy's insanity is what Martha Halsey calls "a sort of lucid madness." He feels he needs to tell everything he has learned about the world that surrounds him, mainly after his fellow-players' trick: "Deliro frente a un mundo que delira/ mientras ríe y se aturde sin saberlo" (p.214). After the terrible orgy, his madness is of a different sort; it has now become daring and courage, so much so that he dares not only to proclaim his views, but also to die for them. Eloy has discovered the evils of this world and dreams of a better one, without war or bombs, etc.,... He very closely resembles H.G. Wells' hero. Toby, who certainly admires Preemby, refers to him in the following terms: "He thinks he's a certain Mesopotamian monarch called Sargon". And then he expounds his views:

> The Distinction of Rich and Poor is to be Abolished Altogether. Women are to be freed from all Disadvantages. There is to be No More War. He gets at the roots of things every time.
> We don't want to be poor and we don't want to be hurt or worried by war, but that's not wanting to end those things. He wants to end them.
> ..., all the great old things, justice, faith, obedience, mutual service. As it was in Ancient Sumeria. He is rather wonderful. (pp.188-189)

Mr Preemby sees the solution to our present civilization in Ancient Sumeria; Eloy in Mars; Don Quixote in chivalry. They are madmen who get to the roots of things.

As Iglesias Feijoo points out, in Eloy we have another "loco lúcido; sus ideales podrán parecer quiméricos pero no puede ignorarse que son los mismos que, ya cumplidos, vimos en el mundo de los investigadores de *El tragaluz*: un mundo sin guerras en el que no se recurra a la fuerza sino que venere 'la vida'."[56]

Eloy's madness then is that sort of disease which has a purpose; that, like Mr Preemby's, is there to yield knowledge for others. Eloy is ready to die, so is Ismael: "Tú te mueres.../ Yo moriré también. Somos dos locos" (p.238). This is the madness which is to be envied.

In *La Fundación* Tomás also creates his own imaginary world, which the spectator shares totally. He genuinely believes that his delusions are real. In his madness he is happy to enjoy a beautiful landscape, an imaginary music, etc: "Es una melodía tan serena como el fresco de la madrugada, cuando asoma el sol. Da gusto oírla en un día tan luminoso como éste. ¡Si vieras como brilla el campo! Los verdes, el lago... Parecen joyas."[57] The presence of his girlfriend, Berta, is an essential part of his delusion. He makes her appear when he needs her. He does not doubt that she will come; her presence depends entirely on his imagination: "¡Yo sé que vendrás!", he tells his imaginary Berta (p.143). Tomás thinks that he is living in the ideal world they had always dreamt of, a world of total happiness: "Es hermoso vivir aquí. Siempre habíamos soñado con un mundo como el que al fin tenemos" (p.163). Like other madmen, he may be deceived, but he is truthful. "¡Nunca he mentido!", he tells his cell-mates (p.198); "Puedo enloquecer, pero mentirte, no... Mentirte, no" (p.231).

Little by little he starts noticing that he is the only one who sees certain things in the cell. His delusion vanishes gradually; his cigarettes, television, music, wine glasses, camera, etc. When he finds out that they have had a corpse in the room for six days, he realizes that none of the others ever heard the "sick" prisoner ask for food and drink. His cell-mates try to wake him out of the unreal dream, of his madness. He is afraid of accepting his own disease: "¿Insinúas que... estoy enfermo?" (p.192). He is reluctant to put the fantasy he has invented to the test; he does not want to awaken from it. When Tulio challenges him to try to open the door of the cell, he says "No me atrevo" (p.175). "No creo que finja. Es que no quiere despertar", Lino remarks (p.210). In his confusion, Tomás thinks that the others are also losing their mind: "¿Es que estamos perdiendo la razón?" (p.211).

Before he finally accepts that he had invented his own world, he turns to Berta. He needs her to prove that his "reality" is not false. But Berta herself is not the same any more:

> Tomás.-Estos locos dicen... que lo van a matar. Pero es
> mentira. Si tú estás aquí, es mentira.
> Berta.-Tú sabrás.
> Tomás.-Ya no sé nada, Berta. ¿Por qué la Fundación es
> tan inhóspita? ¿Tú lo sabes?
> Berta.-Sí. Y tú.

Tomás's Dulcinea disappoints him and so plays an essential role in his cure. The same could be said of Don Quixote's cure. Neither the Dulcinea in the Cave of Montesinos, nor the Dulcinea Sancho presents him with, corresponds to Don Quixote's ideal. Tomás's girlfriend comes to visit him in prison too, but she is extremely different from the girl Tomás has placed in his Fundación, who also becomes mysterious. After her last "visit", Tomás eventually realizes that she had not really been there on that occasion, and therefore that she had never been there at all. "Nunca vino. Estoy delirando" (p.217). Like the Father in *El tragaluz*, and Irene, Tomás was trying to take refuge. As Martín (*Las Meninas*) says, going mad "siempre es un remedio".[58] Tomás could not forgive himself for betraying his colleagues and, after trying to take his own life, he decided to take refuge in his imaginary world of comfort, beauty and serenity. "Tu mente creó la inmensa fantasía de la Fundación: desde el paisaje que veías en el muro hasta el rutilante cuarto de baño", Asel explains to him (pp.227-8). Tomás is surprised that he is able to discuss his own madness: "A eso los médicos lo llamáis locura. Pero si lo soy, ¿cómo lo reconozco?" (p.223). The gradual process of his cure coincides with the understanding of his madness on the others' part. "Tú no estás loco. ¡Tú estás vivo! Como yo", Tulio tells him (p.205). Asel understands and is almost jealous of Tomás's madness:

> Si Tomás no fingía, su mundo era verdadero para él, y mucho más grato que este horror en que nos empeñamos que él también viva. Si la vida es siempre tan corta y tan pobre y él la enriquecía así, quizá no hay otra riqueza y los locos somos nosotros por no imitarle. (p.212)

Don Quixote also knew how to create his own world of greater beauty. One could never say that his life in the world created by his own imagination was not real and tremendously intense. Referring to his beloved Dulcinea, he tells Sancho: "Y para concluir con todo, yo imagino que todo lo que digo es así, sin que sobre ni falte nada, y píntola en la imaginación como la deseo, así en la belleza como en la principalidad, y no la llega Elena, ni la alcanza Lucrecia..." (I,23). Nobody could reproach the knight for having created such a marvellous lady in his imagination. His world, like Tomás's, is real for him and his life is thus marvellously enriched. We could say, with Asel, that those people are mad who do not imitate such madmen, who do not find, like Irene, something marvellous around them.

Tomás realizes that once he is cured, he cannot continue to take refuge in fantasy. However, Asel advises him to retain part of his madness, his "paisaje". "El paisaje sí era verdadero" (p.241). That landscape, the memory of the ideal world which he had imagined, will render him capable of striving to attain it, as will be seen later.

The mad character in *Caimán* is Rosa. She imagines and firmly believes that her daughter Carmela is still alive. Néstor, her husband, tries to make her believe the facts. But not even the fact that a corpse has been found which seems to be Carmela's convinces the anguished Rosa of the reality of her little daughter's death.

Rosa's madness is discussed again and again during the play. "¿Estás loca?", Néstor screams. "¡Eso es lo que tú crees, que estoy loca! ¡Tú quieres sacarme de la locura de creerla viva! ¡Pero no lo conseguirás!"[59], Rosa answers, calling her husband "pobre loco de la sensatez".

Rosa admits to her madness, which is a hopeful one; Néstor's common sense is full of resignation. That is why Rosa resists being sane, refuses to accept reality: in her own world, like in Tomás's, there is room for hope. When Néstor repeats "¿Estás loca?", Rosa admits "¡Sí!" (p.98). She wants to be mad: that is the only way in which she can still hope that her daughter will come back.

Dionisio supports and understands Rosa, because he is also one of those who live in hope. He hopes for "... una mujer imposible... capaz de amar mi pierna destrozada" (p.57). After Néstor's statement "¡El mayor peligro para Rosa es el de no aceptar la realidad!", Dionisio challenges him : "¿Y sabes tú cuál es la realidad?" (p.104). If an objective and well defined reality does not exist, madness and sanity not only "se parecen" but are the same thing. Rosa's obstinate attitude is madness according to Néstor; Néstor's sensible view of the situation is insane according to Rosa. Who is sane and who is mad? How can we judge if we do not know which is the reality? Two interpretations are given of Rosa's departure, as in the case of Irene's. The relativity of madness is again emphasized by Buero, who does not provide an answer for his audience.

In a similar fashion, Don Quixote and Sancho call each other mad. In Part I, Chapter 25, the squire admonishes his master: "... quien oyere decir a vuestra merced que una bacía de barbero es el yelmo de Mambrino, y que no salga de este error en más de cuatro días, ¿qué ha de pensar sino que quien tal dice y afirma debe de tener güero el juicio?" In Chapter 36 he tries to explain that the knight had not killed any giant as he thought, and this time it is his master who accuses Sancho of being mad: "Y ¿qué es lo que dices, loco? ... ¿Estás en tu seso?" But it is madness to try to convince a brave knight who thinks he has just killed a huge and wicked giant, that no giant was in fact involved. In Part I

Sancho suffers what Don Quixote would also agree to describe as "la locura de la sensatez."

It can then be said in general terms that those of Buero's characters who are called "mad", are usually more "discretos" than their accusers. On the one hand, they look at reality with an open mind, disposed to find the truth. On the other hand, many of Buero's "locos" are characterized by their daring, the courage of someone who knows that he has the truth; or by the zeal of someone who has found his or her own world and tries to encourage others to share in its beauty, in its richness.

As will be discussed in Chapter Five, many of those accused of lunacy also possess an immense interest in the life of others. Erasmus states in his *Praise of Folly*:

> He who loves intensely no longer lives in himself but in whatever he loves, and the more he can depart from himself and enter into the other, the happier he is. And when a mind yearns towards travelling out of the body, ... you doubtless and with accuracy, call the state of it madness. ... So far as the love is more perfect, the madness is greater and more delightful. (p.172)

In that sense, it is only normal that those who pursue their own selfish interests and do not want the wretchedness of their lives to be known, accuse those who are generous of being mad.

"La falta que él pensaba que hacía en el mundo su tardanza" made the knight leave his land and launch himself in search of adventures which would earn him the title of "loco". What Don Quixote called "hazañas" the world called "desatinos". In Part II, Chapter 2, Sancho informed Don Quixote of what was being said about both: "... el vulgo tiene a vuestra merced por grandísimo loco, y a mí por no menos mentecato". Don Quixote's calm reply is relevant also to our study of Buero's view of madness:

> Mira, Sancho, -dijo don Quijote-: dondequiera que está la virtud en eminente grado, es perseguida. Pocos o ninguno

> de los famosos varones que pasaron dejó de ser calumniado
> de la malicia.

If Don Quixote earned that "calumny", Buero's "locos" will not be
spared it.

NOTES TO CHAPTER I

1. Fernando Rielo, *Teoría del Quijote. Su mística hispánica* (Madrid: Studia Humanitatis, 1982), pp.68-9.

2. Miguel de Unamuno, *Vida de Don Quijote y Sancho* (Buenos Aires: Espasa-Calpe Argentina, 1946), pp.29 & 30.

3. Rielo, *Teoría del Quijote*, p.124.

4. Unamuno, *Vida*, p.149.

5. Salvador de Madariaga, *Don Quixote. An Introductory Essay in Psychology* (London: Oxford University Press, 1961), p.39.

6. Madariaga, *Don Quixote*, p.109.

7. Anthony Close, 'Don Quixote's Love for Dulcinea: A Study of Cervantine Irony', *Bulletin of Hispanic Studies* 50 (1973), 237-55 (pp.253-4).

8. "Así pues, en la concepción cervantina va implícita la idea de que la locura tiene una significación trascendente, y que el delirio en sí no es sino la idea creadora desviada y pervertida." (Mauro Olmeda, *El ingenio de Cervantes y la locura de Don Quijote* (Madrid: Ed. Ayuso, 1973), p.261.)

9. Otis H. Green, 'El "ingenioso" hidalgo', *Hispanic Review* 25 (1957), p.176.

In his study of *El licenciado Vidriera* Agustín González de Amezúa also maintains that Cervantes was ahead of his time in his notion of madness: "El genio cervantino, aun en estas cosas tan alejadas de la literatura, se adelantó a su tiempo, con atisbos y adivinaciones que los estudios modernos han confirmado como exactos." (*Cervantes, creador de la novela corta española* (Madrid: Consejo Superior de Investigaciones Científicas, 1982), Tomo II, p.169.)

10. Green, 'El "ingenioso" hidalgo', p.177.

11. Juan Huarte de San Juan, *Examen de ingenios para las ciencias* (Madrid: Editora Nacional, 1977), p.40.

12. In *Cuadernos Americanos* (Mayo-Junio 1944), 82-92, quoted by Olmeda, p.259.

13. R.D. Laing, *The Divided Self* (London: Tavistock Publications, 1969), p.37.

14. "I am aware that the man who is said to be deluded may be in his delusion telling me the truth, and this in no equivocal or metaphorical sense, but quite literally, and that the cracked mind of the schizophrenic may let in light which does not enter the intact minds of many sane people whose minds are closed" (Laing, *The Divided Self*, p.28).

15. Huarte, *Examen de ingenios*, p.107.

16. "De un rústico labrador sabré yo decir que, estando frenético, hizo delante de mí un razonamiento encomendando a los circunstantes su salud, y que mirasen por sus hijos y mujer si de aquella enfermedad fuese Dios servido llevarle, con tantos lugares retóricos, con tanta elegancia y policia de vocablos como Cicerón lo podía hacer delante del Senado. De lo cual admirados los circunstantes, me preguntaron de dónde podía venir tanta elocuencia y sabiduría a un hombre que estando en sanidad no sabía hablar; y acuérdome que respondí que la oratoria es una ciencia que nace de cierto punto de calor, y que este rústico labrador le tenía ya por razón de la enfermedad" (Huarte, p.107).

17. "De otro frenético podré también afirmar que, en más de ocho días, jamás habló palabra que no le buscase luego su consonante, y las más veces hacia una copla redondilla muy bien formada" (Huarte, p.107).

18. Huarte, pp.108-9.

In *Don Quixote* Antonio Moreno also reproaches Sansón Carrasco for trying to bring the knight back to his village so that he is cured there. He, however, puts charity before his natural desire to enjoy Don Quixote's follies:
"¡Oh señor! dijo don Antonio, Dios os perdone el agravio que habéis hecho a todo el mundo en querer volver cuerdo al más gracioso loco que hay en él. ¿No veis, señor, que no podrá llegar el provecho que cause la cordura de Don Quijote a lo que llega el gusto que da con sus desvaríos? ... y si no fuera contra la caridad, diría que nunca sane Don Quijote; porque con su salud, no solamente perdemos sus gracias, sino las de Sancho Panza, su escudero, que cualquiera dellas puede volver a alegrar a la misma melancolía" (II,65).

19. Huarte, p.109.

20. "Multi etiam propterea quod ille calor sedi mentis in vicino est, morbis vesaniae implicantur aut instinctu lymphatico infervenscunt; ex puo Silliciae efficintur, et Bacchae, et omnes qui divino spiraculo instigari creduntur, cum scilices id, non morbo, sed naturali intemperie accidit. Marcus civis Syracusanus, poeta etiam praestantior eram dum mente alienatur. Et quibus nimius ille calor remissus ad medio critatem

fit, ii prosus melancholici quidem, se longe prudentiores" (Huarte, p.110).

21. Erasmus, *Praise of Folly*, in John P. Dolan, *The Essential Erasmus* (New York: the New American Library, 1964), p.112.

22. Michel Foucault, *Madness and Civilization. A History of Insanity in the Age of Reason* (New York: Random House, Inc., April 1973), p.80.

23. Roland H. Bainton, *Erasmus of Christendom* (London: Collins, 1970), p.122.

24. A.K. Forcione on *El licenciado Vidriera*, in *Cervantes and the Humanist Vision* (Princeton University Press, 1982), p.263.

25. Cervantes, *El licenciado Vidriera*, in *Novelas Ejemplares* (Madrid: Espasa-Calpe, S.A., 1969), vol.II, p.33.

26. William Shakespeare, *King Lear*, edited by Kenneth Muir (London and New York: Routledge, 1989), p.169.

27. Aeschylus, *The Oresteian Trilogy* (Harmondsworth: Penguin Books, Ltd., 1972), pp.79 & 84.

28. F. García Lorca, *La casa de Bernarda Alba*, edited by H. Ramsden (Manchester University Press, 1983), p.84.

29. Fyodor Dostoyevsky, *The Idiot* (London: J.M. Dent and Sons Ltd., New York: E.P. Dutton & co., 1914), p.25.

30. See *The Idiot*, pp.83, 113 & 147.

31. Maxime Chevalier admits that the prince is a clearly quixotic character, though he does not seem to think that he constitutes a representative example of Cervantes' influence on Dostoyevsky, because the prince's mental disturbance is not caused by reading: "Aparte queda el príncipe Mishkin, figura claramente quijotesca, pero personaje cuyos aturdimientos nada tienen que ver con la locura libresca del caballero manchego. A pesar de que se le suele evocar en cuanto se esboza un paralelismo entre el autor del *Quijote* y el del *Idiota*, Mishkin no representa, a mi entender, caso tan demostrativo de la influencia cervantina en la obra de Dostoievski como los que se citan aquí (Maxime Chevalier, 'Cervantes, Rousseau, Dostoievsky', *Ínsula* 538 (Octubre 1991), 15-16 (p.15).).
I think that the reference to Dostoyevsky's idiot is perfectly justified when the parallels between Cervantes and the Russian novelist are discussed.

32. Olmeda, *El ingenio de Cervantes y la locura de don Quijote*, pp.254-5.

33. *Teatro español actual*, pp.74, 76-8.

34. H.G. Wells, *Christina Alberta's Father* (London: The Hogarth Press, 1985), p.143.

35. Amezúa, *Cervantes, creador de la novela corta española*, p.168.

36. Pedro Laín Entralgo, 'La vida humana en el teatro de Buero Vallejo', in *Antonio Buero Vallejo. Premio Miguel de Cervantes 1986* (Madrid: Biblioteca Nacional, Abril-Junio 1987), 21-27 (p.21).

37. Laín Entralgo, 'La vida humana en el teatro de Buero Vallejo', p.23.

38. Antonio Buero Vallejo, *El terror inmóvil*, Cuadernos de la Cátedra de Teatro de la Universidad de Murcia (Murcia: Secretariado de Publicaciones, 1979), p.35.
(Further references to this play are given after quotations in the text.)

39. Antonio Buero Vallejo, *Casi un cuento de hadas* (Madrid: Narcea, S.A., 1983), p.57.
(Further references are given in the text.)

40. Antonio Buero Vallejo, *Diálogo secreto* (Madrid: Espasa-Calpe, S.A., 1985), pp.49-50.
(Further references are given in the text.)

41. Antonio Buero Vallejo, *La doble historia del Doctor Valmy. Mito* (Madrid: Espasa-Calpe, S.A., 1984), p.40.
(Further references to both plays are given in the text.)

42. In his discussion of *El concierto de San Ovidio* Johnston refers to the relevance Buero attaches to art: "Buero has stressed the dual function of art, emphasizing that while exploding of myth and false assumptions in the name of truth is relatively easy, the real validity of any art form lies in its construction of new possibilities, of images of increasingly relevant ways of focusing faith" (David Johnston, Antonio Buero Vallejo. El concierto de San Ovidio, Critical Guides to Spanish Texts (London: Grant and Cutler, 1990), p.61).

43. Antonio Buero Vallejo, *El tragaluz. El sueño de la razón* (Madrid: Espasa-Calpe, S.A., 1988), pp.116-7.
(Further references to both plays are given in the text.)

44. Bainton, *Erasmus of Christendom*, p.118.

45. Ramón de Garciasol, *Claves de España. Cervantes y el "Quijote"* (Madrid: Espasa-Calpe, S.A., 1969), pp.177-8.

46. Antonio Buero Vallejo, *La tejedora de sueños. Llegada de los dioses* (Madrid: Cátedra, 1988), p.243.
(Further references to both plays are given in the text.)

47. Antonio Buero Vallejo, *Jueces en la noche. Hoy es fiesta* (Madrid: Espasa-Calpe, S.A., 1981), p.73.
(Further references to *Jueces* are given in the text. A different edition is used for *Hoy es fiesta*.)

48. Antonio Buero Vallejo, *Irene o el tesoro* (Buenos Aires: Ed. Losada, 1962), p.170.
(Further references given in the text.)

49. Unamuno, *Vida*, p.106.

50. Unamuno, *Vida*, p.178.

51. E. Ionesco, 'La Farce Tragique', interview by Beatrice Rodaro, April 1986.

52. T.S.Eliot, *The Cocktail Party* (London: Faber & Faber Ltd, 1950), p.111.

53. Halsey, *Antonio Buero Vallejo*, p.97.

Carmen González-Cobos Dávila speaks of "la posible relación de 'el padre' con la loca de *Irene o el tesoro*." "Estas analogías o 'parentescos' tienen que referirse a la posibilidad de que ambos personajes, en su locura, posean la verdad, es decir, la lucidez de pensamiento de que carecen otros personajes demasiado realistas y racionalistas para llegar a ella." (*Antonio Buero Vallejo: el hombre y su obra* (Ediciones Universidad de Salamanca, 1979), p.125.)

54. Enrique Pajón considers another insignificant being, the blind man in *Un soñador para un pueblo* who "llevaba el destino en sus manos". According to Pajón, it is not easy to detect the lucidity of such privileged minds, and he explains why: "Llevar en sus manos, no su destino, sino el destino en general es algo extraordinario, algo que indica grandes poderes que trascienden la normal condición humana; pero el hecho de que ese poseedor sea insignificante y ciego nos avisa de que el fenómeno debe ser interpretado desde perspectivas nuevas. Ese hombre que en apariencia nada significa por desvalido y por marginado tiene poderes que no pueden ser vistos porque intentamos captarlos mediante nuestro yo, centro del mundo." (Enrique Pajón, *El teatro de A.*

60

Buero Vallejo. Marginalidad e infinito (Madrid: Fundamentos, 1991), pp.20-21.)

55. Halsey, *Antonio Buero Vallejo*, p.128.

56. Luis Iglesias Feijoo, *La trayectoria dramática de Antonio Buero Vallejo* (Secretariado de Publicaciones de la Universidad de Santiago de Compostela, 1982), p.378.

57. Antonio Buero Vallejo, *El concierto de San Ovidio. La Fundación* (Madrid: Espasa-Calpe, S.A., 1986), p.138.
(Further references to both plays are given in the text.)

58. Antonio Buero Vallejo, *Historia de una escalera. Las Meninas* (Madrid: Espasa-Calpe, S.A., 1989), p.243.
(Further references to both plays are given after quotations in the text.)

59. Antonio Buero Vallejo, *Caimán. Las cartas boca abajo* (Madrid: Espasa-Calpe, S.A., 1981), p.73.
(Further references to both plays are given after quotations in the text.)

Chapter II
DREAMS
The inspiring power of the world created by the imagination

According to Ramón de Garciasol, *Don Quixote* would not be possible without his dreaming, whether or not his dreams are realizable.[1] Both in English and Spanish "dream" and "sueño" indicate involuntary and voluntary states of unconsciousness or semi-consciousness variously interpreted by religion and psychology; and, at the same time, aspiration, as in the formulation of ideal constructs. In Don Quixote's case, his experience in the Cave of Montesinos is often interpreted as a dream in the first sense of the word. However, when we refer to Don Quixote as a dreamer, we usually mean that he has ideals, aspirations. Buero's interest in exploring semi-conscious states of mind probably shows more of a twentieth-century post-Freudian concern with the interpretation of dreams.[2] But in many of Buero's characters we also find a very special capacity to dream, not in the literal sense of the word, that is, when sleeping, but in the metaphorical sense of a very particular ability to see beyond the present state of things, and also in the sense of having, and behaving according to, what the world considers a fantastical ideal without foundation. They are individuals who are not afraid of being different, even if that means that they have to put up with general contempt. In his doctoral thesis David Johnston deals with the subject of dreams when tracing Unamuno's powerful influence on Buero. He maintains that in the work of those two authors, dreams are seen "not solely as a device for exploring the inner and, for both authors, more authentic realm of experience of their characters, but also as the expression of a particular view of human nature."[3] For both authors, not only "the authentic, the heavily personalized life is the dreamed life", but it is precisely dream and imagination which "take man closer and more rapidly to the truth by circumventing rational theory and by re-creating the original experience from which the theory has been distilled" (pp.167 & 169). "Dreaming is a creative ability which enables man to project his uniqueness into the world" (p.178). The inner world is in fact more real, more genuine. According to both Unamuno and Buero, therefore, "without dream and imagination man is doomed to failure" (p.190). In that sense of the word dreamers, we are dealing with characters who have ideals. They have often been described as "contemplatives". I would not, however, agree with the use of such a term if it were to connote in any way some sort of inactivity or passivity. As we shall see, the term "dreamer" can correctly be applied in a derogatory sense to some characters who refuse to act. But the real dreamers, the true "contemplativos" in Buero's plays are also, and maybe as a consequence, active.

In order for contemplation to be authentic, in order for it to be quixotic, it must necessarily lead to action. An individual who sees more, who is able to look deeper, to penetrate the reality around him, takes on the responsibility of speaking out, of helping others to discover what he himself grasps, what he knows by virtue of a special intuition, and, above all, the responsibility of acting according to what he so clearly sees to be the truth.

Don Quixote, or rather the Don Quixote of Part I, believes firmly in his ideals, possesses convictions according to which he acts at every moment. Chivalry constitutes his religion. Moreover, nobody would think of a Don Quixote enclosed within the physical limits of his library, taking flight only in his fantasies and in his powerful imagination. We picture him in action, in battle, fighting for his ideals, even when that strong determination involves abnegation, poverty and self-sacrifice. He can do anything without complaint, because his contemplation is real, authentic, absorbing. The images that his fantasy depicts also inspire him with courage. Sancho does not follow his master's impulses in Part I, simply because his imagination does not transform reality in the same fashion. As Unamuno so accurately points out, Don Quixote "no fue un contemplativo tan sólo sino que pasó del soñar a poner por obra lo soñado."[4]

Don Quixote would not be the work it is if the dreamer had not put his dreams into practice. And Buero, as we will see, does not admire dreamers for their dreams, but for their efforts to make those dreams come true.[5]

"Dream" has, of course, a negative sense. And it is particularly in that sense that the dreamers in Buero's plays are accused of being "soñadores", that is, of wasting their time entertaining absurd and impossible ideas. They are reproached for being dreamers, "dreamers" here being synonymous with "deluded", "gullible", "ilusos".

Both Penélope and Anfino are dreamers in *La tejedora de sueños*. But in the Queen of Ithaca we find the dreamer "par excellence", she "weaves" dreams. What or who does she dream of in this innovative interpretation of the *Odyssey*? For Penélope, her dreams are all she has, her whole life. When she is forced to stop dreaming, her life loses all its content, its meaning. Anfino is the only confidant of her dreams; and both know their content. In the second act Penélope confesses to him: "Las mujeres no sabemos razonar, pero soñamos. Y ahora debo decirte yo mis sueños... Porque yo sueño ahí dentro..., muchas cosas. Y tú tienes que saberlas" (p.157). Her dreams are the intimacy of her soul, expressed in the embroidery in Laertes's shroud. Ulises, her husband, was part of her dreams only in their first years. After that, she dreamt of Anfino, of her ideal man, the "hombre de sus sueños". That is why she offers to show her embroidery, her soul, to him. When she finds out that the stranger is really Ulises, she tries to prevent him from seeing the shroud: "*Instintivamente se refugia en la puerta del templete, como protegiéndola*" (p.189).

Penélope dreams of an honest, lovable, faithful man, and Anfino could fulfil her dreams. Anfino himself wants to behave according to the ideal that she has created in her dreams: "Te quiero, Penélope, pero lucharé sin ventajas. Porque yo sé que es así, en el fondo, como tú me has soñado ahí dentro" (p.176).

Penélope can be reproached with passivity. She does not make up her mind to act, to accept Anfino and face the consequences. That is why Dione refers to her with these words: "Ella no sabe ser reina. Deja que dilapiden sus riquezas y se refugia ahí a soñar... Piensa en ti durante el día, cuando teje... y luego desteje por las noches" (p.152). She does not dare to choose Anfino among all the other suitors. She weaves her dreams but unravels them at night. Dione is right to say that she is weak. "Débil en el fondo, incapaz de ocuparse de los asuntos de palacio... Soñadora" (p.151). The term "soñadora" is used here in the negative sense mentioned above. Penélope does not act. "Porque nada, ¡entiéndelo bien!, ¡nada!, había ocurrido entre Anfino y yo antes de tu llegada..., salvo mis pobres sueños solitarios", she tells her husband (p.202). Her dreams, her contemplation, are passive; they do not lead her to action.

The cloth she was embroidering, "¡mis sueños! Mis sueños, que luego debo deshacer todas las noches, por conseguirlos definitivamente algún día" (p.160), is incinerated together with Anfino's corpse.

Anfino is also a dreamer, but he is as passive as Penélope. He does not dare to defy the other suitors. He sees the queen as eternally young and beautiful but he is ready to wait for years... His dreams, again, do not bring about action. For him "la muerte es nuestro gran sueño liberador" (p.194). His dreams cannot be fulfilled in his lifetime. The dreams of both Anfino and Penélope are unproductive. It will be seen that Ulises is a purely active character, one who is not able to dream at all. But one would agree with him when he accuses his wife of "soñar y tejer estérilmente ahí dentro" (p.197). Neither Penélope nor Anfino has been brave enough to risk breaking a lance in defence of their ideals. Their dreams do not incite to action. They cannot be considered quixotic heroes.

In *Irene o el tesoro* we find in Irene another indisputable dreamer, but in an altogether different sense. Buero uses Unamuno's lines as an epigraph:

El secreto del alma redimida:
vivir los sueños al soñar la vida. (p.124)
(*Cancionero*)

Like Penélope, Irene lives in her dream world, but she is absorbed by it. She cannot distinguish between dream and reality.[6] The real world for her is the one in which she is happy, the one that Juanito the "duende" offers her: "¡Hijo mío! ¡Tú sí que eres verdad! ¡Tú eres más verdad que todos y que todo!" (p.139). Like Daniel, Irene has discovered that we are surrounded by something mysterious, marvellous, that is worth exploring. And once it is found we want to remain in it. Irene cannot live without the marvellous, as La Voz says: "Ella no puede vivir sin lo maravilloso" (p.193).

Daniel is the only one who tries to understand Irene. He also confesses himself a dreamer:

Ya sabes que no soy más que un pobre soñador. Y todos los soñadores sabemos que el mundo no es sólo esta sucia realidad que nos rodea: que en él también hay, aunque no lo parezca, una permanente y misteriosa maravilla que nos envuelve. (p.176)

Irene was always prone to the marvellous. She is not only taking refuge in her dreams. She always sought to find the mysterious side to reality. "¿No te gusta a ti que las cosas sean maravillosas? Yo sé que lo son", she tells Sofía in the first act (p.139).

She never wakes up from her dreams. She refuses to go back to the miserable world of the wretched Dimas, Justina and Aurelia. They know nothing of the marvellous: they are too concerned with their own welfare, with money and comfort. They cannot see the golden coins that read "goodness" because their eyes are blind.[7] That is why Irene is happier than ever when her ideals come true, her dreams materialize, in spite of the fact that she is the only one who seems really to appreciate the marvellous. She does not want to abandon the world of Juanito; she is absorbed by it. Referring to quixotic idealism in his *Meditaciones*, Ortega y Gasset quotes Flaubert: "El ideal sólo es fecundo -entiéndase moralmente fecundo- cuando se hace entrar todo en él. Es un trabajo de amor, y no de exclusión."[8] Irene feels she ought to communicate her happiness to those she loves. She tries to make Sofía see Juanito. She cannot keep this marvel to herself. She wants to be understood, but when Juanito suggests that she go with him, she is determined to leave and so she does. Irene follows the path that Juanito points out to her, she goes in search of the definitive union with the world she has begun to enjoy in her visions, in her dreams.

The borderline between dreams and reality is blurred in the play, for the spectators or readers too. Even Juanito, the "duende", doubts that he is real. But we are inclined to prefer Irene's reality, marvellous and bright, to the miserable life that Dimas and his family lead.

The doctor, Campoy, compares Irene to Don Quixote: "Don Quijote era hombre y veía gigantes con quienes combatir. Ella es mujer y puede ver un duende o un niño a quien besar" (p.163). She discovers the marvellous around her, creates a new world for herself, a world which, as Juanito suspects, exists only in her imagination. In that colourful and fantastic world she finds liberation from her misery, her sadness. And, ironically, she frees the family from the real danger: Dimas, who was truly the mad one after all, and is put into the madhouse by his own wife.

In the case of *Un soñador para un pueblo*, we have to do with a completely different kind of dreamer. Esquilache has no visions; he does not imagine a "duende" beside him, as Irene does. But Esquilache also lives for something which is not himself: he has ideals, "ilusiones", and in that sense he is called a "dreamer". Buero presents an Esquilache who tries to serve the Spanish people. Esquilache himself expresses one of his ideals with the following words: "Si Dios nos ayuda,

a la vuelta de unos años el país tendrá gente apta para todo."[9] One of
his aims is to educate the Spanish people. For this reason, Pilar de la
Puente Samaniego thinks that Esquilache's dreams are possibly the most
generous: "Entre todos los soñadores de Buero, sea quizá Esquilache el
de horizontes más amplios: sueña una España mejor. Es ya el soñador
puro que no mira sus intereses, sino que busca el bienestar de un
pueblo, y un pueblo que ni siquiera es el propio".[10] He considers that
they have not yet come of age, but he is trying to help them to grow up.
These are what Ensenada calls "tus ilusiones" (p.111).

On the other hand, the prime minister cannot stand corruption. His
wife doña Pastora is a frivolous woman who tries at all costs to benefit
from her husband's position. She wishes to be close to the powerful,
but wants to have nothing to do with her husband's ideals of service and
self-sacrifice. The marriage is really crumbling and all attempts at
communication between Esquilache and his wife prove vain. In the midst
of such failure, Esquilache is determined to dream: he makes up his mind
to end this ridiculous situation, asking the king to grant him a
separation from his wife and to take from his two sons the privileges the
king had bestowed on them by reason not of any personal merit but only
of doña Pastora's insidiousness. His wife appears as the opposite of a
true Quixote, unable to see beyond her own wealth and welfare. She
looks down on her husband's ideals because she is too concerned with
her own ambitions: "Ya he hablado demasiado. Le temo a tu quijotismo.
Por lo demás, no presumas tanto de idealista. Lo que pasa es que tienes
miedo" (pp.115-6).

Esquilache continues to trust others. "No es más que un niño
envejecido... Un niño que todavía quisiera confiar en los demás", he
says of himself (pp.121-2). He does not renounce his ideals. The king
has understood him and holds him in high esteem precisely because he
has ideals: "¿Sabes por qué eres mi predilecto, Leopoldo? Porque eres
un soñador" (p.150). He wants to dream along with Esquilache and to
be surrounded by dreamers, by men with ideals. He is also presented
as a king who lives to serve his subjects. Nevertheless, he himself
wonders if everthing is a useless dream, if the Spanish people realize all

the sacrifice that both Charles III and his favourite minister are making for them. "¿Hemos soñado, Leopoldo? ¿Hay un pueblo ahí abajo?" (p.195). The king, however, always knew it was worthwhile to dream. He himself considers such dreamers to be the solution to the great problems of the country: "España necesita soñadores" (p.150).

Buero is obviously concerned with the problem of Spain. We discover in this aspect his close connection with the writers of the Generation of 98.[11] In his *Vida de Don Quijote y Sancho*, Miguel de Unamuno remarks that Spain needs the quixotic spirit and asks God not to let Sancho lose his faith.

> Consérvale a Sancho su sueño, su fe, Dios mío, y que crea en su vida perdurable, y que sueñe ser pastor allá en los infinitos campos de tu seno...; ¡consérvasela, Dios de mi España! Mira, Señor, que el día en que tu siervo Sancho cure de su locura, se morirá, y al morir él se morirá su España, tu España, Señor.[12]

Spain needs *dreamers*, Quixotes who generously risk their lives for an ideal, and Sanchos who believe and preserve their faith. As Azorín suggests at the end of *La ruta de Don Quijote*, a "vena ensoñadora"[13] is indispensable for the realization of ambitious human enterprises, and, without it, peoples and individuals head inevitably for decadence. Unamuno and Azorín, together with Ortega, give us a hint for the interpretation of the quixotic features found in some of Buero's characters. Those who see the truth, those who contribute solutions to the problems they see, possess those "ojos soñadores" that Azorín mentions, even though sometimes those eyes are physically blind.

As Esquilache puts it, a person with ideals lives for something other than himself; that is the reason for his greatness: "¡El hombre más insignificante es más grande que tú si vive para algo que no sea él mismo!", he tells Ensenada (p.201). He is ready to continue to uphold his ideals even if they call him "loco". To Ensenada's "¿Estás loco?", Esquilache answers: "¡Envidia también mi locura, Ensenada! ¡Y vete!" (p.203). Esquilache is, therefore, a dreamer. He is compared to Don

Quixote, as Irene was, but in a totally different sense. Irene had created her own fantastic world in order to escape from the hostile world that surrounded her. But Esquilache is a dreamer because he has ideals and dedicates all his effort to them, forgetting himself. He is more quixotic than Penélope and Anfino, on the other hand, because he has given everything for his dreams. Penélope and Anfino did not make any significant effort to make those dreams come true. Esquilache is a man with ideals but also a man of action. Though his dreams seem useless, though he seems to have been defeated, he is victorious, like many other dreamers.[14]

In *El concierto de San Ovidio* two indisputable dreamers, two contemplative characters, can be analysed. David is an idealistic character, but in two different senses. On the one hand, he is without any doubt a contemplative. He has been a music-lover since his childhood and he describes himself as a thinker. He tried to learn what he heard, thinking at night for hours: "Pensar ha sido mi placer desde niño", he acknowledges in the third act (p.120). Johnston points out that David "is identified virtually from the start as a dreamer. He has collected less than the other beggars because 'se me pasó el tiempo', the first hint in the play that David will be, at least in the first instance, the contemplative who stands in opposition, as always in Buero's theatre, to the ruthless and grasping man of action."[15] It is only normal for a blind person to devote most of his time to thinking; his physical shortcomings force him to orientate most of his activity towards the imagination. In that sense, David is not an exception. But we also learn that he dares to think more than his friends in the hospice; he is more aware of their dignity and tries to teach them to appreciate it. David himself tells them: "Siempre habré pensado yo lo que no os atrevíais a pensar. Siempre aprenderé yo cosas que vosotros no os atrevéis a saber" (p.27). His friends do not dare to learn more. Some of the other blind men have already accepted without further question that they are useless. That is, in their case, a comfortable attitude to take. Being incapable of working, they must resign themselves to being beggars; they need not commit themselves to undertaking any more ambitious enterprises. While Elías states sadly "No servimos para nada", we read in the stage direction that "*David deniega en silencio, irritado y conmovido*" (p.25). David is, therefore, a contemplative character who knows the reality of his blindness but attempts to improve his life. His lack of sight saddens him deeply but he is not hoping for a miracle, as Ignacio was. He yearns to progress, to play the violin, to show his blind friends and the sighted that they are men, and not sick animals:

> Hermanos, hay que poner en esto todo nuestro empeño.
> ¡Hay que convencer a los que ven de que somos hombres
> como ellos, no animales enfermos! (p.27)

Another characteristic of this idealistic temperament is that it leads the character to speak out; his voice rises without any sort of fear, even though he knows he is always exposed to misunderstanding. David's scream "¡Estáis muertos y no lo sabéis! ¡Cobardes!" (p.28), reminds us of Unamuno's words when making his apology for Don Quixote:

> ¿Tropezáis con uno que miente?, gritarle a la cara:
> ¡mentira! ¿Tropezáis con uno que roba? Gritarle: ¡ladrón,
> y adelante! ¿Tropezáis con uno que dice tonterías, a quien
> oye toda una muchedumbre con la boca abierta?, gritarles:
> ¡estúpidos y, adelante! ¡Adelante siempre![16]

Unamuno also remarks that Don Quixote is a contemplative, because only "contemplativos" dare to attempt an undertaking like his. We could say the same of David. Only a person who thinks, who has ideals, is able to bear misunderstanding, solitude, hostility. Of course, when crying out the truth without inhibition, he will have to face insults, reproaches. Like the knight errant, David is accused of being a dreamer, an "iluso". He is trying in vain to convince his friends to work hard in order to become a real orchestra. The others refuse to react. They are unable to see beyond their own misery. "Me creéis un iluso" (p.28), says David, and he is right. What he is suggesting is not an impossible task, but it is challenging, committed; the others refuse to attempt. Valindin ("... tú sueñas con algo imposible", p.41), Lucas ("¿Cuándo vas a dejar de soñar?"), Nazario ("Lo que tú quieres es un sueño", p.97), have doubts about the feasibility of such project. David is reproached with madness on several occasions.[17] Valindin calls him insane quite emphatically and insistently. Lefranc refers to some of David's actions as "locuras": "Son locuras, como las de antes" (p.41). Valindin screams in one of his frequent fits of anger: "¡No me digas que ese lunático se ha rebelado otra vez!" (p.53). He may think that he is in fact doing the blind inmates of the hospice some good, but he is only pursuing his own benefit. As Iglesias says, "Valindin podrá hablar de su buen corazón y emocionarse cuando se refiere a su labor con los ciegos... Todo ello no es más que palabrería de charlatán de feria, nunca mejor dicho, y su interés por los ciegos no tiene nada ni de humanitario ni de filantrópico."[18] He calls David "lunático" because he rebels, because he dares to tell the truth. Valindin does not know anything about the tragedy of the blind: he will never be able to understand that a blind man might have professional ambitions, desires to improve his own life style. That is why he talks to David with cruel disdain: "Tú estás loco y a los locos se les encierra" (p.104); "Me diviertes, loco" (p.112). Donato understands what that "locura" is. "Dicen que está loco porque sabe más que ninguno de nosotros" (p.48). This echoes La Voz's statement in *Irene*, which brings to mind once more the madness-wisdom paradox: "La locura de los hombres puede ser sabiduría."

David knows his situation perfectly well but he is not dismayed. His mind does not cease to work, which is why he detects the truth. He is the only one who realizes that the "wings" on Gilberto's helmet are not wings but donkey ears; and that the big wooden bird on stage is a peacock, the symbol of foolishness:

> No son alas. Y el pavo real es el emblema de la necedad.
> (...) Es el animal que pintan al lado del más necio de los
> reyes (...) el rey Midas, a quien le nacieron orejas de
> asno por imbécil. Tú eres el Rey Midas, Gilberto. Y lo
> que llevas en la cabeza son dos orejas de burro. (p.71)

David does not hesitate to think; that is why he does not mind speaking the truth either.

But I have said that David is a dreamer in a second sense. He is a dreamer in the negative sense of the word. His friends know that he dreams of his damsel, like Don Quixote. He longs for Melania de Salignac, a rich and blind lady. "An actual historical character who had apparently overcome her blindness, she represents for David a psychological bulwark against the pervasive chorus of disbelief and mockery, and he accordingly surrounds her name with a quixotic devotion."[19] Donato talks to Adriana about Melania when referring to all those things that David, but nobody else, dares to think:

> Él sabe que hay una mujer... ¡una mujer muy bella, señora! Tan bella como vos... No la conoce, pero sabe que vive en Francia, y que está ciega. (p.49)

David's words about Melania have an unquestionably quixotic echo:

> Pues sí, ¡entérate! ¡Para ella hablo y para ella toco! Y a ella es a quien busco... A esa ciega, que comprendería... ¡Dios mío! (p.92)

> Ella pelea en mí, y vence en mí, y yo vivo y respiro en ella, y tengo vida y ser. (*Quixote*, I,30)
> ... pues cuanto yo he alcanzado, alcanzo y alcanzaré por las armas en esta vida, todo me viene del favor que ella me da y de ser yo suyo. (I,31)

All his friends know that David finds in that dream a respite from his sadness. The thought of the blind lady who can read and compose music, fills his moments of solitude. For this reason, they do not trust him any more. They are all aware of the fact that he entertains impossible dreams. Any other ideal, any goal to be aimed at, has in their eyes the same proportions as Melania de Salignac, in whose existence nobody believes. David himself acknowledges that he once dreamt in order to forget his fear:

Os decía que yo antes soñaba para olvidar mi miedo.
Soñaba con la música, y que amaba a una mujer a la que ni
siquiera conozco... Y también soñé que nadie me causaría
ningún mal, ni yo a ellos... (p.113)

Both Don Quixote and David seem to have heard of the perfections and
virtues with which their beloved is endowed; they have never really
seen them. Don Quixote had also said: "Sólo estoy enamorado de oídas
y de la gran fama que tiene de hermosa y discreta" (II,9). Dulcinea is
also an image, an incarnation of perfections which Don Quixote
attributes to her. After their visit to El Toboso, however, the knight
even doubts that he is ever going to be able to see her at all. Don
Quixote had invented Dulcinea because he needed someone to inspire his
actions. "Dulcinea is to Don Quixote what Oriana is to Amadís, or
Polinarda to Palmerín, the goddess that dominates his thoughts and
inspires his acts."[20] Like the knight, David also dreams of a lady who
inspires his acts, but Melania is supposed to be real, her perfections
really exist. However, she belongs to a higher social class and he can
hardly hope to meet her at all, as Adriana comments to David almost
savagely, calling Melania "bachillera ridícula" and "damisela soñada",
and encouraging David to look for a "mujer de carne y hueso"
(p.52).[21]

Though Don Quixote doubts that he will ever see Dulcinea, his belief
in the ideal perfections that she embodies does not waver. Similarly,
though David realizes that it may be silly to love a woman he has never
met, he does not lose his faith in the feasibility of the project that she
inspired.

Not even David knows the significance of his own dreams. And this
is where Valentín Haüy, our second dreamer in El concierto, is relevant.
David dares to think that the blind will some day be able to read and
write, and to play and compose music. But he can do nothing to achieve
it. He tries to make his friends organize an orchestra, but fails,
because he does not have the means. Nevertheless, the humiliation that
David and the others suffer sparks off the efforts of Valentín Haüy,
whom Valindin calls "¡un loco! ¡un misántropo en esta edad de

filántropos!" (p.81), to achieve what David dreamed of. He is the man who will put into the hands of the blind books that they themselves will have printed, who will make them read and write, and finally play harmonious concerts. It is not an easy task, he says, but they will achieve it little by little, with considerable effort and because they themselves are determined to do it:

> Yo era un desconocido sin relieve: Valentín Haüy, intérprete de lenguas y amante de la música. Nadie. Pero el hombre más oscuro puede mover montañas si lo quiere. (p.125)

Without faith in the ideal and the will to make it come true, no dream can be realized. By introducing Haüy, Buero makes it clear that David's dreams, which many of those around him jeered at and deemed unreal, were in fact realizable in not too distant a future.

In *Aventura en lo gris* the character who dreams also sees the truth more clearly. Silvano is called a "soñador" several times, and he acknowledges that he is a dreamer. He is of course accused of being mad. "¿Está usted loco?", Alejandro asks him, also calling him "trastornado".[22] But Silvano is the one who uses his mind. After all, he is the intellectual, not Alejandro, who just strives to survive. Alejandro reproaches the ex-professor with madness from the beginning. The sergeant does it in the last act: "¿Se ha vuelto loco, profesor?" (p.217). This time he is labelled "loco" because he wishes to stay in order to save the life of Isabel's baby. Such brave, heroic actions are often called madness. But Silvano's madness, like Ana's, is "redentora", for they both save a life. The contrast between the contemplative and the active is very clearly expressed in the play. However, we are interested now in discovering the scope of Silvano's dreams. In Alejandro's words, Silvano is "un contemplativo inconfundible". It is true that Silvano is a "contemplativo". He himself refers to his dreaming: "Yo sueño mucho. Y estos días, con la debilidad, casi a todas horas... incluso con los ojos abiertos, me traspongo a veces y empiezo a ver cosas" (p.157). Silvano is referring to daydreaming, a common experience. But he analyses the significance of his dreams. It is in dreaming that man knows his most intimate attitudes and feelings, that he comes to know himself. That is why he considers dreams so important. "¿Es que quizá no debiéramos todos aprender a soñar?"; "Aprender a soñar sería aprender a vivir". Silvano then suggests that those who do not know how to dream, do not know how to live. In order to understand Silvano, it will be useful to look at his recurring dream:

> Hay un sueño que se repite con frecuencia... Me encuentro en un campo inmenso y verde inundado de agua tranquila. A mi lado pasan seres muy bellos que sonríen. Matronas arrogantes, muchachas y muchachos llenos de majestad, ancianos de melena plateada y niños de cabellos de ámbar. Son todos como ángeles sin alas. (p.158)

Silvano, a historian, longs for peace. He knows the history of warfare, and desires peace and justice. A dream takes place in the course of the play, and he refers again to the angelical creatures. He is afraid that they will never come. That is why he prefers to die.

It is clear that dreaming, in some of Buero's characters, is a productive activity which grasps and interprets new aspects of reality. In this play one whole section becomes a dream. In actual fact the dream, in which all the characters except Goldmann participate, turns out to be very revealing, crucial to the interpretation of what really happens that night. In it, Ana reveals her real feelings for Goldmann, her resentment, the malice she bears towards him, which she had never openly confessed to Goldmann, except in a few complaints. After that night, she will not be afraid of telling Goldmann the truth. We all have the experience of how strong a determination, how distinct an impression, a vivid dream can leave in our mind. Ana finds in Silvano somebody who will be able to help her, to understand her. She too is searching for a quiet and peaceful valley, and Silvano can help her to find it. In her dream, Ana endeavours to hold Silvano's hand, and desperately seeks his help:

¡Ten piedad de mí! ¡Dame una palabra de ánimo! ¡Con él estoy sola y llena de frío! ¿Voy a seguir sola? Todo puede borrarlo una palabra tuya. ¡Una palabra, Silvano, una sola palabra! (p.157)

She had not admitted to herself that she had seen in him somebody who would help her, but in the dream her most intimate desires run riot. Even the next morning Ana will not react. But by means of the dream we learn that Ana is a generous person. She wants to give and to share her desires with somebody who also knows how to give. She recognizes in Silvano a kindred spirit and during the dream she begs for help. "Baja y te daré mis sueños", she promises. "Si bajas te los doy. ¡Baja! Las enfermeras dan. Yo quiero dar. Él nunca da." The dream is a revelation for us: we learn the extent to which Ana's life with Alejandro must have been a martyrdom. She sees in him only a man of action whose shoulders are red with blood: "Sus hombros son rojos. Chorrean rojo" (pp.176-7).

Silvano also reveals his feelings openly in the dream. He has already watched Ana, and he is now encouraging her not to be afraid of Alejandro: "¡No le temas!" (p.183). He has seen very quickly in Ana somebody who can understand him and share his ideals, his desires for peace, his dreams. And it is precisely in the dream that they both come to know each other's most intimate desires.

Silvano, the dreamer, is the only one who is ready to discover the identity of the girl's murderer. He has no energy, only the strength that his dreams provide. In the dream the truth has been revealed. The person who knows how to dream also knows how to live. The man of action cannot get away with murder, precisely because Silvano has been alert in his dream: "Aunque al final sea el soñador quien desenmascare al hombre de acción" (p.208).

Ana had forgotten how to dream because she had lived with Alejandro for so long. She needs the dreamer to make her understand that she should not be afraid, that she can do without Goldmann, that she has to be both brave and sincere with herself if she is to make her dreams a reality.

In *Mito* we find another contemplative character. Eloy is the real Quixote of the play. The Quixote of the performance played by Rodolfo addresses his Sancho in the following terms: "Ah Sancho bueno, tu alma simple y pura/ aún quisiera soñar junto a la mía/ en una España llena de ventura" (p.139). Is the solution to all the problems of Spain contained in *Don Quixote*? According to Ortega y Gasset,

> si algún día viniera alguien y nos descubriese el perfil del estilo de Cervantes, bastaría con que prolongásemos sus líneas sobre los demás problemas colectivos para que despertáramos a nueva vida. Entonces, si hay entre nosotros coraje y genio, cabría hacer con toda pureza el nuevo ensayo español.[23]

But the real Quixote of the play is not the one in the performance, that is, Rodolfo, but Eloy. He seems to be the only one who sees the truth clearly. He feels they are all being deceived by the government, and he guesses that there is some hidden reason behind those "ensayos de defensa atómica" (p.150). He is not content with the explanation "Muchos" give him and he faces up to them. Magda Ruggeri Marchetti remarked on Eloy's special capacity to penetrate the reality around him, precisely because of his condition as a "soñador". The same can be said of many other dreamers. As we saw, David also understood the reality around him better than the others; he too had dared to dream of the ideal.[24]

The electrician states: "El pobre sueña en fantasmas" (p.151). Eloy imagines that there will be a better world, that the "visitantes" will come to save humans from their own insanity; that they have already arrived and that he has talked to them. Eloy lives in the reality of his dreams. He himself says that he "sueña en otro cielo y otros astros/ la humanidad que aquí hemos violado" (p.219). He is not only dreaming of "una España llena de ventura." He goes as far as saying that humanity cannot be found on earth any more and he feels he has to denounce this fact.

Marta is also wrapped in mystery, the "luz de una presencia sobrehumana" (p.160). She encourages Eloy to live his dream intensely. She is in fact part of it when she says: "Piensa que fue tan sólo un bello sueño/ nuestro encuentro. Mas ya no necesitas/ la voz del yelmo. Con el sueño basta" (p.167). The dream is sufficient. For Marta there is also a "yelmo" and not a "bacía". She is part of Eloy's dream.

Though Ismael says that he and Eloy dreamt together once (p.171), he does not seem to understand Eloy at all and accuses him of being a dreamer: "Serás un soñador/ si el escrúpulo no ahogas/ y a actuar no te decides" (p.172). His remark reminds us of Verónica's advice in *Llegada*: visions are useful only insofar as they lead to action.

Eloy suffers a disillusionment very similar to Don Quixote's. After Rodolfo's joke, he sees with more clarity the corruption that he was trying to denounce. Rodolfo accuses Eloy of pessimism when he describes the future that awaits the world. Then Eloy feels he must refer to the present: "En él los hombres a entender empiezan/ que no tienen más dios que el hombre mismo" (p.215). While Simón and Eloy are supposed to be aloft on a flying saucer in Buero's updating of the Clavileño episode, we contemplate a devastating picture of corruption, of the irrationality of human behaviour. Eloy is deeply humiliated, but he has learned a great deal.

His dreams give Eloy a great strength, an extraordinary courage. He feels like a "legión". He is convinced that he must speak and so he does, even though few listen and many laugh at him. He is also able to defend Ismael, to save the fugitive's life. Eloy now understands his own world fully and one can say that he dies a hero.

But I have said before that he suffers a very quixotic disillusionment. After the pretended flight to Jupiter, Eloy starts to doubt his own visions:

> Sé bien que no hay bondad en lo que ha hecho. A hacerme pasar hambre, ha preferido matar mi alma. Darme la evidencia de que soy un imbécil y un iluso. Pues bien, alégrese. Lo ha conseguido. Tal vez mi flaco juicio no distingue lo real de lo soñado. (p.214)

Don Quixote also doubted after his experience in the Cave of Montesinos.
The absurdities in the adventures in the cave make the knight-errant
wonder, not only about the reality of that particular experience, but
about his own capacity to see things as they are. In the same way, Eloy
feels he is stupid and "iluso", after Rodolfo plays the joke on him. He
feels unsure about himself, about all the ideals he had dreamt of before.

Don Quixote himself explains the nature of his experience in the
cave:

> ... y estando en este pensamiento y confusión, de repente
> y sin procurarlo, me salteó un sueño profundísimo; y
> cuando menos lo pensaba, sin saber cómo ni cómo no,
> desperté dél y me hallé en la mitad del más bello, ameno y
> deleitoso prado que puede criar la naturaleza ni imaginar la
> más discreta imaginación humana. (II,22)

In Chapter 25 he questions Maese Pedro's prophesying ape about the
truth of the adventures in the cave. "... Yo para mí tengo, con perdón
de vuestra merced, que todo fue embeleco y mentira, o, por lo menos,
cosas soñadas", Sancho had said. Don Quixote is not adamant this time;
his answer is hesitant: "Todo podría ser...; pero yo haré lo que me
aconsejas, puesto que me ha de quedar un no sé qué de escrúpulo." He
admits Sancho's doubts because he is doubting himself, and he wants to
be certain that his experiences there were real.   He looks for
reassurance from Sancho at the end of Chapter 41, refusing to believe
his squire's experiences when riding Clavileño unless Sancho accepts his
account of the Cave episode: "Y llegándose don Quijote a Sancho, al
oído le dijo: -Sancho, pues vos queréis que se os crea lo que habéis visto
en el cielo, yo quiero que vos me creáis a mí lo que vi en la Cueva de
Montesinos. Y no os digo más". In Chapter 62 he again asks Antonio
Moreno's enchanted head whether the adventures in the cave were true
or just a dream. At this stage in Part II Don Quixote has already begun
to lose heart, and he shows that the episode in the cave has for long
been a sore point. As in the case of the ape, he does not get a straight
answer: "A lo de la cueva, hay mucho que decir; de todo tiene". The

ape had also said that "parte de aquellas cosas eran verdad y parte mentira" (II,25).

Obviously, Don Quixote is not at ease. From the beginning there had been a disagreement regarding the time he had spent in the cave. Sancho thought that his master had been in it for a bit longer than an hour; Don Quixote reckoned he had been there for three days. From that moment, Don Quixote was uncertain. He himself had said that he fell into a profound sleep. Everything seems to point to the fact that he was fast asleep. And his story seems to be the description of a typical dream. But the stories the knight had actually dreamt were as real to him as all his other delusions. If he admitted to the fact that he had only been dreaming on that occasion, the totality of his knightly existence would come to nothing. If that fabulous and fantastic story turned out to be a dream, the knight would have to admit that he had been deceived all along, that he had been dreaming all the time.

Eloy goes through a very similar experience. After the joke Rodolfo plays on him, he doubts not only the reality of that particular experience but his own capacity to apprehend reality. That is why he sadly admits that the incident of the flying saucer has killed his soul. The episode in the cave killed Don Quixote's soul to a similar degree. The death of his soul is more gradual, but the Cave of Montesinos adventure is undoubtedly a key moment in the process of the knight's decline.

The electrician very affectionately calls Eloy "¡Don Quijote!" (p.223). Eloy is in actual fact the true Quixote of *Mito*, because, in spite of his own sorrows, his innermost doubts, he dares to go on dreaming, and to act with the courage of a hero. Don Quixote, vacillating seriously after he asked the ape about the Montesinos adventure, dares to fight the puppets. Chivalry is still in his soul. Eloy also dares to go on speaking about "¡Nuestro tiempo!" (p.215). He bravely tries to save Ismael, risking his own life in the process. His dreams are, therefore, not useless.

In the Francisco de Goya of *El sueño de la razón* we find another dreamer worthy of the adjective "quixotic". From his dreams he draws an enviable fortitude and interior vigour.

Goya's dreams are nightmares. "Sueña pesadillas", Arrieta states (p.124). In them the painter has glimpsed the ugliness, the misery in which the Spain of his time is plunged. That is why Arrieta himself notices that Goya's black paintings are "de satírico". Satire depicts reality as distorted. What for Arrieta is satire, maybe an exaggeration, for the painter is a vision of reality, probably much more terrible because of the depth of his intuition. After all, nightmares present something frightening, but not necessarily unreal.

The black paintings are Goya's means of expression: his painting constitutes his language. Like the real dreamers, Goya dares to speak, to communicate, he refuses to be deprived of his language. He wants to speak out the truth, even when this is a horrifying one: "Delaciones, persecuciones... España. No es fácil pintar. ¡Pero yo pintaré!" (p.130). It is not easy to tell the truth, but he dares because his dreams are clear.

When showing Arrieta the painting of the flying creatures, the painter exclaims: "Es de una colección a la que llamo 'Sueños' aunque son más que sueños" (p.136). His paintings represent more than dreams, maybe because they are an interpretation of reality.

Arrieta tells Duaso that "el sueño de la razón produce monstruos." But he corrects himself at once: "Tal vez no siempre..., si la razón no duerme del todo" (p.193). Perhaps Goya's dreams, because his reason never sleeps, are much closer to reality than the others are ready to admit. That is why in, some cases, his paintings are bitter, because reality is also bitter.

The painter is concerned about Spain, like Esquilache, Velázquez and Larra. Perhaps we shall have to affirm once more that Spain needs dreamers. Spain requires real Quixotes.

Goya, like Irene and Julio, tries to escape from a hostile atmosphere, from human misery. He imagines his own Dulcinea: "Un pobre solitario como yo puede soñar que una bella mujer... de la raza misteriosa... le llevaría a su montaña a descansar de la miseria humana" (p.137). In Goya's dreams there is also hope of salvation. He has clearly detected the tragically corrupt situation of the country, and he has denounced it without fear. His nightmares are the reflection of Spain at the painter's time. But there is another kind of dream with room for hope. "Sí, en 'Asmodea' hay una esperanza, pero tan frágil... Es un sueño" (p.184). The situation of the country is discouraging. Nevertheless, Goya, like Eloy, like the real Quixotes, has depicted its salvation: in this case, flying creatures who will come to save us from our own misery. Firstly, with his nightmares he denounces the corruption, the ugliness of the society around him. However, Goya can also entertain hopeful dreams. Once he has identified the problem, in his dreams he sees a solution. The painter, old and tired, still retains his hope. One of his dreams consists of his "hombres-pájaro": "Lo he pintado estos días, cuando he comprendido que no vuelan por arte mágica, como yo creí, sino con artificios mecánicos" (p.134). Buero knows that this particular dream has proved to be prophetic. Very significantly, Leonardo Da Vinci is mentioned by Goya in the play as another designer of flying machines: "¿Cree que se podrá volar así? (*Arrieta deniega.*) Leonardo pensó un artificio parecido. (*Arrieta inicia signos.*) No voló, pero acaso volemos un día". Like Esquilache's and Haüy's dreams, Goya's have been realized.[25] We have also seen that the Father in *El tragaluz* is considered by the Investigadores as a privileged mind who foresaw the importance of asking the "pregunta tremenda". Buero views his dreamers from a future time and thus proves them right, showing that their dreams were valid, even prophetic. Only dreamers can foresee salvation while fully aware of the corruption that surrounds them, because they see and know more.[26]

We have seen that dreams take Irene to a radiant, bright new world. In *Llegada de los dioses*, by contrast, Julio in his visions sees a totally distorted reality; his hesitant and bitter spirit leads him to a mistrust of others; his dreams reveal to him a part of the truth, which is not insignificant, but which often seems miserable, repugnant.

Irene, as Campoy remarked, was trying to take refuge in her dreams in order to run away from a hostile atmosphere, from her own sad memories. But Julio, who also wants to hide from the hostile world that surrounds him, finds in his dreams a world full of bitter and heartrending cruelty. But let us examine how much truth Julio is able to grasp in his dreams. Julio "sees", imagines, "pinturas en movimiento", "fantasmas". He says that, above all, he sees himself. He had always been very insecure, hesitant. With his blindness and Verónica's help, he will learn to know himself, he will acknowledge his own mistakes. Above all, those violent, esperpentic pictures, show him the truth about his family, his society, the world that surrounds him. "Tú sabes más que todos ellos. Y más que yo", Nuria tells him (pp. 253-4). Julio himself confesses that he sees better since he became blind. "Y a ellos también los veo mejor" (p. 245).

Like Don Quixote, Julio transforms reality in his imagination. But Don Quixote, as Unamuno states, "redeems" other characters, transforms them in order to dignify them. He refers to the "mozas de partido" as "doncellas". Julio, on the contrary, plunges the others into the reality of their misery, judges them with cruelty. He clearly distinguishes between the visions that assail him, and those he himself maliciously conjures. He often laughs at the characters around him by imagining them with grotesque features:

> Verónica.-Cuando charlabas con ellos te has reído varias
> veces.
> Julio.-Sí. (*Ríe.*) Sí.
> Verónica.-Imaginabas.
> Julio.-Sí.
> Verónica.-¿Lo que querías?
> Julio.-Sí, por fortuna. (*Breve pausa.*) ¡Lo prefiero así,
> Verónica! Esos otros fantasmas que a veces se me imponen,
> ¿de dónde vienen? (...) Parece como si fuesen ellos
> quienes me imaginasen a mí. ... a veces parecen traerme
> advertencias oscuras... Prefiero las fantasías que yo mismo
> discurro. Las que me hacen reír.
> Verónica.-Las que tú dominas.
> Julio.-Sí.
> Verónica.-Caricaturas. (pp. 243-244)

Julio does not need to make an effort to find the truth. He already knows part of his father's past, and one of his imagined victims continuously appears before his eyes. When he makes up his mind to force his father to confess the truth of his life, a half-naked man appears. Julio is assailed again, almost against his will. The more his father talks, the more clearly Julio sees the man's wounds:

> *Flaco, macilento, despeinado, con barba de días y oscuras ojeras, muestra su tronco, brazos y cara atrozmente cubiertos de innumerables surcos y llagas, de los que parten largos regueros de sangre coagulada.* (p.275)

Those vivid dreams are his strength, the source of his courage: "(*Considera la imagen del torturado y se acerca a su padre.*) ¿Cómo le torturaste, padre?" (p.276).

When Julio recovers his sight for a few minutes, he starts to doubt the truth of his visions. He then suspects that they may just have been hallucinations. Significantly, the same person who saw himself as "implacable", does not believe now that his father had performed such monstruous acts. In the real light, he sees Felipe with new eyes: "Parece imposible que hicieras aquello... ¿Lo hiciste realmente?" (p.332). He does not believe that the negative visions he had while blind could correspond to reality: "También eran mentira las que veía ciego" (p.331). Verónica tries to convince Julio that there is a part of the truth in his visions. Not all of them were faithful to the true facts; the reality that he saw in his blindness was completely distorted by his wild imagination. But there existed also a part, and not a small one, of the truth in those moving paintings: Nuria was the daughter of Felipe, not his god-daughter; Felipe had tortured, had behaved cruelly. Julio also saw Nuria's toy as her coffin and it proves to be the cause of her fatal accident; Verónica realizes that the vision of Nuria's toy as a coffin is an involuntary one, one of those which, according to Julio, seem to bring him "advertencias oscuras": "No eran fantasías voluntarias, ¿verdad? Éstas te han asustado" (p.300). But it is not true that Felipe continued torturing, or that, as Julio chooses to suspect, Felipe and Verónica are deceiving him, taking advantage of his blindness. Julio, in order to discover and penetrate the evil of the world around him in all its depth, has deprived it of all its beauty. "No debes deformarle para juzgarle", Verónica advises him (p.249).

Verónica is certain that the pictures which occasionally terrify him will make him grow up. Thanks to them, Julio has discovered his own misery. His dreams have also given him strength, the courage to speak out.

Tomás, another dreamer, goes through different stages in *La Fundación*. At the beginning of the play we find him immersed in the beautiful reality hat his fantasy has created, "...por debilidad y para huir de una realidad que te parecía inaceptable" (p.226). His recovery is a gradual process, like that of Don Quixote, who, disconcerted by some unusual elements in his experience in the Cave of Montesinos, starts doubting his own perception of reality. Tomás begins by thinking he is being cheated by the others, but he also ends up doubting his own perception as the different elements his imagination has added to the poor cell gradually disappear, ending with the curtain. The last time he thinks he has seen Berta in their room, he has had a real dream, which he later believes to be true. But when he clearly sees that Berta is not in the "bathroom" and that she could not have come in, he realizes that he has always imagined her presence in the room. Before this final disillusionment, however, Tomás's imagination has begun to work in a different direction: he has begun to think of a hopeful future when everything will be finished and they will be able to see their girlfriends again. Tulio says to Tomás: "Un día recordaremos todo esto entre cigarrillos y cervezas. Diremos: parecía imposible. Pero nos atrevimos a imaginarlo y aquí estamos." They are not hiding behind a new fantasy but hoping for a better future. They still have fears, but these dreams lead Tomás to the awakening, the tremendous growth of his character. That is why Tulio exclaims: "Sueña, Tomás. Me arrepiento de habértelo reprochado. Es nuestro derecho. ¡Soñar con los ojos abiertos! Y tú los

estás abriendo ya. ¡Si soñamos así, saldremos adelante!" (p.205). Like
Goya, Tomás has two types of dream; he dreamt in order to escape
reality, the reality of his own cowardice. But Asel wants to help him to
dream of a better world, to be a dreamer in the good sense, a productive
dreamer. As Verónica with Julio, Asel does not want Tomás to forget
everything he has dreamt. "Has soñado muchas puerilidades pero el
paisaje que veías era verdadero" (p.241). Tomás will only be able to
create a better world if he is able to dream of it first. Tomás will grow
up; he will even lose his fears, he will follow Asel's advice: "Duda
cuanto quieras pero no dejes de actuar" (p.240). The Tomás at the end
of the play is ready to face danger, pain and hard work, death; he is
full of hope. He is ready to act because he has dared to dream.

In *La detonación*, Buero's Mariano José de Larra is also accused of
being a dreamer. Dolores reproaches him "¡Deja de soñar!"[27] But he
has a very deep and genuine passion for truth: he wears no mask.
Larra is determined to make an effort to deepen his knowledge of human
miseries, in order to seek solutions for them.

His nightmares are an attempt to understand those who suffer. In
his first "vision", not really a dream, he sees Pedro carrying his
fourteen-year-old son in his arms. The writer sees his deep and bloody
wound. Not very long after this he has another vision. In this case he
is part of a firing squad and he is forced to shoot. "Yo nunca... he
fusilado", he exclaims (p.141). He even shakes the old lady to see if she
is really dead. Larra tries to understand that nobody can possibly
escape the responsibility for these killings. From the beginning he
maintains that it is essential to know the world where one lives. "Debo
conocerlo", he says to his father (p.47). Don Mariano warns him: "En
España ya no hay más que cobardes y verdugos. Te aconsejo la
cobardía" (p.48). Though, as Pedro says, Larra is impatient, he is not
cowardly, and in his dream he sees himself as one of the executioners.
Everyone is to blame for the bloodshed. Gallego too admits: "También
los nuestros fusilan sin dar cuartel. Todos somos caínes" (p.124). In
his vision, Larra screams "¡Es un crimen repugnante!", but he shoots.

His dream is an expression of his belief that "el mal somos nosotros...
todos nosotros" (p.145).

Larra also remembers a real nightmare he had. He has not been able
to forget so vivid an image. He dreamt that Juanín came again bringing
a repulsive puppet, which turned out to be Larra's daughter, Adelita.
She had no ears. He cannot forget the fact that many children had been
left with no ears during the Carlist war, and he sees his own daughter
in that pitiful state.

The writer has a special gift for penetrating reality. That is why he
suffers with those who suffer. In that same nightmare his right hand
and his tongue are mutilated. He is left without his instruments,
without his tools to speak the truth. The graphic images of Calatrava
cutting his tongue and Díaz mutilating his hand are only the reflection
of what the writer actually feels, as he himself says later: "Sé lo que
digo. Clemente Díaz es ahora censor y me ha hablado muy claro. Es
como si me hubiesen cortado la mano y la lengua" (p.185).

Larra's satire is sharp and caustic precisely because he knows the
reality that he criticizes perfectly well. His experience of it is not,
however, direct, but through intuition, through the marvellous strength
of his dreams.

Buero uses a similar device in *La doble historia*, where Mary Barnes
imagines her own son being mutilated by her husband. She has never
actually seen torture being inflicted on anyone; she has only read about
it. Her vision gives hers a much deeper understanding of Daniel's "job"
and of her ex-pupil Lucila's situation.

Dreams or hallucinations are never irrelevant in Buero's plays.
Lázaro, for example, suffers from an auditory illusion: he frequently
hears a telephone ringing, which nobody else can hear. One could say
that it does not help him to come to terms with the truth: at the end of
the play Lázaro still hesitates to believe that he behaved like a coward.
His two different memories are still there and he cannot make up his mind
to choose one or the other as truthful, in spite of Amparo's help. He is
not prepared to bear the suffering that the acceptance of the truth
might bring. Nevertheless, the ringing phone, though it has not shown

him all the truth about himself, has been the source of the discovery of other truths: the fact that Silvia died; that Fina, Lázaro's sister, knew it, and hid it from him out of selfishness; that Germán, who boasted that he was an altruist, a generous soul concerned for the welfare of others, has acted basely. As we will see, Germán is one of those "activos" who do not know how to dream.

Lázaro has not yet found his own truth but, as the phone goes on ringing even more insistently at the end of the play, we are left with the hope that one day, perhaps not too distant, Lázaro will find out and face the reality of his own cowardice, as Tomás succeeds in doing. Then there will be in his imagination only one version of the story that torments him: the real, the truthful one. The spectator is also encouraged by Buero to listen to his or her "teléfono interior". As he himself says, it is not an easy task, but that is the purpose of some writers' work: "...cabe desear que empiecen a preocuparse, o sea a sentir -metafóricamente- su teléfono interior. Para eso escribimos algunos escritores nuestras obras" (Letter).

Eugene Ionesco has stated: "Un uomo che non sogna e un uomo malato. La funzione del sogno e indispensabile, la funzione dell'imaginazione e altrettanto indispensabile".[28] Buero's "¡Si soñamos así saldremos adelante!" seems to be his view of this world of dreams, the dreams that give reality its true meaning.[29] As we have seen, those dreams can present themselves as terrible nightmares: the understanding of cruel reality can bring about sorrow and suffering; but, in some cases, it causes the strengthening of lost hope and the firm determination to act.

To say "Spain needs dreamers" is to affirm that Spain could do with men who are not afraid of accepting reality as it is, of seeing beyond it and losing the fear to act. To be "soñadores" would then mean to commit oneself to the truth. One could therefore say of Buero's authentic dreamers what Unamuno said of Don Quixote: "Pasó del soñar a poner por obra lo soñado."

NOTES TO CHAPTER II

1. "El que los sueños no sean realizables no quiere decir que se haya de renunciar a ellos. De otro modo sería imposible el *Quijote*" (Ramón de Garciasol, *Claves de España. Cervantes y el "Quijote"*, p.167). Garciasol dedicates the section "El *Quijote*" to Buero with these words: "**Para Antonio Buero Vallejo, príncipe moral y quijoteador**" (p.149).

2. In his frequent use of oneiric episodes (in *Irene o el tesoro, Aventura en lo gris, La doble historia del doctor Valmy, El sueño de la razón, Llegada de los dioses, La Fundación, La detonación, Jueces en la noche, Diálogo secreto, Lázaro en el Laberinto*), the post-Freudian Buero differs remarkably and notoriously from Cervantes, who only uses one "real" dream. We will see that some of Buero's characters have oneiric experiences which in some cases are prophetic, in the sense that Freud described: "Popular opinion is but little affected by scientific judgement, and is not concerned as to the sources of dreams; it seems to persist in the belief that nevertheless dreams have a meaning which relates to the prediction of the future and which can be discovered by some process of interpretation of a content which is often confused and puzzling ... One day I discovered to my great astonishment that the view of dreams which came nearest to the truth was not the medical but the popular one, half involved though it still was with superstition" (Sigmund Freud, *The Standard Edition of the Complete Psychological Works*, translated and edited by James Strachery (London: The Hogarth Press and the Institute of Psycho-analysis, 1971) vol.V, pp.634 & 635).

Though the interpretation of dreams constitutes a modern concern, the popular belief that Freud refers to is supported by even Biblical sources; see for example Matthew 1. 20-21, 2. 13 and 27. 19., where God Himself uses the means of dreams to communicate important messages to men. See also Pedro Meseguer, S.J., *The Secret of Dreams*, translated by Paul Burns (London: Burns & Oates, 1960), especially chapters I ('Dreams in History') and IV ('Telepathic, Prophetic and Mystic dreams'), which in its section IV on "dreams as vehicles of divine communication" (pp.160-162), provides various examples of theophany in dreams: Jacob's ladder (Genesis 28. 10-16), Salomon's dream (I [III] Kings 3. 4-15), etc.,.

3. This view, Johnston says, derives from the anti-rational tendencies of modern philosophy and from the Spanish tradition "reflected supremely in the novel by Cervantes who, in *Don Quijote*, depicted reality as forged by as many viewpoints as there are individuals" (p.165).

4. Unamuno, *Vida*, p.31.

5. It is not only their dreaming that makes Buero's characters quixotic, but their striving to attain what seems unattainable: "More mystical than rational, Buero's dreamer-protagonists strive like 'pequeños Quijotes' for the seemingly impossible" (Martha T. Halsey, 'The Dreamer in the tragic theater of Buero Vallejo', in *Estudios sobre Buero Vallejo*, p.48).

6. Johnston deals extensively with this play and draws a parallel between Irene and Unamuno's Quixote. "The idea that man lives most authentically in the world of transcendental reality, in the realm opened up by dint of quixotic faith, is central to *Irene o el tesoro*" (p.178). Since Irene starts seeking refuge in her daydreaming, using what Johnston calls "the quixotic ability to salvage her life lyrically from the destructive circumstances which threaten to swamp it" (doctoral thesis, p.172), her life acquires new vitality which "derives from the intensity of her 'soñar', a form of salvation that appears to draw freely upon Unamuno's reworking of Don Quijote" (p.175).

7. In her dreams Irene is also able to find "goodness". As in Don Quixote's case, it is Irene's dreams - Johnston says - "which permit her to nurture her faith in 'la bondad de la vida'... Goodness is a quality that Unamuno also associated with the dreamer" (p.177).

8. Ortega y Gasset, *Meditaciones del Quijote* (Buenos Aires: Espasa-Calpe Argentina, S.A., 1942), p.21.

9. A.B.V., *En la ardiente oscuridad. Un soñador para un pueblo* (Madrid: Espasa-Calpe, S.A., 1988), p.107.
(Further references to both plays are given after quotations in the text.)

10. Pilar de la Puente Samaniego, *A. Buero Vallejo. Proceso a la historia de España* (Salamanca: Ediciones de la Universidad, 1988), p.38

11. In his prologue to *Visión de España*, Azorín speaks of love for Spain among other necessary - and very quixotic - virtues which he was advised to put into practice as a writer: "No pierdas la confianza en la vida; no desesperes nunca; no sientas jamás -y menos en la declinación de la vida- asimiento por las cosas del mundo; sé generoso; da largamente tus energías creadoras y sé franco con la amistad, con los menesterosos; no niegues nunca a ningún perseguido, injustamente perseguido, tu amparo; ama a España; procura reflejar en tus libros -en esos libros que yo deseo que escribas- el ambiente moral, el paisaje los hombres de España" (José Martínez Ruiz, *Visión de España* (Buenos Aires: Espasa-Calpe Argentina, S.A., 1948), p.13).
 Carl W. Cobb says of Antonio Machado, another writer of the Generation, that "he was thinking, and thinking seriously, about Spanish problems ... Machado, like Ganivet and Unamuno before him, is calling for a return to the development of serious and virtuous men, in the ancient sense of the words" (Carl W. Cobb, *Antonio Machado* (New

York: Twayne Publishers, Inc., 1971), pp.31 & 32). Antonio Machado admits that the problem of Spain fascinates him: "A veces me apasiona el problema de nuestra patria y quisiera... Hay un ambiente de cobardía y mentira que asfixia ... Hoy quiero trabajar, humildemente, es cierto, pero con eficacia, con verdad. Hay que defender a la España que surge, del mar muerto, de la España inerte y abrumadora que amenaza anegarlo todo" ('Carta sin fecha a J.R. Jiménez' in Antonio Machado, *Campos de Castilla*, edited by Antonio Fernández Ferrer (Barcelona: Editorial Laia, 1982), p.76).

Iglesias Feijoo has remarked on Buero's concern for Spain: "Si Buero habla muchas veces del hombre y su problema metafísico, nunca deja de pensar en su propio país. España es uno de sus grandes temas y, aunque en esta obra [*En la ardiente oscuridad*] parezca haberlo excluido, no deja de tenerlo presente: 'Algunos de mis dramas sin localización concreta poseen, no obstante, fuertes problemas españoles. "En la ardiente oscuridad" se encierra un manojo muy diverso de significaciones: pretende reflejar entre ellas nuestra resistencia a la crítica y al movimiento' "(*La trayectoria*, pp.85-6).

Ricardo Doménech says that Buero's historical plays "buscan las raíces secretas, subterráneas, de lo que en nuestro tiempo ya es tópico llamar el problema de España" (*El teatro de Buero Vallejo*, p.202).

Pilar de la Puente refers to the influence of Cervantes on Buero, particularly through the Generation:
"La generación del 98 supo llevar este modo de ver y entender el mundo de Don Quijote a una interpretación de la historia de España como posibilidad realizable en una generación posterior. ... El autor ha reconocido en varias ocasiones que han influido en él tanto los pensadores como los creadores. Heredero del espíritu del 98, Buero se presenta como el autor más representativo de lo que España puede ser y del papel que debe hacer en el mundo que se está edificando, de la verdad histórica, en el sentido orteguiano de la palabra, que día a día se está haciendo" (*Antonio Buero Vallejo. Proceso a la historia de España*, p.157).

Finally, David Johnston says that "en sus indagaciones de lo que constituye la experiencia española, se puede encontrar a Buero Vallejo entre escritores como Larra y Machado" ('Introducción' to *Música cercana* (Madrid: Espasa-Calpe, 1990), p.16).
(Further references to this play and to Johnston's introduction will be given after quotations in the text.)

12. Unamuno, *Vida*, p.266.

13. Azorín, *La ruta de Don Quijote*, p.68.

14. "Esquilache himself - like Penélope, Ignacio, David, Silvano, and perhaps Irene - goes down to outward defeat. **Like Don Quijote**, the dreamer is defeated by a reality which seems unchangeable. In his struggle, however, he shows his true greatness - his unyielding and inflexible urge to strive toward the ideal, to attain the seemingly

unattainable. We see the irony of man's limitations, but overshadowing this is his nobility - his integrity and refusal to compromise. The dreamer's outward defeat thus signifies his inward victory. As is the case in all tragedy, moreover, his outward defeat implies the survival of his inner ideals and hopes" (Halsey, 'The Dreamer...', p.61).

15. Johnston, *Antonio Buero Vallejo. El concierto de San Ovidio*, p.67.

16. Unamuno, *Vida*, p.18.

17. Johnston says that "it is perhaps the inevitable lot of anyone who stands against the received wisdom of an entire system that he or she will be branded insane. Accordingly, David is held to be 'peor que Gilberto' by his companions, and Haüy's outraged intervention during the concert is dismissed as the rantings of a drunkard" (*Antonio Buero Vallejo. El concierto de San Ovidio*, p.74).

18. Iglesias Feijoo, *La trayectoria*, p.305.

19. Johnston, *Antonio Buero Vallejo. El concierto de San Ovidio*, p.75.

20. Anthony Close, 'Don Quixote's Love for Dulcinea...', p.239.

21. Victor Dixon refers to what he regards as "otra ironía, ... el hecho de que Melania de Salignac, que según David, 'está aquí. En Francia... En algún lugar... que ignoro' en 1771, había muerto en 1766 (D. Diderot, *Oeuvres philosophiques*, Paris, Garnier, 1964, p.154). Pero no sería extraño que David ignorara que su Dulcinea del Toboso, 'la mujer más hermosa de la tierra', para quien hablaba y para quien tocaba, además de ser una 'damisela remilgada' no era ya 'una mujer de carne y hueso'" ('*Pero todo partió de allí...: El concierto de San Ovidio* a través del prisma de su epílogo').
According to Johnston, "it is Adriana who ultimately leads David from the infinitely rich world of quixotic imagination into the challenge of the real world. David's crucial journey from dream to action is, therefore, paralleled by the creation of a more meaningful set of personal relationships" (*El concierto de San Ovidio*, p.75).

22. Antonio Buero Vallejo, *Hoy es fiesta. Aventura en lo gris* (Madrid: Ed. Magisterio Español, S.A., 1974), p.144.
(Further references to both plays are given after quotations in the text.)

23. Ortega y Gasset, *Meditaciones*, p.97.

24. Magda Ruggeri also remarks on Eloy's contemplative nature: "Considerato pazzo e motteggiato dai suoi compagni è l'unico che si è reso conto ('reparó') della vera natura di ciò che accade attorno a lui. Anche se attraverso il mitico mondo dei dischi volanti, egli ha l'esatta

percezione delle tendenze positive e negative nel mondo. Si noti che in ventinove versi appare nove volte il verbo 'reparar' e che in quattro interventi Eloy ripete la forma 'he reparado'.

È un'ennesima valorizzazione del sogno e del sognatore: essi riescono ad immaginare e desiderare, benché attraverso questo mezzo, il bene, la fine dei problemi e delle sofferenze, l'amore, anche se con l'intervento di esseri provvidenziali come i marziani." (*Il teatro di...*, p.147)

25. In that sense Derek Gagen compares David's and Esquilache's dreams: "David's dream contrasts with the sordid reality of life in eighteenth-century Paris. But the spectators know that there has been progress: the dreams both of David here and of Esquilache in *Un soñador para un pueblo* have been partially fulfilled" ('"Veo mejor desde que he cegado": Blindness as a dramatic symbol in Buero Vallejo', *Modern Language Review*, vol. 81, 3-4, (1986), 633-646, p.644).

26. "Pero como todo soñador, Goya puede ver lo que otros no. Al fondo de 'El Santo Oficio' ha pintado un sol que brilla, por más que sepa que la escena está en tinieblas y que la gente que cree ver con claridad se engaña. Él puede sentir lo sombrío del momento, pero sabe que el sol brilla lejos, detrás de una montaña, para el futuro. Junto con Buero, Goya cree que algún día, guiado por su Asmodea esperanzadora, el hombre podrá sobrevolar la miseria terrenal hacia la montaña desde donde se ve el amanecer" (J.W. Kronik, 'Buero Vallejo y su sueño de la razón', in *Estudios sobre Buero Vallejo*, p.258).

27. A.B.V. *La detonación. Las palabras en la arena* (Madrid: Espasa-Calpe, S.A., 1979), p.189.
(Further references are given after quotations in the text.)

28. 'Il discorso di Ionesco sullo stato del teatro nel mondo', *Giornale* (18-IV-76).

29. On considering Buero's achievement in *El sueño de la razón*, Kronik has also called Buero himself "soñador": "Sólo al recapacitar sobre la obra, o al afrontarla en la lectura, se pone de manifiesto que aquí, como en ocasiones anteriores, junto al técnico experto, ha trabajado un autor que tiene que decirnos algo profundo e importante y que nos atañe a todos, un dramaturgo serio, preocupado y soñador" ('Buero Vallejo y su sueño de la razón', p.261).

Chapter III
ISOLATION
The quixotic alienation of the individual

Don Quixote sometimes feels extremely lonely. In order to bear his moments of solitude, it is necessary for him to rely on his courageous character, on his will. The knight has to go on alone, even if he manages to attract others by the example of his bravery.

He has to suffer a "bitter solitude". John J. Allen makes the point that Don Quixote's use of language separates him from the rest of the characters. Many of those whom he meets simply do not understand Don Quixote's language: "Cervantes presenta el contacto inicial de don Quijote con los otros personajes a través de la ambigüedad inherente al lenguaje mismo. No sólo no están de acuerdo los personajes en cuanto a la naturaleza del mundo que le rodea (gigantes/molinos), sino que ni siquiera llegan a entenderse entre sí."[1] Sancho gets used to his master's vocabulary and is able to discuss things related to the life of knights and squires: "No entendían los cabreros aquella jerigonza de escuderos y de caballeros andantes, y no hacían otra cosa que comer y callar y mirar a sus huéspedes, que con mucho donaire y gana embaulaban tasajo como el puño" (I,11). But sometimes Don Quixote's words are beyond his understanding also: "Y antojósele hacer aquel inútil razonamiento a los cabreros, que sin respondelle palabra embobados y suspensos le estuvieron escuchando. Sancho asimismo callaba y comía bellotas..." Thus Don Quixote often talks in vain, either because he is not understood or because no one is there to listen to him any more. In Part I, Chapter 43, Maritornes plays a trick on Don Quixote, and Cervantes makes it clear that the knight suffers on his own:

> Don Quijote que sintió la aspereza del cordel en su muñeca dijo: Más parece que vuestra merced me ralla, que no que me regala la mano: no la tratéis tan mal, pues ella no tiene la culpa del mal que mi voluntad os hace, ni es bien que en tan poca parte venguéis el todo de vuestro enojo: mirad que quien quiere bien no se venga tan mal. Pero todas estas razones de Don Quijote ya no las escuchaba nadie, porque así como Maritornes le ató, ella y la otra se fueron muertas de risa, y le dejaron asido de manera que fue imposible soltarse. (I,43)

On that occasion, as on similar ones, Sancho is of no help: "...allí fue el llamar a su buen escudero Sancho Panza, que sepultado en sueño y tendido sobre el albarda de su jumento no se acordaba en aquel instante de la madre que lo había parido." Cervantes often stresses the fact that other characters are bored by Don Quixote's words and explanations: "Cansábanse los compañeros, que con el preguntante venían, del coloquio que con Don Quijote pasaba". In the following chapter, the inn-keeper explains to the newcomers that there is no need to pay any heed to the knight because his words do not make any sense:

> "Cualquiera que dijere que yo he sido con justo título encantado, como mi señora la princesa Micomicona me dé licencia para ello, yo le desmiento, le reto y desafío a singular batalla." Admirados se quedaron los nuevos caminantes de las palabras de Don Quijote; pero el ventero les quitó de aquella admiración diciéndoles quién era Don Quijote, y que no había que hacer caso dél, porque estaba fuera de juicio. (I,44)

When Sancho makes his way to El Toboso, leaving his master in expectation of news from his beloved Dulcinea, the knight sends the squire off in these terms:

Ve, amigo, y guíete otra mejor ventura que la mía, y
vuélvate otro mejor suceso del que yo vengo temiendo y
esperando en esta **amarga soledad** en que me dejas. (II,10)

Mainly in the second part of the novel, its hero suffers a melancholic and
unbearable loneliness: "Cuéntase, pues, que apenas se hubo partido
Sancho cuando don Quijote sintió su soledad, y si le fuera posible
revocarle su comisión y quitarle el gobierno, lo hiciera" (II,44). One
could say perhaps that Don Quixote was already alone, and that he felt
that solitude more deeply when his squire left him.[2] After Sancho's
departure Don Quixote has no one who understands him, and many
people who constantly make fun of him. After the episode with the cats,
"quedó Don Quijote acribillado el rostro, y no muy sanas las narices. ...
A todo esto no respondió Don Quijote otra palabra, sino fue a dar un
profundo suspiro" (II,46). The jokes played on him are increasingly
brutal and abusive, and Don Quixote has no one to console him.
Cervantes ends Chapter 48 with the following words, emphasizing the
knight's solitude after Sancho's departure: "Duró la batalla casi media
hora, saliéronse los fantasmas, recogió doña Rodríguez sus faldas, y
gimiendo su desgracia, se salió por la puerta afuera sin decir palabra a
Don Quijote, el cual, doloroso y pellizcado, confuso y pensativo, se
quedó solo..." (II,49).

Sancho Panza means so much to Don Quixote that we could never
affirm that the knight, once he has engaged his squire, is alone in
absolute terms. It is hard to accept Madariaga's view that Don Quixote's
feeling following Sancho's departure to Barataria is not only of sadness
but also of envy ("Sadness and a certain harshness due to offended
pride, with a touch of shame-faced envy"). Sancho and his master come
to know each other so well that one could almost say that one possesses
part of the other. Madariaga himself deems Sancho to be "a
transposition of Don Quixote in a different key", and Don Quixote and
Sancho "true brothers" who share a "fraternity of soul which unites
them." If this is the case, strictly speaking Don Quixote is not really
alone. There is a battle, however, that he has to fight on his own, the

one against "this undercurrent of doubt, this inner enemy, the most formidable of all he ever fought," which "will accompany him throughout his whole heroic life."[3] Unamuno's words remind Don Quixote of his solitude:

> Estás solo, mucho más solo de lo que te figuras, y así no estás sino en camino de la absoluta, de la completa, de la verdadera soledad. La absoluta, la completa, la verdadera soledad consiste en no estar ni aún consigo mismo. Y no estarás de veras completa y absolutamente solo hasta que no te despojes de ti mismo, al borde del sepulcro. ¡Santa soledad![4]

The awareness of alienation, of individual isolation, has been especially intense in twentieth-century life and literature, not only in Buero but in many other authors. Walter Kaufmann defines alienation as "estrangement from other men - usually from one's society. If anything at all could be said to be alienation 'par excellence', this would be it."[5] Though, as he puts it, "alienation is neither a disease nor a blessing but, for better or worse, a central feature of human existence", he realizes that "the experiences widely associated with that term are often held to be distinctive characteristics of our time, of our capitalistic societies."[6] Richard Schacht remarks on the fact that "social commentators contend with growing frequency that 'alienation' is one of the greatest problems confronting us today."[7] One reason for the continuing appeal of *Don Quixote* is that the problem of isolation is anticipated to an extraordinary degree by its hero. Buero also has admitted that at times he himself has been possessed by a feeling of isolation. As a writer, he feels alone: "Se me está tratando de arrinconar... Quizás un día podrán conmigo" (Interview). He recognizes that isolation is a universal human experience:

> La soledad es un ingrediente muy frecuente en el ser humano, y puede ser una de las formas de su destino trágico, de modo que por esta razón en mi teatro aparecen solitarios, o solitarios a la fuerza. Esto puede tener relación con don Quijote, pero también con muchas otras

cosas. La soledad es una vivencia humana frecuentísima en la vida humana y en la literatura. (Interview)

I propose to analyze the isolation in which some of Buero's characters find themselves. Firstly I will discuss those characters whose isolation is due to lack of understanding on the part of others, to a failure to transmit their ideals and ambitions. Secondly, there are characters who are in a way responsible for their own isolation; this is the case of Silverio and Lázaro, who made a mistake in the past which prevents them from communicating. In Chapter Six, I will also deal with those characters whose selfishness isolates them, renders them unable to communicate successfully.

I will refer first of all to Ignacio, in *En la ardiente oscuridad*. He is sincere in that he openly expresses his desire to see. The other blind inmates cannot understand him at the beginning, and he is considered a danger to the institution. But Ignacio does not resign himself to accepting their point of view, does not remain quietly in the background. He is a rebel, ready to stand alone: "Y aunque no haya ninguna mujer de corazón que sea capaz de acompañarme en mi calvario, marcharé solo, negándome a vivir resignado, ¡porque quiero ver!" (p.36). Ignacio speaks of his calvary, which is significant. Theologians affirm that the feeling of solitude suffered by Christ at Calvary is not comparable to any human sorrow, no matter how deep. Even though Ignacio compares his suffering to that of Christ at Calvary, he is ready to bear it. Ignacio, like David, is no doubt a Christ figure who has to undergo a similar agony, and who - as Johnston says - claims "a Christlike intent 'a traer guerra y no paz', a burning desire to force others onto the difficult path to knowledge about themselves and about their world."[8] Nevertheless, Buero himself points out in his 'Comentario' that Ignacio is not a messiah:

El Ignacio de mi obra anhela la "luz", pero no la tiene ni la tuvo. Con esto queda claro que no es un mesías aunque su actuación sea parcialmente mesiánica; no puede serlo porque es un pobre ser humano cargado de pasiones

encontradas, que busca la luz... sin ser, a veces,
demasiado bueno.[9]

Part of Ignacio's suffering and solitude is also caused, as will be seen in
some further cases, by the others' lack of understanding of his sorrow.
The other inmates cannot share in his agony. Juana tries to understand
it:

> Juana.-No se propone nada. Sufre... y nosotros no
> sabemos curar su sufrimiento. En el fondo es digno de
> compasión. (p.58)

That lack of understanding is also a barrier between Carlos and Ignacio.
"El mayor obstáculo que hay entre tú y yo está en que no me
comprendes", Ignacio tells Carlos on one occasion (p.69). Carlos rejects
Ignacio's apologies and refuses to accompany him. He does not intend
to break down the barrier that separates them:

> Ignacio.-(*Cansado*). No discutamos más. Y dispensa mis
> ironías. No me agradan, pero tú me provocas demasiado.
> Lo siento. Y ahora, sí me marcho, pero va a ser al campo
> de deportes. La noche es agradable y quiero cansarme un
> poco para dormir. (*Serio*). Las maravillosas estrellas
> verterán su luz para mí aunque no las vea. (*Se dirige al
> chaflán.*) ¿No quieres acompañarme
> Carlos.-No.
> Ignacio.-Adiós.
> Carlos.-Adiós.(...) ¡No, no quiero acompañarte! Nunca te
> acompañaré a tu infierno. ¡Que lo hagan otros! (p.73)

This is perhaps the climax of the play in that it seems clear that
there is not going to be an understanding between them, although
Carlos, ironically, will go to the hell he was trying to avoid, whereas
none of the others will. Ignacio and Carlos have tried to make each
other see the truth of their own convictions. Ignacio is firmly convinced
of the truth he is pursuing. He is not afraid of loneliness. Though he
would like others to follow him, he has an iron will and dares to walk
alone if nobody is willing to accompany him.

However, one should not forget that Carlos will accept that loneliness also. I will deal later with the influence that some strong-willed characters exert on others, but we need now to consider that Carlos, who knows Ignacio's sorrow and decides to kill him out of envy and jealousy, has already accepted part of Ignacio's tragedy. When the latter dies, Carlos is left in the most absolute solitude. One presumes that Juana will try to understand him, but she will never come to terms with the crime, even if Carlos has the courage to confess it. He accepts her return to him with a smile which shows no real happiness: "*Carlos la acoge con una desencantada sonrisa*" (p.82). Juana may never mean the same to him any more. Doña Pepita will never reveal the murder. She would not disturb the peace of her husband's institution. But she abhors the crime even though she does not want to punish it or to incriminate Carlos. "A veces, Carlos, creemos hacer un bien y cometemos un grave error", she tells him at the end of the play (p.84). But Carlos himself now rejects Doña Pepita's help, refusing to accept any affection or consolation that she might give him:

> Doña Pepita. -... Se nos acercan personas que nos quieren y sufren al vernos sufrir, y no queremos entenderlo... Las rechazamos, cuando más desesperadamente necesitamos descansar en un pecho amigo...
> Carlos (*Frío*).-Muchas gracias por su afecto, que es innecesario ahora.

Undoubtedly, any attempt to help him becomes a useless consolation in the face of the terrible agony which has already invaded his soul.

Don Pablo is too weak to provide Carlos with any moral support or consolation. After telling Ignacio's father about the supposed "accident", he will prefer to forget about it. The inmates want the peace they enjoyed before.

Carlos is then left in the deepest solitude: alone with his tragedy, alone with the terrible responsibility for his crime. The end of the play seems to be the beginning of Carlos's loneliness. He is left alone on stage with the corpse of Ignacio. He knows that the other inmates who were once attracted by Ignacio's behaviour and words, have left him: "Muerto Ignacio, sus mejores amigos le abandonan; murmuran sobre su cadáver" (p.84). But he cannot leave Ignacio now. He inherits Ignacio's loneliness, which is now incurable:

> *Después avanza hacia el cadáver. Ya a su lado, en la suprema amargura de su soledad irremediable, cae de rodillas y descubre con un gesto brusco la pálida faz del muerto, que toca con la desesperanza de quien toca a un dormido que ya no podrá despertar.* (p.87)

Maybe from now on he will become the one who will draw others by his example, but he will also have to bear the bitter loneliness of his calvary.

In *Madrugada* we learn that Amalia and Mauricio did not say to each other everything they needed to know; their lack of communication separated them. Amalia blames her own shyness, "esta maldita vergüenza mía que nos ha impedido a los dos crear la confianza necesaria..."[10] But Mauricio was also very reserved. That is why, Amalia explains, she did not say too much and did not talk to Sabina either while he was alive:

> Amalia.-(...) Mauricio era muy callado y me enseñó a serlo. Apenas hemos tenido, tú y yo, ninguna confidencia. Puede que ni te hayas llegado a dar cuenta de que..., desde hace algunos meses..., estábamos muy distanciados. (p.13)

Amalia and Mauricio spent "meses espantosos de frialdad" and she had to bear them by herself. In her search for the truth she now has an ally. Sabina immediately states: "La creo a usted, señora" (p.14). Sabina's support does not completely relieve her sorrow, her fear, but does lighten her suffering.

> Amalia.-¡Sabina! ¡Tengo miedo!

Sabina.-Ánimo, señora.   Entre las dos todo será fácil.
(p.16)

Yet,in spite of Sabina's support, Amalia has to go through the agony of
trying to find the truth by herself.   That night she is alone in her
suffering, which is even more difficult to bear as she has to put on a
display of strength and self-confidence which she lacks. Only when she
is left alone on stage do we understand how miserable she feels.

> Amalia.-Ahora iré. (*Lorenzo entra en el comedor. Amalia se
> recuesta contra la puerta del gabinete, rendida. Leandro da
> unos pasos hacia ella.*) ¡Por favor! (*Leandro se vuelve y
> entra en el comedor, bajo la mirada de Paula, que sale tras
> él. Breve pausa. Amalia se ha hundido. Cierra los ojos.
> Luego, con trabajo, cruza lentamente hacia el comedor.
> Antes de llegar, el reloj comienza a dar la hora. Son las
> cinco en punto. Amalia se vuelve y lo mira sobresaltada,
> escuchando, llena de temor, las cinco campanadas.*) (p.42)

Amalia cannot but doubt everyone.   She cannot even trust her niece
Mónica, who is obviously inclined to help her and to sympathize with
her. She is too afraid. Mónica too feels lonely, as she is not able to
make her aunt understand that she is on her side.   Amalia is too
frightened to trust anyone at all:

> Amalia.-No. No puedo decírtelo...aún. ¡Porque también
> yo dudo de ti! (*Se separa bruscamente agitada.*)
> Mónica (*Triste*).-Todo es inútil. Estoy sola.
> Amalia (*Dura, sin mirarla*).-También yo lo estoy. Y él.
> Todos lo estaremos hasta que la noche termine. (...) Entre
> tanto, suspicacia, mentira y soledad. (p.46)

Mónica's attempts to approach her aunt are vain, and so are Leandro's:

> Leandro (*Dolido*).-No me crees.

> Amalia.-¡No quiero creer a nadie! (p.49)

That night, when she needs to find out the truth, Amalia cannot rely on anyone, cannot seek any consolation. Sabina's attempt to offer her some support relieves somewhat her excruciating fear. Once she has found out the information she wanted, she can also trust Mónica, who had always been on her side. But Amalia still feels her husband's absence, will find it hard to forget.

> (*Tímida, se le acerca Mónica, sin atreverse a tocarla. Al fin, dice con mucha dulzura:*)
> Mónica.-Tía...
> Amalia (*Con la voz quebrada por el llanto*).-¡Mauricio!...
> ¡Mauricio! (p.79)

Nevertheless, Amalia's solitude is not absolute. There are people she can trust. Sabina was with her at the beginning and Mónica accompanies her at the end. And, above all, she has found the truth.

In *Un soñador para un pueblo* Esquilache also is immersed in the most terrible solitude. But he, like Amalia, finds somebody who would like to help, to relieve his loneliness in some way.

> Esquilache.-Perdóname. He pensado mal de ti. Pero ahora sé que me has defendido en la calle, sin miedo a la impopularidad ni al peligro.
> Fernandita.-(*Sonríe*) Yo soy del pueblo. No me preocupa ser impopular.
> Esquilache.-(*La conduce a un sillón y él se sienta en el otro.*) Déjame mirarte con nuevos ojos. ¡Ah! Es maravilloso. Ya no estoy solo. Ya tengo una verdadera amiga.

Esquilache, the king's right hand, a married man, has to find the relief for his solitude in this poor servant, a girl "del pueblo". Before that he felt alone. His wife ceased to love him long ago and is too busy with her social life. They form another one of those couples between whom there is only silence or bitter words. Even Fernandita realized that the relationship between them had cooled considerably:

Fernandita.-Yo empecé a pensar mucho en su merced desde
un día en que visitó a la señora marquesa en su gabinete y
ella lo trató con mucho despego... Vi a su merced abatido,
tan solo, que...
Esquilache.-*Certo*. (*Le toma las manos*) Desde hace años.
(*Melancólico*) Y ahora, surges tú... (pp.158-9)

He has Fernandita's affection and compassion but lacks what a public
man most needs, the gratitude of his people:

Esquilache.-(...) La ciudad más sucia de Europa es ahora
la más hermosa gracias a mí. Es imposible que no me lo
agradezcan. (p.160)
(...) Todo es ingratitud. (p.188)

"Todos me abandonan", he tells Fernandita (p.183). At one stage he
even fears that the king himself has abandoned him too: "El Rey.-
Comprendo... Has llegado a creer que te abandonaba. Pero ¿cuándo he
abandonado yo a mis amigos?" (p.192).

Then he has to leave the country that he has learnt to love, his
friend the king, and Fernandita, who belongs to the Spanish people.
His wife awaits him in Italy. He is again condemned to silence or
bitterness, all for the sake of the Spanish people who have abandoned
and misunderstood him.

In *Las Meninas* we find the royal painter surrounded by his family,
friends and admirers, though also by enemies. Doña Cristina herself
respects and defends Velázquez, and her father the king cannot hide his
profound admiration for the painter. Despite all this, Velázquez is a
lonely character; he himself states to his wife that he is alone, without
"alguien que me ayude a soportar el tormento de ver claro en este país
de ciegos y de locos. Tienes razón: estoy solo" (p.130). This emphatic
statement is revealing. The one who sees clearly is tormented by that
vision and needs somebody who can see ("que vea"), who can
understand with him. Velázquez acknowledges the fact that he needs to
feel accompanied: "Es triste no saberse pasar sin enseñar lo que uno
pinta. No es vanidad: es que siempre se pinta para alguien... a quien

no se encuentra" (p.127). In spite of all the people around him, he does not seem to have found one who can do something to relieve his solitude. Not even his wife doña Juana is able to help him, even though she tries to convince him that he does not need to feel sad. To her "No estás solo, Diego", her husband answers with a blatant prevarication: "Ya lo sé, Juana." His "¡Soy el hombre más acompañado de la tierra!" (p.128) is highly ironical, especially since it is followed by her disloyalty. Juana shows Nieto the painter's Venus, fully aware that she is betraying her husband ("No debo traicionarle", p.138). His own wife has not been able to understand him and so he cannot trust her. He explains: "... hube de resignarme a que no entendieras. (...) No te guardo rencor, Juana... Has sido una compañera abnegada, a pesar de todo. Mas ya no puedo fiar en ti" (p.208). Shortly after, she assures her husband: "Diego, estoy contigo...", but this statement is followed by "¡Ah!... ¡No te comprendo! ¡Nunca podré!" (p.209). She loves her husband but does not understand the painter. Buero specifically demands from the actors a series of gestures which will enable the spectators to appreciate Velázquez's solitude. His hands seek each other. Unable to trust anyone, he wrings his hands in despair. Doña Juana hates looking at his hands, which once sought hers, when they are seeking each other, because this gesture is indeed revealing of her husband's lack of trust in her. After telling her that he needs somebody who can appreciate and understand his work, the painter "se toma lentamente la mano izquierda con la derecha y se la oprime, con un gesto que doña Juana no deja de captar" (p.127). When he listens to his wife's complaints that he does not love her any more, "oprime de nuevo su izquierda con su derecha" (p.128), "se vuelve a oprimir las manos". She knows that something has been lost, that her husband does not see her as his confidant any more: "Pero antes, Diego, yo era tu confidente. Me sentaba a tu lado como ahora y tú buscabas mi mano con las tuyas... Míralas. Desde tu vuelta se buscan solas" (p.129). She even accuses him of unfaithfulness, which the painter cannot tolerate, "oprimiéndose con furia las manos" (p.130).

The marquis obviously causes the same feeling in don Diego;

> *Sale* [el marqués] *por el fondo sin dignarse responder a la apresurada reverencia de Pareja. Velázquez suspira y de cara al proscenio, se oprime las manos.* (pp.145-6)

As for Nieto, he denounces Velázquez to the Holy Office; and doña Marcela slanders him before the king.

The reason for the painter's solitude is once again that he is not afraid of the truth. He himself admits: "La verdad es una carga terrible. Cuesta quedarse solo" (p.152). He does not accept the hypocrisy of the palace, and that is why he has to remain alone, even though he finds it arduous.

There are only two people who alleviate the painter's solitude for a short period of time. We see the painter letting the king's daughter hold his hand: "*Le toma una mano. Velázquez se estremece*" (p.153). And he definitely does not feel alone when Pedro returns after so long. He is the only one who makes the painter feel really accompanied and understood, though very briefly. He makes don Diego forget his solitude because he understands his paintings, even though he is almost blind. "Durante estos años creí pintar para mí solo. Ahora sé que pintaba para vos", the painter tells him (p.163). After Pedro, in spite of his poor sight, asks the painter to let him see his new sketch, Velázquez himself touches Pedro's arm ("*le toca el brazo*"). He will have to face his wife's lack of understanding again as she cannot accept that Pedro is the most important person for her husband. Don Diego "*se oprime con fuerza las manos*" as he gives her instructions as to how to treat his guest (p.187). The painter now knows whose hands he can hold with complete confidence:

> No. Ya no os puedo dejar. Venid. Dadme la mano. (*Pedro se la tiende tímidamente. Ante la trastornada mirada de su esposa, Velázquez la oprime, conmovido.*) (p.189)

When his wife asked him what his hands were seeking, the painter answered that he needed someone who could understand his painting. Until that person appears his painting itself is isolated: "Es mi pintura la que se siente sola" (p.128). That is why Pedro is the only person who can relieve the painter's solitude. The gesture of Velazquez's grabbing Pedro's hand significantly ends the first half of the play, indicating to what extent Pedro's company radically changes the painter's life, and how his friend's absence will mean a return to his former isolation. After Pedro's sudden death, his solitude, his sadness, are much more profound, maybe definitive ("Era mi único amigo verdadero", p.237). In spite of his having been able to communicate with the king, to tell him the truth about his court, to teach his daughter a lesson, to obtain permission to go ahead with his masterpiece, the painter's tears and words tell us that he will still be lonely. The last words that he utters and the final words of the play are "Pedro... Pedro" (p.244). Pedro was the only person able to understand him, able to share his overpowering desire to paint.[11]

After his trial, the painter again wrings his hands. However, María Teresa takes them and this time puts his palette in them ("*Le desenlaza suavemente las manos y le da la paleta*").

> Velázquez.-(*Se arrodilla y le besa la mano.*) ¡Que Dios os bendiga!
> María Teresa.-Sí... Que Dios nos bendiga a todos... y a mí me guarde de volverme a adormecer.
>
> (*Retira su mano y sale, rápida, por el fondo. Velázquez se levanta y mira su paleta, que empuña.*) (p.242)

She leaves him too, but understands that the painter's hands will only stop seeking each other when they are not empty but using his tools, even if he has to paint in isolation. His painting thus becomes his way of transcending his solitude by communicating with others, including ourselves.

David in *El concierto de San Ovidio* also suffers the anguish of solitude.[12] He himself explains why he cried: "Lloré en la barraca... y sabía que todos me miraban. Pero ¿qué importaba? Yo estaba solo... Estoy solo" (p.89). He feels alone too. Only to a limited extent can we say that Donato is comparable to Pedro or to Sancho. The two blind men are very close and Donato is initially ready to support and defend David, as can be seen in the moving scene in which the others agreed to attempt to form an orchestra, even if their only reason for doing so is to get more food or women:

> David.-¡Donato, han dicho sí! Un sí pequeñito, avergonzado, pero lo han dicho. (*Le pone la mano en el hombro y Donato la estrecha conmovido.*) ¡Lo conseguiremos! (p.29)

But Donato does not provide much support in so far as he is the weakest and the one who needs to be helped. He is not faithful to his friendship with David. It is true that Donato also defends him at times ("¡Yo le creo!", p.48), but he does not want to run any risks. He is terrified by Valindin and prefers to give in rather than rebel ("¡No!...Ceder...Ceder..."). David is prepared to yield for Donato's sake, does not want to make him suffer ("Dadme mis anteojos, Adriana. Ponedle los suyos al muchacho, vamos a ensayar", p.74). But David is left with nobody, and also has to die on his own. Adriana tries to help him and to understand him; she attempts to defend him from Valindin:

> Valindin. ¡Ya era hora! (*Vuelve al centro, seguido de Adriana y los seis ciegos.*) ¿Por qué... tan tarde?
> David. Porque...
> Adriana. (*Le interrumpe.*) Porque me retrasé yo. (p.65)
>
> (...)
>
> Adriana.¡Tú sabes que yo os he defendido, que he intentado ayudaros! ¡Tú lo sabes, David! Debes admitir que lo sabes. (pp.88-9)

She offers to help him to carry his burden: "Déjame ayudarte a llevar esa carga" (p.118), but Adriana and David cannot remain together. They could have understood each other but they too have to separate. They are violently pulled apart by the police: "*Latouche y Dubois tiran de ellos para separarlos ... Aún quedan por un instante duramente soldadas las manos de ambos, que Latouche separa de un postrer tirón*" (p.123). The hope of being rid of their isolation vanishes again. Adriana too is left on her own.

Donato will also have to suffer an "irremediable soledad", as did Carlos. He is abandoned by Adriana.

> Donato.-¡Tenéis que creerme!
> Adriana.-¡Judas!
> Donato.-¡Tenéis que creerme! ¡No podré vivir si no me creéis! ¡No me abandonéis, os necesito!... (*Adriana le escupe en la cara. Él se estremece violentamente. Ella le vuelve la espalda y sale rápida...*) (p.124)

We know through Valentín Haüy that, years later, he refuses to talk about the past: "...nunca responde" (p.125). We also know that "siempre va solo" (p.126). He has inherited David's adagio, which he plays to seek consolation in his agony, just as Carlos repeats the words of Ignacio at the end of *En la ardiente oscuridad*.

Valentín Haüy too is a misunderstood character who is rejected. When he goes into the "barraca" and sees the show the blind musicians offer, he condemns it aloud. Since the rest of the cruel audience want to enjoy the show, they try to get rid of him immediately.

> Voces.-¡Fuera! ¡Que lo echen!
> (...)
> Voces.-¡Que se calle! ¡Que sigan tocando! ¡Fuera!
> Latouche.-¡Salid ya!
> Damisela 1ª.-¡Sí, sí, que se vaya!
> Latouche.-¡Fuera de aquí! (pp.80-1)

Thereafter he dedicates thirty years to his project. One imagines that the response of other people of his time would not have been very encouraging, as it was not for David, and that he needed to work on his own for many years. He says at the end of the play: "A veces pienso que nadie reconocería hoy en mí a aquel mozo exaltado de entonces, porque los años y las gentes me han fatigado." People of the same sort that he encountered in the "barraca" that night when the course of his life changed have probably exhausted him, have left him alone with his work. That is his merit: that he has been ready to dedicate his entire life to a task that most of his contemporaries would have deemed impossible. He does not even have the satisfaction of seeing his solitary task accomplished. He hopes it will be achieved, but he cannot be sure that he will be there to see it: "Si se les da tiempo, ellos lo conseguirán, aunque yo haya muerto" (p.125). Haüy's isolation yields fruit while Valindin's does not because he is of course isolated by his own selfishness.

Solitude becomes nearly complete isolation in the case of El Padre, in *El tragaluz*. He is a character who suffers the torture of knowing his son Vicente only too well, who never recovered from the suffering that the death of Elvirita caused him. Patricia O'Connor remarks:

> La obra, de hecho, se ve muy enriquecida por esta metáfora de la soledad del hombre ético atrapado en un mundo egoísta y cruel. **Algo similar es la cruz soportada por Don Quijote,** un personaje con quien el padre tiene mucho en común.[13]

The Father has to carry the cross of knowing the cruel world that surrounds him, and he does it in isolation. He knows, and does not seem to be able to communicate. His wife suffers part of his isolation, though she tries to cope with it in a different way. However, she misses the time when he used to talk to her normally: "(*Mario sale. La madre se vuelve hacia su marido, pensativa.*) Si pudiéramos hablar como hace años, me contarías..." (p.66).

The father kills and does not hide his action because he is not aware of any guilt: to him it is a matter of justice. He judges and executes the sentence that he believes to be the fairest.

At the end of the play he is left in absolute isolation. Mario tells Encarna: "Ahora está tranquilo" (p.106). He is now quiet but maybe more lonely than ever. He is not even allowed to use his scissors and has to use his hands to cut out his figures. His wife, who had patiently looked after him for years, will not find it easy to forget the death of her favourite son. The Father is thus left confined, in his own world, in his loneliness.

Eloy in *Mito* also feels alone, even though he is at times accompanied by a multitude of characters. He complains before the "visitantes": "Pero, hermanos...,/ mi **soledad** es grande y tan **amarga**..." (p.164). But his "visitantes" do not save him from the suffering. He would not be a hero if he did not have to endure it. Not even Marta's encouraging words ("Eloy, ya nunca más te sientas solo", p.166), provide him with any consolation. The electrician also calls him "solitario": "No hay misterios, Eloy, y está usted solo. / Acompañado de alucinaciones, / como buen solitario, pero solo" (p.193).[14] Marta's gentle voice, which had tenderly tried to console him, ends up resounding in Eloy's ears: "Al soportar la prueba que te aguarda.../ sentirás que estás solo...Solo...Solo" (p.225). Marta's and the electrician's words echo those Unamuno addressed to Don Quixote. In fact, at the moment of his real trial, Eloy will be utterly alone, but he will triumph, transcending his solitude by risking and then losing his life for Ismael.

Eloy's solitude seems to be even more bitter than Don Quixote's. We know that Sancho and his master were inseparable. R.M. Flores says that "Sancho's devotion to, and love for his master, are proverbial".[15] Simón does not seem to show such affection for Eloy at all. In fact, he can be quite rude at times. "¡Y aún el hideperra/ sigue mezclando berzas con capachos!" (p.212), he says referring to Eloy, with words directly taken from Sancho but which the squire applied to the author of their story: "Yo apostaré -replicó Sancho- que ha mezclado el hi de perro berzas con capachos" (II,3).

Simón is also able to cry when Eloy is about to die but one could not say that his words "¡Vea lo que le traigo! Su remedio.../ Esto le va a curar... Usted lo sabe..." (p.239) are fully sincere. He is sorry at his friend's death but does not become one with him.

It is very true that, together, Quixote and Sancho add up to a whole greater than the two parts ("Kafka saw them as originally one single being").[16] In spite of his occasional rudeness, very similar to that of Simón, Sancho truly shows his master his loyalty:

> Sancho wins his island, loses it disillusioned, and still continues by the side of don Quixote. From which we see that there has been growing between these two something deeper, something which was of course already there, latent in these two heroes at birth: the fraternity of soul which unites this strange master and this singular servant. (p.136)

If we cannot talk about that "single being" in the case of Simón and Eloy, neither can we find that "fraternity of soul". It is true that Eloy calls Simón brother, as Don Quixote did Sancho ("¡Hermano!/ ¡Dime que fue verdad! ¡Que lo recuerdas!/ ¡Tú escuchaste las notas siderales!"). But Simón replies doubtfully: "Quizá es que me zumbaban los oídos". Moreover, Simón does not have a chance to show his loyalty, his detachment from material profit, as he never manages to become a "burgomaestre": "Ni seré burgomaestre/ ni chamberlán de platillos./ Seguiré soltando gallos, cobrando mi escaso sueldo,/ y renegando y bufando" (p.221). When Eloy most needs the consolation of a friend, the company of somebody who could believe with him, Simón abandons him:

> Eloy. No te vayas, Simón.
> (Simón entra en su camerino y cierra con un portazo.)
> No me abandones. (p.222)

One could not really say that Simón plays a major role in Eloy's world. Sancho is a parallel to Don Quixote, "bringing out the main figure and enriching the design of the whole." As we have seen,

Madariaga goes as far as saying that "Don Quixote and Sancho are true brothers and their maker planned them after the same pattern" (p.122). The same could not be said of Eloy and Simón. That is why Eloy's loneliness is far more bitter than that of Cervantes' hero. Eloy does not find much consolation in the one he addresses as "hermano" but who calls him "hideperra". As R.M. Flores remarks about Sancho, we can find unkind words about Don Quixote and occasional though infrequent threats to abandon his service, "but such fluctuations and extemporaneous remarks are only to be expected in a true-to-life literary character."[17] We would never hear Simón saying something like "Le quiero como a las telas de mi corazón, y no me amaño a dejarle por más disparates que haga" (II,13). All he manages to say when he is asked whether he is Eloy's friend is "No mucho" (p.200); "En nada puedo ayudarle/ y me encuentro muy cansado" (p.199).

The only consolation Eloy finds is in his imagination. He faces death on his own, but knowing that he has managed to give something, to act. His last words are "Simón, no hay que llorar, pues no estoy solo.../ Yo canto a una galaxia muy lejana" (p.239). He knows he has not died in vain because "los actos son semillas... que germinan..." (p.238).

The old painter Goya is physically isolated by his deafness. He hears women's voices telling him that he is alone:

Mujer (*Su voz*). Estás solo.

Las dos mujeres (*Sus voces*). Estás solo.

Goya is alone with his thoughts, the noises of his mind, the miaowing of his imagination:

(Óyese de pronto un suave maullido. Goya se detiene sin volver la cabeza, y a poco sigue pintando. Otro maullido. El pintor vuelve a detenerse. Los maullidos menudean: dos o tres gatos los emiten casi al tiempo. Goya sacude la cabeza y, con la mano libre, se oprime un oído. Silencio.

El pintor arroja las gafas sobre la mesa, se despoja de la
bata y vocifera, con su agria voz de sordo.) (pp.120-1)

This is what Goya has to bear when he is left alone. Nobody can help him, because they do not hear the terrible noises. There is no consolation for him. Another of his torturing thoughts is that he will never see Mariquita again. Once Arrieta leaves the room, Mariquita's voice comes to the painter's mind:

> (*Arrieta asiente, se inclina y sale, acompañado de Leocadia.*
> *Los latidos siguen oyéndose sordamente y su ritmo semeja*
> *al de un corazón cansado.*)
> ¡Nena!...¡Mariquita!... ¿Dónde estás?...
>
> Mariquita (*Su voz*). Ya no me verás más...
>
> (*Goya escuchó con creciente zozobra. Los latidos, ya muy*
> *débiles, dejan de oírse. Silencio. El pintor se pasa la mano*
> *por la frente y suspira.*) (p.141)

He cannot share his anguish with anyone because, like many of Buero's lonely characters, he would like to find a confidant but finds it hard to trust anyone. Fr Duaso and Arrieta consider themselves Goya's friends. "A don Francisco le quedan sólo dos amigos", Arrieta says to Duaso (p.188). And the painter appreciates their friendship. Arrieta is certainly welcomed by Goya "con efusión" (p.129), and Leocadia reminds the doctor that he once took the trouble of learning sign language to communicate with Goya. The painter entrusts Arrieta with the meaning of some of his black paintings, and even with his ideas about the flying creatures whom he once saw, and who might come back to save the human race from its misery. Though Arrieta does not fully believe him, Goya appreciates his friendship: "Pero usted es un médico (*Se acerca por detrás y le oprime los hombros.*) Y un amigo" (p.185). He offers the doctor help, his own house to hide in, so that they could both be less lonely: "¡Podría pasar con nosotros la Nochebuena! Sacudiríamos penas y luego... se quedaba usted. (*Tímido*) Estaríamos los dos menos solos..." (p.186). Fr Duaso also comes out of friendly concern, and he genuinely intercedes for his friend and "paisano" before the king when he realizes he has been badly abused. Though this seems to be real friendship, and Goya admits that he needs it ("... yo estoy tan necesitado de expansión...", p.139), real communication does not take place. Goya admits the existence of a barrier between himself and the others, and in this he obviously resembles Silverio: "Por eso quiero tanto a la gente; porque nunca logro entregarme del todo, ni que los demás se me entreguen. Los quiero porque no puedo quererlos" (p.183). However, he also recognizes an incapacity to communicate in the others; he says to Fr Duaso: "A veces creo que los demás están más sordos que yo" (p.163). There is an implication that we are all fundamentally alone. Arrieta suggests that the problem of isolation is not only Goya's but an essential aspect of the human condition. Goya cannot at first understand him, but soon implies, grimly, that he agrees:

> ¿Sordos todos? (*Arrieta asiente*). No le comprendo...
> (*Arrieta va a accionar. Goya lo detiene con un ademán.*)
> Sí. Sí le comprendo. Pobres de nosotros. (*Arrieta suspira.*) (p.184)

When communication is lacking, dark thoughts arise, as happens to Juan and Adela in *Las cartas boca abajo*. Goya too is afflicted by bad thoughts. He seriously suspects that Leocadia is being unfaithful to him. His mind has created a very convincing story that he cannot but believe. He does not want to listen to the voices and would like to believe that the thoughts that assail him are caused by his deafness. But they continue to torment him.

> (... *Leve, múltiple, insistente, el coro de misteriosas risas puebla la soledad del anciano. Goya se detiene para escucharlas, menea la cabeza y continúa pintando.*)

These voices are clearly projections from his own isolated psyche. "¡No escucharé!", he says, but the voices keep on trying to tell him something.

> Mariquita (*Su voz*). No. (*Goya se interrumpe en el acto y atiende*). Usted no puede acallar las voces.
> Goya (*Inclina la cabeza*). Es la sordera.
> Mariquita. No lo cree.
> Goya. La sordera.
> Mariquita. Yo le aviso de las cosas que suceden y que no ve...
> (...)
> Goya. No quiero escuchar. (pp.173 & 174)

He does not want to listen but he still has to hear the voices which insistently remind him that he is alone:

> Mujer. No busques, moribundo. ¿Qué te queda ya en la tierra? Ni siquiera nosotras,...
> (...)
> Mujer. Estás solo.
> (...)
> Las dos mujeres (*Sus voces.*) Estás solo.
> (pp.174 & 175)

Goya's isolation is also reflected in his failing ability to communicate sexually with Leocadia. She says to Arrieta that Goya does not even speak to her much: "Conmigo apenas habla, pero habla con alguien... que no existe" (p.124). When they discuss the relationship of the painter with his mistress, "Las fisgonas" appears. "¿No se da cuenta? Esas dos mozas se burlan... del placer de ese pobre imbécil", Leocadia explains to Arrieta. The man in the painting cannot communicate sexually and enjoys sex by self-stimulation. It is a reflection of the situation of Goya himself, who has stopped seeking sexual intercourse. Leocadia says that he used to be "un gran lobo" (p.127), but he has now lost his vigour: "Me busca todavía..., muy de tarde en tarde. ¡Dios mío! Meses enteros en los que me evita por las noches y ni me habla durante el día... Porque... ya no es tan vigoroso..." (p.127). When asked by Arrieta the meaning of "Las fisgonas", Goya answers: "Claro que me siguen encalabrinando las mozas. Aún no soy viejo. Como entonces no, conforme. Pintar me importa cada vez más y me olvido de ello ... No tema por mi salud. A mí no me parte un rayo. ¡Y no quiero hablar de indecencias!" (p.138). His recourse to masturbation, "el vicio solitario", becomes a further expression of Goya's inability to communicate with others.

He cannot escape from his own mind. And he has to leave Spain, alone, forever unsure as to whether his suspicions about Leocadia were true: "Nunca sabré" (p.213). His mind, his imagination, his thoughts, isolate him and he is left with uncertainty, with doubt. According to John W. Kronik, this constitutes the greatness of Buero's protagonist: that he is condemned to live alone with his suffering. Kronik says that

> la grandeza de Goya -no su grandeza de artista, sino la del hombre en cuanto creación literaria de Buero- reside en el ininterrumpido vivir a solas con su sufrimiento. No es la sordera la verdadera tragedia de Goya, bien que sea la sordera el síntoma y símbolo de su tragedia. Peor que la sordera física es la soledad en que se encuentra.[18]

At the start of *La Fundación*, Tomás seems to himself and to us to be accompanied. He holds a conversation with the sick man in bed, and is visited by his girlfriend Berta. Eventually, he - and we - realize that he is alone, that he has been imagining his non-isolation, that his conversation with the man in bed and Berta's visit were delusions. The audience is obliged to share his isolation, along with everything else he experiences. Tomás is truly on his own but does not notice for a while. Though Berta does not really visit him in his cell, he makes her come; though the prisoner in bed is dead, he makes him talk. When Tomás is joined by his companions, he is isolated from them by his condition. He cannot talk about Berta's visits without provoking a reaction of laughter and incredulity in his cell-mates, which he does not understand. He constantly tries to please them but he does not find that easy either. "A veces es difícil contentaros", he tells them (p.171). He realizes that he is watched by the others, who talk about his progress, even before he has any awareness of his own disease. Though he holds Asel in high esteem, he says to him: "¡No entiendo tu jerga!" (p.177). He gradually realizes that the others know something of which he is not aware, and this confuses and isolates him even more: "Ya estoy harto de crucigramas. Tus palabras me confirman que vosotros sabéis algo que yo ignoro. ¡Porque todas estas cosas extrañísimas que aquí pasan me sorprenden a mí, no a vosotros! Y exijo que me las expliquéis" (p.179). He is visited by his girlfriend, another Berta who does not seem to know anything about his "Fundación", who is crying, Tomás does not know why; he is the only one who hears the complaints of the sick prisoner and finds no explanation for this either. Though Asel is genuinely trying to cure him, he at one stage suspects that Tomás is feigning a diseased mind in order to inform on his cell-mates, and he transmits his suspicion to the others. "¡Otra vez me excluís de vuestros secretos!", Tomás complains (p.197). He cannot even trust Asel now: "¿Os habéis propuesto que mi cabeza estalle? ¿Es a mí a quien pretendéis destruir?... Asel, ¿ya no puedo confiar ni en ti?" (p.211). Tomás is thus isolated by his own madness first, and then by their suspicions of him. The company Tomás sought in Berta also vanishes. He desperately needed company, and, as Asel himself tells him, his mind invented a doctor because he needed one.

But Asel too says that he feels alone. The root of his isolation lies in the fact that the others cannot really understand the nature of his solitude: "Vosotros no podéis comprender lo solo que me siento" (p.210). Communication was beginning to take place and total understanding on the part of the others could have happened had they been given the time. Tomás's cure had to follow its course, but one can easily see that a process of identification was taking place, partly because Tomás and Asel experienced their weaknesses in the same way. "Ya no me siento huérfano", Tomás says (p.255). Once cured of his illusion, and having learnt his own weakness, he has also acquired a strength, a confidence, that Asel has taught him, has instilled in him, to such an extent that he considers him his father. Had he lived longer, Asel too would probably have felt less isolated.

From the beginning of the play, it can be appreciated that Asel is different; he looks at things from a different angle. Tomás himself notices it. "Es un tipo desconcertante", he tells Berta (p.141). When trying to cure Tomás, he is on his own. He often has to persuade the others to wait, to be patient, not to precipitate a crisis in Tomás that would be more harmful:

> Asel.-(...) ¡Si pudierais tener todos un poco más de comprensión!... Ya sé que no es fácil. Una vez más os ruego que confiéis en mí, sin provocar palabras innecesarias... Ya estoy hablando demasiado. Respirad, calmaos, pensad... Y después, ¡por favor!, sigamos. (p.174)

Asel has a vast experience of human weakness, in part because he is obviously older than the others, as Buero specifies in his stage directions: "*Asel es el mayor de todos: unos cincuenta años, tal vez más. Cabello gris, expresión reflexiva...*" (p.144). He has also experienced the difficulty of trying to change things and not being able to achieve much. He would like to continue working but, at the same time, he is exhausted:

> Asel.-¡Debemos vivir! Para terminar con todas las atrocidades y todos los atropellos. ¡Con todos! Pero en tantos años terribles he visto lo difícil que es. Es la lucha peor: la lucha contra uno mismo. Combatientes juramentados a ejercer una violencia sin crueldad... e incapaces de separarlas, porque el enemigo tampoco las separa. Por eso a veces me posee una extraña calma... Casi una alegría. La de terminar como víctima. Y es que estoy fatigado. (p.220)

His exhaustion is caused by his isolation, which thus resembles Haüy's. Asel is tired of waging an endless battle on his own. He could have found a companion in Tomás. "No estás solo, Asel", he had told him "*con afecto"* (p.210). But he prefers to end his life rather than face the possibility of experiencing his own weakness again by betraying his friends. He wants to give them the opportunity to continue the struggle and, perhaps, to lead a better life.

Larra is separated from those who wear a mask because they cannot communicate openly; they are not sincere. But the image of his servant Pedro keeps recurring. The writer is in a way constantly accompanied by his presence. Larra himself wonders why he keeps appearing, even at a time when logically he should not be there.

> Pedro.-¿De frac, señor?
> Larra.-*(Mirando hacia donde salió su padre.)* De frac.
> *(Empieza a despojarse de la levita. Súbitamente irritado se vuelve.)* ¿Por qué tú?
> Pedro.-1826. Usted está en Madrid.
> Larra.-*(Mientras abandona la levita y el criado le pone el frac.)* ¡Antes de casarme no tuve criado!
> (...)
> Larra.-*(Colérico)* ¿Pues qué haces aquí? *(Pedro se encoge de hombros. Su señor deja de mirarlo y baja la voz.)* (p.52)

Larra seems to be irritated by the presence of his servant. But, as Pedro remarks, if he keeps appearing, it must be because Larra needs him. Pedro himself does not know why he is playing a major role in the drama that Larra is re-creating.

> Larra.-¿Y tú eres un personaje?
> Pedro.-Y tú otro. El principal, quizá.
> Larra.-¿Quizá?
> Pedro.-¿No me estás dando demasiado papel?
> Larra.-Cierra esa boca.
> Pedro.-No puedo. (p.63)

Pedro cannot be quiet because Larra needs to listen to him. Larra's lonely psyche is projecting him. The servant is both "company" for the writer and a measure of his lack of it, because he keeps reminding Larra that he, a servant, has been the only one who could understand him, who was sufficiently honest to tell his master what he thought of him. Pedro did not need to wear a mask. He is the person whom many of the lonely characters need: someone who listens. That is why Larra cannot do without him, why he can be visible when Larra is not. "Mientras yo esté, tú también estás", Pedro tells him. As long as Pedro is there, Larra is present too, because Pedro is a projection of Larra's need of him.

Larra felt bitterly lonely when he realized that nobody could understand his writings: it was like talking to nobody, like a nightmare, and so he wrote:

> Escribir como escribimos en Madrid es tomar una apuntación, es escribir en un libro de memorias, es realizar un monólogo desesperante y triste para uno solo. Escribir en Madrid es llorar, es buscar voz sin encontrarla, como una pesadilla abrumadora y violenta. Porque no escribe uno siquiera para los suyos. ¿Quiénes son los suyos? ¿Quién oye aquí? (p.89)

He had no one at his side; he was misunderstood by Pepita and abandoned by Dolores, who lied to him to protect her own honour. Larra knew that he needed somebody, and he felt exhausted, as he told Espronceda:

> Larra.-Los dos estamos fatigados. Y casi anulados.
> Espronceda.-¡Yo no!
> Larra.-Sí. Porque somos muy semejantes. Para pelear sin desmayo, necesitamos a otro ser... que nos falta.
> (pp.115-6)

He knew that he needed to be supported. And it was only Pedro, one Christmas Eve, who was able to listen, to encourage him, but also to speak the truth to him. He was one of Larra's readers as well:

> Larra.-Así te encontré una noche en que todo se había vuelto contra mí. Encendí el quinqué y te dije... (*Calla. Levanta el rostro.*)
> ¿Qué haces aquí?

Pedro.-Puede... que le dijera: si sus murrias le han dejado
sin amigos en Nochebuena, podemos distraernos aquí, con
Adelita y cantando asturianadas. Yo sé hacerlo.
(pp.169-70)

Pedro offered his company. He realized that Larra had been left alone
precisely on that night when you want to be surrounded by your family.
Pedro also remarked that the writer in a way isolated himself. Once
again, lack of communication, silence, make bad thoughts arise: "Como
el señor está tan solo... ¡Y por eso no entiende a los demás!" (p.170).
Larra was amazed at his servant's straightforwardness, and his
ability to understand him. Thus Pedro is in fact the only person to
whom he can afford to open his heart: "Y háblame como si fuera un hijo
tuyo" (p.171). Pedro reminds us of Sancho in Part II, trying to
encourage his master not to lose hope, faith in himself. Like him, Pedro
cannot prevent his master from falling into despair, but he offers his
friendship, his understanding.

Pedro.-(*Con simpatía.*) Yo tampoco quiero hacerle daño.
En este artículo no hay más que ideas negras... (*Se acerca
y le palmea el hombro con rudo afecto*) ¡A sacudírselas!
(*Señala el bufete.*) Y a no pensar en esa caja amarilla.
(*Larra se estremece.*) Y menos, hablar de ella en los
papeles. ¿Y qué es eso de que Madrid es un cementerio, y
de que media España murió de la otra media ?
Larra.-¿Tampoco hay que escribir esas cosas?
Pedro.-¡Sí, pero sin desanimarse! (pp.173-4)

Pedro can actually understand Larra's suffering because he too has had
to endure very hard times. In spite of the support Pedro tried to
provide, which he now remembers, Larra does not change his mind; he
is already too despairing. He does not listen to his servant's insistent
"¡Hay que apretar los dientes y vivir! Hay que vivir ... Hay que vivir"
(p.176), and "¡Ánimo! ... ¡Ánimo!" (p.178). It is too late, he is
already sunk in misery. But Pedro was the only one who really tried to
understand him, to encourage him to live.

At the end of Part II, Sancho too tried to relieve the knight's sorrow. Larra says "Estoy perdido", and Don Quixote: "Pero, ¿qué digo, miserable? ¿No soy yo el vencido? ¿No soy yo el derribado?". Sancho encourages him: "Déjese deso, señor (...): viva la gallina, aunque con su pepita" (II,65).

Larra complains that Pedro cannot understand his suffering: "Tú no puedes comprender mis sufrimientos" (p.174). So does Don Quixote: "Yo velo cuando tú duermes; yo lloro cuando tú cantas; ...De buenos criados es conllevar las penas de sus señores, y sentir sus sentimientos, por el bien parecer siquiera" (II,58).

Both Pedro and Sancho do their best to encourage their masters to live. "La mayor locura que puede hacer un hombre en esta vida es dejarse morir, sin más ni más, sin que nadie le mate, ni otras manos le acaben que las de la melancolía" (II,74), says Sancho. "Hay que vivir", says Pedro. He affirms after the *detonación* that his master lacked patience, resilience. Pedro had learnt to be strong: "No acertó a aprender lo que yo ya me tenía bien sabido antes de conocerlo: que es menester un aguante inagotable. Murió por impaciente" (p.193). Larra dies exhausted, with the fatigue suffered by many solitary characters who struggle on their own. However, neither Larra nor Don Quixote is completely alone: they can rely on their faithful companions. Pedro and Larra appear together. Likewise, one somehow cannot imagine Don Quixote without his squire, even though, at times, they argue hotly.

There is indeed a great difference between those who are alone because of their uprightness, because they are not corrupt, and those who are in a way the makers of their own solitude, who are to blame for it. It is possible to speak of a lonely Silverio in *Hoy es fiesta*, though he is surrounded by many other characters and loved by his wife. He has not managed to confess to anybody what he supposes to be his guilt. He deeply understands the problems of his neighbours, which he tries to solve. He tenderly loves his wife Pilar, even though she is in a way the cause of his sorrow. But there exists a barrier between them which Silverio himself has raised. Buero says in his 'Comentario' that "esta

pareja viene a representar un drama de incomunicación."[19]   There
would be no more suffering if his wife forgave him, if she knew she had
something to forgive.

The virtual saviour of them all finds himself in the most profound
isolation when Pilar dies: "Pero estoy solo. Tú lo eras todo para mí y
ahora estoy solo" (p.103). He had not done anything to save her child's
life, and at the end of the play he has to see his wife die too. While Pilar
was alive there was hope for him to break down the barrier between
them; when she dies he is left with the most terrible uncertainty. He
will never know whether she would have forgiven him or not. Even
though he has been able to help some of his neighbours, nobody knows
his terrible sorrow. Buero also refers to his self-centred nature, which
separated him from his neighbours.

> En cuanto a Silverio, es una individualidad disonante, que
> no logra sintonizar con su prójimo ni compartir sus
> problemas. Es éste el drama real de numerosas personas,
> relegadas a su soledad cordial, por pura deficiencia
> psíquica o por exceso de egoísmo. A Silverio lo mantiene,
> pese a sus esfuerzos en contra, distante de sus sencillos
> vecinos, y a través de la sordera de su mujer viene a
> adquirir expresión escénica y a culminar en el fracaso de la
> comunicación que más desea y más teme, la que debiera
> unirle con Pilar, y a Pilar con él. Que Silverio padece un
> serio defecto social, es evidente; que su egoísmo tiene gran
> parte de culpa en el defecto, él mismo lo reconoce, como
> reconoce su dificultad para relacionarse con los demás.[20]

Thinking of the past, Silverio admits his own egoism: "Era un imbécil,
pero sobre todo, un completo egoísta" (p.115).

Silverio's best friend, Elías, does not manage to get out of him the
reason for his sadness, for his lack of happiness:

> Elías.-(...) ¿Qué te ocurre?
> Silverio.-No lo sé.
> Elías.-¿Estás procupado por...ella?   (*Silverio sonríe
> tristemente y da unos pasos sin contestar. Levemente
> molesto*) ¡Di que sí! ¡Antes reventar que hablar!
> Silverio.-(*Medio en broma, pero triste.*) Es...mi secreto.

Elías.-(*Suave.*) Entonces ya me lo contarás. Los secretos se cuentan siempre. (*Silverio deniega, melancólico.*) (p.70)

He is not able to tell his secret, the root of his isolation, not able to share it. Neither does he tell Pilar, who realizes that he has chosen to suffer by himself. Act Two ends with a clear manifestation of Silverio's incapacity to share his suffering:

> Pilar.-¡No grites, calla! (*Busca nerviosamente en su bolsillo y saca el cuadernito y el lápiz, brindándoselos.*) ¡No sufras solo! ¡Dime esa cosa horrible que estás diciendo!
> Silverio.-(*Mira el cuadernillo con un anhelo y un temor ilimitados.*) Si me atreviera... (p.85)

Pilar offers to share his suffering too but does not succeed in making him speak or, at least, not in time.

Silverio's isolation is different from that of other characters in that there is no obvious lack of understanding on the part of the people who surround him. He simply has not been able to communicate his anguish to the person who could absolve him from his sin, or to anybody else. There is no possible consolation for someone who does not express the reason for his suffering. That is the root of his "soledad radical", which in his case goes hand in hand with an apparent gift for relating to others very successfully at a merely superficial level. Buero summarizes the causes of Silverio's isolation as follows:

> Silverio fue una persona que cometió un error, y ese error, como es una persona sensible y con un sentido autocrítico pronunciado, le pesa desde que lo cometió. Esto es lo que determina su soledad. Porque ese error que cometió, como es natural, no se atreve a confesárselo a nadie que le pueda oír y entender, y sólo se lo confiesa a su mujer, que es justamente la que no puede oír ni entender, cree él, aunque de hecho tal vez ella tenga una cierta intuición, mayor de lo que él supone, en cuanto a la insuficiencia o deficiencia que él puede tener. Pero eso determina también una **soledad radical** por parte de Silverio, que tampoco es

incompatible con su elevado índice de comunicación con los demás. (Interview)[21]

Lázaro is another such lonely character who, though not an "activo", is in some degree responsible for his own isolation. Just as Goya was alone with his miaows, Lázaro is alone when the telephone rings and he is the only one to hear it. His niece and nephew beg to be allowed to remain beside him:

> Coral.-Tío, yo te cuidaré a ti durante toda la vida. Porque nunca me casaré ni querré a ningún hombre; seguiré a tu lado y tocaré para ti.
> Mariano.-Soy torpe, ingenuo. Y siempre necesitaré papás. No dejes tú de serlo.[22]

But he does not accept what he reckons to be their pity: "No quiero vuestra lástima. Dejadme atrás y aprended a marchar solos" (p.145).

Amparo is the only one who can help him to discover what happened, to face the tragedy of his cowardice if necessary. But she also leaves him alone, wants to let him find out by himself:

> Amparo.-Sí... Llegar a saber qué ocurrió... Lázaro... Tú solo.
> Lázaro.-¡Nadie puede crecer sin la ayuda de otro!
> Amparo.-Ya has tenido la mía. Mi compañía no te serviría de ayuda sino de... morfina.
> Lázaro.-¡No puedo entenderlo! (*Desesperado*) ¿Por qué te vas? (pp.152-3)

He is left with the sound of the phone again. He is "invadido por el terror". The only company he will have will be the terrible masked characters of his imagination. He has to suffer the agony of his solitude. Amparo is gone. Mariano and Coral look up to him too much. He needs to listen to the telephone alone. Mariano de Paco puts it as follows:

Pero si Julio se encuentra con la ayuda de Verónica
("¡Moriremos caminando!") y Fabio, en *Diálogo secreto*, con
la de Teresa ("Buscaremos juntos"), que le hace ver que la
doncella del cuadro quizá venza al tiempo y a las
hilanderas, Lázaro ha de someterse para siempre, expiando
su culpa, a la convivencia con la fingidora Fina y a su
propio terror.[23]

As will be seen in the last chapter, the "activos" also isolate
themselves; they are isolated by their selfishness.[24] They end up in
their own little world of ambition, and in some cases, the punishment
they suffer for their lack of concern for others is utter isolation.

Don Quixote is not isolated through his own lack of love but through
lack of understanding on the part of others. He suffers his loneliness
when he is occasionally abandoned by his squire, or when he is sad and
nobody seems to be able to relieve his suffering; nobody can fight his
most difficult battle: the one against his doubts. But, throughout the
novel, he learns that he can rely on Sancho, he comes to know his
loyalty and faithfulness in spite of his fluctuations.

Some of Buero's characters, also alone, are able to rely on other
characters, have their Sanchos. The various relationships have been
analysed: Amalia-Sabina, Mónica; Esquilache-Fernandita; Velázquez-
Pedro; David-Donato, Adriana; Eloy-Simón; Larra-Pedro. But most of
them, in the moments of despair, cannot really rely on anyone to provide
them with much support. The lack of understanding, the lack of
communication, silence, lead to an isolation that is "irremediable". That
is why at the end of some plays we hear a hopeless utterance like
"¡Mauricio!... ¡Mauricio!" (*Madrugada*), "¡Pilar, Pilar!" (*Hoy es
fiesta*), "Pedro... Pedro" (*Las Meninas*). The characters are deprived
of the only person who could understand or redeem them.

Even though Don Quixote feels "legión", there are moments of
discouragement that he - like Ignacio, Carlos, Amalia, Silverio,
Esquilache, Velázquez, David, Haüy, El Padre, Eloy, Goya, Asel,
Larra, and Lázaro - needs to face by himself, either because nobody is

able to sympathize with him, or because he must be the one to lead the way.

NOTES TO CHAPTER III

1.   John J. Allen, 'El duradero encanto del *Quijote*', *Ínsula* 538 (Octubre 1991), 3-4 (p.3).

2.   According to Azorín, great souls are also solitary souls: "Hay en esta campiña bravía, salvaje, nunca rota, una fuerza, una hosquedad, una dureza, una autoridad indómita que nos hace pensar en los conquistadores, en los guerreros, en los místicos, en las almas, en fin, solitarias y alucinadas, tremendas, de los tiempos lejanos" (*La ruta de Don Quijote*, pp.42-3).

3.   Madariaga, *Don Quixote*, pp.177, 121, 122 & 114.

4.   Unamuno, *Vida*, pp.22-3.

5.   Walter Kaufmann, 'The Inevitability of Alienation', in Richard Schacht, *Alienation* (London: George Allen & Unwin Ltd., 1970), p.XXIV.

6.   Kaufmann, 'The Inevitability of Alienation', pp.XIV & XV.

7.   Schacht, *Alienation*, p.LIX.

8.   Johnston, *Antonio Buero Vallejo. El concierto de San Ovidio*, p.77.

9.   Buero's 'Comentario' to *En la ardiente oscuridad*, pp.86-7.

10.   Antonio Buero Vallejo, *Madrugada* (Madrid: Alfil, 1960), p.15. (Further references to this play are given after quotations in the text.)

11.   Though Pilar de la Puente compares the role of Pedro Briones to that of Sancho, she seems to think that Buero's dreamers are very different from Don Quixote:
"Sancho supo comprender y creer las 'locuras' de don Quijote, que no se cree, aún después de terminar malparado en todas sus aventuras, que lo que le dictó su mente fuera falso. El tipo soñador de Buero difiere con mucho del personaje cervantino. Sin embargo, podría establecerse cierto parangón entre Velázquez-Pedro Briones y Don Quijote-Sancho, sobre todo cuando el mismo Buero ha llegado a decir que se cree 'hijo directo' de Cervantes" (*A. Buero Vallejo. Proceso a la historia de España*, p.65).

12.   "David struggles unsuccessfully until the end, both to convince his complacent companions that his dreams are possible and to force Valindin to permit him to attempt to realize them. Like Ignacio he is the activist who brings not peace, but war, to all around him. Like Ignacio, also, he is a solitary figure, for his anguish is understood only by Adriana,

the mistress of Valindin, who herself has suffered much" (Halsey, 'The Dreamer...', p.56).

13. Patricia W. O'Connor, 'Confrontación y supervivencia en el *El tragaluz*', *Anthropos*, p.XII.

14. Magda Ruggeri describes Eloy's solitude in the following terms: "Gli chiedono anche di esser certo dell'utilità della lotta e del trionfo finale anche se si troverà solo, senza contatti con questa 'legión' e senza segni tangibili dell'attività delle forze del bene. Egli deve credere e sperare contro ogni speranza, contro le fredde affermazioni del pragmatismo scientifico senza che si insinui in lui il dubbio che si tratti di allucinazioni [Note: Non si dimentichi che **solitudine ed allucinazioni sono esperienze personali di Buero Vallejo**]" (*Il teatro di...*, p.137).

15. R.M. Flores, *Sancho Panza through 375 years* (Newark: Juan de la Cuesta Hispanic Monographs, 1982), p.129.

16. E.C. Riley, *Don Quixote* (London: Allen & Unwin, 1986), p.60.

17. R.M. Flores, *Sancho Panza through 375 Years*, p.130.

18. He expands on the painter's isolation: "Peor que la sordera física es la soledad en que se encuentra. Vive apartado en su quinta. Le abandonan los amigos. Se le separa de sus hijos y de sus nietos. Sus criados huyen. Ya no recibe encargos de retratos. El pueblo, envilecido, le amenaza. El régimen le violenta. Rodeado de hombres y de hechos hostiles, viviendo en una España cuya faz horrorosa no reconoce, irremediablemente solo, es lógico que se hunda en un mundo de voces y de monstruos, que sueñe, y que el miedo se apodere de él" (Kronik, 'Buero Vallejo y su sueño de la razón', p.255).

19. Buero's 'Comentario' to *Hoy es fiesta* (Madrid: Escelier, 1957), p.103.

20. 'Comentario' to *Hoy es fiesta*, pp.103-4.

21. In *Hoy es fiesta* Buero explores the mystery of communication between human beings. Martha Halsey says that "Buero Vallejo is concerned with the theme - so important in twentieth-century literature - of the radical solitude of the individual and his seeming inability to communicate meaningfully. We see the constant conflict which seems to characterize human relationships and the barriers which separate man from his fellow human beings. Indeed, effective communication or unity with other individuals often appears virtually unattainable" (*Antonio Buero Vallejo*, p.42).

22. Antonio Buero Vallejo, *Lázaro en el Laberinto* (Madrid: Espasa-Calpe, S.A., 1987), p.141. (Further references to this play are given after quotations in text.)

23. Mariano de Paco, 'Introducción', p.23.

24. Carmen González-Cobos talks about these two kinds of isolation when referring to love in Buero's tragic characters. Those who do not really love, isolate themselves. Others are isolated in spite of loving because they are not understood: "El amor se erige, pues, en la base necesaria de las relaciones humanas y su negación puede conducir a la destrucción espiritual del individuo. La ausencia de este sentimiento conduce a la más absoluta incomunicación, que puede tener un alcance familiar, y, en muchas ocasiones, llega a tener una dimensión social. (...) Sin embargo, hay que hacer una aclaración con respecto a la soledad que rodea a aquellos personajes que permanecen fieles a este sentimiento del amor y que también saben conectar con la colectividad. Estos personajes también se encuentran solos pero no porque hayan fallado a sus convicciones éticas y humanitarias. Al contrario. Su soledad procede del hecho de no ser comprendidos en absoluto por el resto de la sociedad. Luchan solos contra la injusticia social y en defensa del hombre y de su libertad. Son seres distintos y anormales con respecto a las normas que la sociedad ha establecido. Por eso están aislados" (*Antonio Buero Vallejo: el hombre y su obra* (Ediciones Universidad de Salamanca, 1979), p.61).

Martha T. Halsey also remarks that "this lack of comprehension and communication is often the result of man's spiritual blindness - the egoism which prevents sympathy, compassion and charity" (*Antonio Buero Vallejo*, p.42).

Enrique Pajón includes among the solitary characters others like Tío Blas, Mauro, Dionisio and Gaspar; these characters, he says, are surrounded by an aura of mystery: "Encontramos también otros personajes que, sean o no carenciales viven esa especie de marginalidad que resulta de no estar integrados en el núcleo social de la obra. A este tipo pertenece, por ejemplo, el Tío Blas de *El terror inmóvil*, Mauro de *Las cartas boca abajo*, o, incluso, Dionisio de *Caimán* y Gaspar de *Diálogo secreto*. Son personajes que evocan siempre en nosotros una especie de sentimiento de misterio... Esos solitarios sienten la soledad, pero no pretenden superarla integrándose en el grupo de quienes los rodean; integrarse de esa manera equivaldría a la aniquilación propia. Esos personajes son solitarios en nuestro mundo porque su mundo es otro, y hacia ese otro mundo es hacia donde Buero pretende conducirnos" (*El teatro de...*, p.19).

I find it hard to accept that Mauro wants to remain alone and should do so, because it seems to me that in the play he is constantly striving to "integrate".

Chapter IV
FAITH
The power of attraction and transformation of quixotic confidence

The source of Don Quixote's daring is the great confidence he has in himself and his ideals. At least in the first part of the novel, he does not doubt his own strength. He dares to undertake the most dangerous adventures because he trusts his own power: he believes himself invincible. In Part I, Chapter 5, he emphatically states: "Yo sé quién soy ... y sé que puedo ser no sólo los que he dicho, sino todos los doce pares de Francia." And again in Chapter 25 he says: "Yo valgo por ciento".

The Argentinian poet Carlos Suárez highlights Don Quixote's faith, calling him "the knight of faith". Don Quixote does not allow anyone to question either his faith or his passion for freedom. Inspired by Carl Jung's psychology, Carlos Suárez maintains that the knight had to descend into a spiritual wilderness to discover his own psyche. Through madness, Don Quixote becomes a knight of faith. The highest human attainment - Suárez says -, beyond pleasure, beauty or morality, is this faith, the integration with one's own soul. The achievers of this are knights of faith.[1]

Don Quixote's faith in his own ideal is combined with a strong will to carry it out. He is truly determined to become a hero. As Ortega y Gasset states in his *Meditaciones*, "la raíz de lo heroico hállase en un acto real de voluntad."[2] Don Quixote's will is imbued with the ambition to be a hero, capable of accomplishing dangerous adventures; he wants to be involved in enterprises that will earn him the title of hero. His faith alone would not have impressed others without the firm will to put the ideal into practice. On the other hand, according to Ortega this will means an arduous and constant struggle:

> No creo que exista especie de originalidad más profunda que esta originalidad "práctica", activa del héroe. Su vida es una perpetua resistencia a lo habitual y consueto. Cada movimiento que hace ha necesitado primero vencer a la costumbre e inventar una nueva manera de gesto. Una vida así es un perenne dolor, un constante desgarrarse de aquella parte de sí mismo rendida al hábito, prisionera de la materia. (p.121)

Aranguren emphasizes the knight's will, his "ánimo esforzado". The essence of adventure lies in "la voluntad de vivirla, y no en la suerte de encontrarla."[3] His will remains unbreakable though his faith weakens. The world as the stage for his adventures gradually vanishes, but something remains which cannot be destroyed: his will. According to Aranguren, doubts had always been there. He doubted not only the world as a possible arena for his adventures, but even his being a real knight. "Lo único que en el fondo de esa duda queda es la nuda voluntad de quizá imposible realización."[4] Commenting on the Marcela episode, Knud Togeby remarks on "la acometividad barroca del parlamento de don Quijote, pura acción, pura fuerza, puro querer".[5] The power of Don Quixote's will is also applied to his own beliefs, his faith: he has a firm will to believe. J.B. Avalle-Arce and E.C. Riley make the point that, had Don Quixote not doubted the adequacy of his ideal before the Cueva de Montesinos adventure, his dream would not have shown him the legend of Montesinos and Durandarte in such a poor light.

> Lo que es verdaderamente heroico acerca de esto, y trágicamente humano a la vez, es que don Quijote impide con toda la fuerza de su voluntad que este tipo de datos se cuele hasta llegar a flor de la conciencia. Si esto llegase a ocurrir, su ideal de vida se derrumbaría en el acto, y las ruinas sólo formarían un montón de bufonadas.[6]

Don Quixote is not always mocked and jeered at. We have seen how Cervantes often makes it clear that no one listens to him. However, at times he knows how to attract the attention of his listeners, who hear him very willingly; and his courage is indeed admired by many. Someone like him necessarily instils his zeal into some of those who have to do with him. The faith and confidence of the knight provide his squire with security too; being close to his master, Sancho considers himself protected, safe from any danger. In Chapter 23 Sancho very gracefully begs Don Quixote:

> ...en apartándome de vuestra merced, luego es conmigo el miedo, que me asalta con mil géneros de sobresaltos y visiones. Y sírvale esto que digo de aviso, para que de aquí adelante no me aparte un dedo de su presencia.

As we saw in the section on madness, if the knight is accused of being mad, so is the squire considered crazy by the barber and the priest:

> Decía esto Sancho con tanto reposo, limpiándose de cuando en cuando las narices, y con tan poco juicio que los dos se admiraron de nuevo, considerando cuán vehemente había sido la locura de don Quijote, pues había llevado tras sí el juicio de aquel pobre hombre. (I,26)

And again in Chapter 47 Sancho is told:

> ¿También vos, Sancho, sois de la cofradía de vuestro amo? ¡Vive el señor que voy viendo que le habéis de quedar tan encantado como él, por lo que os toca de su humor y de su caballería!

On going back to his village after the second sally, Sancho refers to himself as "un hombre honrado, escudero de un caballero andante buscador de aventuras" (I,52). Don Quixote had asked him: "Te ruego, Sancho, que tengas buen ánimo, que la experiencia te dará a entender el que yo tengo" (I,19). Sancho has now witnessed his master's

138

courage, his dauntless nerve; that is why he believes in chivalry, so much so that he intends to live by it. The squire himself is well aware of his profound transformation, of the deep influence that his master has exerted on him: "Algo se me ha de pegar de la discreción de vuestra merced", he tells Don Quixote (II,12). In the letter he writes to his wife he says: "Don Quijote, mi amo, según he oído decir en esta tierra, es un loco cuerdo y un mentecato gracioso, y que yo no le voy en zaga" (II,36).

Undoubtedly, the fact that Sancho so easily assimilates his master's teachings as a faithful and docile disciple, is due not only to his simple nature but also to the powerful and attractive personality of the knight. They shout at Don Quixote in Barcelona:

> Tú eres loco, y si lo fueras a solas y dentro de las puertas
> de tu locura, fuera menos mal; pero tienes propiedad de
> volver locos y mentecatos a cuantos te tratan y comunican.
> (II,62)

As Salvador de Madariaga points out; "the faith of the knight, after supporting his own spirit, feeds the spirit of the servant." When in doubt Sancho "has but to draw on his master's faith, while the knight of the Sorrowful Figure must draw his out of the well of his own spirit by sheer strength of will" (p.135).

Not only Sancho believes in him. Other characters too want to be assisted. Maybe the most obvious example is Doña Rodríguez, who introduces herself to the Knight of the Sad Countenance with the following words:

> Doña Rodríguez, la dueña de honor de mi señora la
> duquesa, que con una necesidad de aquellas que vuestra
> merced suele remediar, a vuestra merced vengo. (II,48)

After telling him the story of her daughter's disgrace, she says:

> Quería, pues, señor mío, que vuestra merced tomase a
> cargo el deshacer este agravio, o ya por ruegos, o ya por

armas, pues según todo el mundo dice, vuestra merced
nació en él para deshacerlos, y para enderezar los tuertos
y amparar los miserables.

It was obviously on her own initiative that she asked the knight for
help. It was not arranged by the Duke and Duchess because they
themselves are surprised when they see her coming in to talk to Don
Quixote:

> ... descubrió el rostro de doña Rodríguez, la dueña de la
> casa, y la otra enlutada era su hija, la burlada del hijo del
> labrador rico. Admiráronse todos aquellos que la conocían,
> y más los duques que ninguno; que puesto que la tenían
> por boba y de buena pasta, no por tanto, que viniese a
> hacer locuras. (II,52)

Doña Rodríguez and her daughter are not part of the joke, as they knew
nothing about Tosilos either; both of them shout on seeing him:

> Este es engaño; ¡engaño es éste! ¡A Tosilos, el lacayo del
> duque mi señor, nos han puesto en lugar de mi verdadero
> esposo! ¡Justicia de Dios y del Rey de tanta malicia, por no
> decir bellaquería! (II,56)

She does not doubt that Don Quixote is the person to solve her problem,
and she trusts him completely.

Similarly Maritornes, the inn-keeper and her daughter, go to him
seeking help: "Socorra vuestra merced, señor caballero, por la virtud
que Dios le dio, a mi pobre padre; que dos malos hombres le están
moliendo como a cibera", screams the inn-keeper's daughter (I,44).

Don Quixote is trusted because his faith is strong; and, when it
weakens, his will is even stronger. This is what inspires in others faith
in him, and in themselves.

Some of Buero's characters also instil their eagerness, their ideals,
into other characters to whom they relate. It is not easy to escape the
influence of the one who does not doubt, who has clearly seen the truth,

because he transmits it with the example of his strength and confidence.[8]

Let us consider Ignacio. The awareness of his own limitations, and his ardent desire to see, totally absorb him. He refuses to live in the fiction that the others believe, that they are normal. Other external elements do not worry him at all: he is not concerned about what the others might think of him. That is why he does not mind using his stick or worry about his clothes. After his arrival a change clearly occurs in the institution. The other blind students start to neglect their clothing, as doña Pepita notices:

> Doña Pepita.-Hay un detalle que aún no lo sabes. Muchos estudiantes han empezado a descuidar su indumentaria.
> Don Pablo.-¿Sí?
> Doña Pepita.-No envían sus trajes a planchar..., o prescinden de la corbata, como Ignacio. (p.74)

Ignacio acknowledges: "... no renunciaré a ninguna conquista que se me ponga en el camino. ¡A ninguna!" (p.55). He is obviously aware of his power of attraction and is ready to use it. We have already seen that he is prepared to remain alone, if nobody wants to accompany him in his agony. But it is precisely his confidence, that faith which can even hope for a miracle, that produces the contagion.[9]

Ignacio's faith is accompanied by a strong will and, as in Don Quixote's case, it becomes a proselytizing faith, which is very powerfully influential, even without meaning to be so. "No intento nada" - Ignacio assures Carlos. "Me limito a ser sincero, y ese contagio de que me hablas no es más que la sinceridad de cada cual" (p.54). Elisa's words, however, show that Ignacio is capable of much more. When referring to the change in Miguelín, she says:

> Elisa.-¡Preferiría que me engañase con otra chica!
> Juana.-¡Qué dices, mujer!
> Elisa.-Sí. Esto es peor. Ese hombre le ha sorbido el seso y yo no tengo ya lugar en sus pensamientos.
> Juana.-Creo que exageras. (p.57)

Obviously, Ignacio has been talking to Miguelín and the others. "Supongo que no dejará de hablar en todo el día. Y aun así, tiene que faltarle tiempo", don Pablo guesses (p.74). There is no other way to explain the quick and radical change in Miguelín. Carlos soon notices Ignacio's power too: "Posee una fuerza para el contagio con la que no contábamos" (p.41).

Ignacio does not bother to feign a happiness that he does not genuinely feel, does not disguise his bitter sorrow. That is why he awakens the sincerity of the others, their hidden sorrows, their sadness. The sincerity of each would not have woken from a prolonged lethargy if Ignacio's had not inspired them, if he had not only walked alone but resolutely, confidently, almost arrogantly. It is precisely Carlos, who initially appears more stubborn, more determined to restore the peace of the institution at all costs, who proves to be the heir of Ignacio's anguish. Juana feels sorry for Ignacio, probably discovers something attractive, different, in him; and the others are more or less fascinated by his rebelliousness. However, neither Juana nor Miguelín nor any of the other inmates, is permanently changed. Ignacio's influence on them is transient. Juana begins to change, so much that Elisa tells her: "Es inútil luchar. ¡Es más fuerte que todos! ¡Nos lo está quitando todo! ¡Todo! ¡Hasta nuestra amistad! ¡No te reconozco!... ¡No te reconozco...!" (p.59). Carlos also notices the change in her; he says to Juana: "Siempre nos dijimos nuestras preocupaciones... ¿No quieres darme el placer de compartir ahora las tuyas?" But she answers evasively: "¡Si no estoy preocupada!" (p.39). In spite of all this, as soon as she knows that Ignacio is dead, she throws herself into Carlos's arms ("se arroja en sus brazos sollozando"), promising him that she will confess everything:

> ¡Sí, sí! Tengo que confesarte muchas cosas... Me pesan horriblemente... Pero mi intención era buena, ¡te lo juro! ¡Yo nunca he dejado de quererte, Carlos! (p.83)

Miguelín also separates gradually from Elisa, allured by Ignacio's conversation. When Ignacio and Carlos argue, Miguelín sides with Ignacio, and we hear him shouting "¡Un tanto para Ignacio!" (p.50); "¡Segundo tanto para Ignacio!" (p.51); "¡Tercer tanto para Ignacio!" (p.52). Elisa has to suffer his indifference. But, as Juana herself remarks, Miguelín's enthusiasm is only transient:

> Volverá. No lo dudes. Él te quiere. ¡Si, en realidad, no ha pasado nada! Un poco indiferente tal vez, estos días..., porque Miguelín fue siempre un veleta para las novedades. Ignacio es para él una distracción pasajera. (p.57)

In fact, after Ignacio's death, Miguelín and Elisa go back together immediately: "*Miguelín le rodea fuertemente el talle. Poco a poco, Elisa reclina la cabeza sobre el hombro de Miguelín*"; "*... Miguelín y Elisa enlazados. Él va serio y tranquilo. Ella no puede evitar una sonrisa feliz*" (pp.81-2). And Miguelín certainly sounds most detached from his admired friend: "Sí. Ha sido lo mejor que le podía ocurrir. Era muy torpe para todo" (p.82).

Many other inmates are influenced by Ignacio's presence and words. Doña Pepita notices the external signs of that internal change. She is also the only one who can see them lose their confidence in their own abilities, because of their new awareness of their limitations:

> ¡Se ha caído usted ya dos veces, Miguelín! Eso está muy mal. Y a usted, Andrés, ¿qué le pasa? ¿Por qué no se lanza?... Vaya. Otro que se cae. Están ustedes cada día más inseguros. (p.55)

Andrés, Alberto, Pedro, the girls, listen to Ignacio, fascinated. But the change they undergo is superficial. Doña Pepita explains to Carlos:

> Yo creo que esos retoños carecen de importancia. Si
> Ignacio, por ejemplo, se marchase, se les iría con él la
> fuerza moral para continuar su labor negativa. (pp.74-5)

And she is right. Besides Miguelín's, we hear other disillusioned voices after Ignacio's death:

> Andrés.-Acaso se trate de un suicidio, don Pablo.
> Alberto.-(...) Ya sabemos que era muy torpe para todo.
> (p.80)

But Carlos, the exemplary student, is the one who inherits Ignacio's affliction, his overwhelming desire to see. By killing Ignacio, Carlos hopes to be rid of that anxiety, but in fact Ignacio's anguish recurs in Carlos with even greater strength. Carlos becomes Ignacio in that regard: the yearning for sight, the awareness of an unattainable beauty, of the existence of light, are not dead; they live in Carlos now, and killing the one who inspired them does not remove the anguish.

We do not know whether Carlos will make up his mind to be sincere, to transmit his sorrow, his thoughts, to the other inmates. Neither do we know whether Sancho decided on a pastoral life, as he suggested to Don Quixote by his deathbed, whether he really became his master's successor. But there is no doubt that Don Quixote was able to transmit his desire to his squire, whose will is now transformed. Likewise, Ignacio leaves his anguish in Carlos.

Riquet also works in Leticia a complete, almost miraculous transformation. The simple but beautiful princess was accustomed to scorn and laughter from her relatives and the others in the palace. Riquet, in his ugliness, has faith in himself, and defies the corrupt atmosphere of vile interests in the court. He assures the princess on their first encounter: "Si fueseis tonta, señora, no lo sabríais. Para creerse, a veces, necio, hay que ser muy inteligente. ¿Nadie os lo ha dicho nunca?". He consoles her affectionately: "Sólo estáis... un poco acobardada por la falta de cariño" (p.47).

Riquet even transforms his beloved's eyes; Leticia, who was horrified at the sight of his ugliness, will confess: "Estaba ciega"; "Eres mi amado que he esperado llena de pena durante años, y que al fin ha venido... para abrir mis ojos."

But Leticia also admits that her faith is based on Riquet's belief in his own ability; if Riquet were to doubt, so would the princess:

> Si dudas de ti, ¿cómo tendré yo fe? Lo intento, pero no siempre lo consigo. ¡Ayúdame! Tú serás para mí el hombre más gallardo, como lo eres ahora..., mientras quieras serlo. (p.87)

Faith and will go hand in hand once more. If the will to believe disappears, faith vanishes immediately. When Leticia loses heart, Riquet must make her confidence spring forth again: "Tú me dijiste que tu fe dependía de la mía... Estoy tratando de crearla otra vez. ¡Ayúdame!" (p.117). The ugly prince needs to "re-create" the princess's faith, but in order to do so, he needs to believe firmly that he can turn Leticia into an intelligent princess; and, above all, that Leticia's eyes will see in him a handsome prince. What he calls "nuestra prueba de fe mutua" (p.88), really depends on his own faith, because Leticia's confidence rests on Riquet's.

We often see Don Quixote reassuring his squire in his newly acquired faith. In that test of faith Sancho is victorious: there is no shade of doubt in his faith by the end of the novel. But Sancho's spirit is fed by the faith of the knight. Like Leticia, sunk in sadness, Sancho too might tell his master: "Sólo tú tienes el poder de abrir mis ojos" (p.133).

Silverio is also able to transform some of the other characters around him, maybe because, as Elías says, he is "un tipo como no hay dos" (p.48). Pilar tells her husband that she has changed her life, filled it with serenity: "Y esa sonrisa que veo en las cosas es la tuya... La tuya, que ha hecho que todo sea risueño para mí". Pilar thanks Silverio for his help, for his patience, for his affection:

Ahora ya puedo decirte: gracias. Gracias por tu cariño y
por tu paciencia inagotable. Sé que has tratado de hacerme
olvidar a nuestra pobre nena... Ni un sólo día la he
olvidado, pero tú has logrado que la recuerde sin dolor.
(pp.53-4)

Daniela too will have to thank Silverio. She seeks advice and
consolation first from Fidel, but does not find it: "Acuérdate siempre de
que recurrí a ti... y me fallaste" (p.63); "Sigues tratándome como a una
niña... a quien se le enseñan juguetes para consolarla. Pero yo ya no
soy una niña" (p.64). Only when she decides to confide her sorrow to
Silverio are her spirits raised; Silverio does not look away, as Fidel has
done: "*Daniela mira a Silverio con los ojos muy abiertos. Él la
corresponde con una mirada expectante*" (p.96), and he knows how to
encourage her, how to tell her what she needs to hear. She recovers
her courage. She said "Todo está perdido" (p.110). But now Silverio
tells her: "Yo sé que estás dispuesta a afrontarlo todo. ¿Verdad?" "Sí",
Daniela answers (p.112).

Fidel too is transformed by Silverio. He is introduced by Buero as
"*un muchacho de aspecto encogido*" (p.32), and his external appearance
is the reflection of his nature. Silverio makes him gain confidence in
himself by entrusting him with a relevant task, by relying on him. At
the end of the play we can appreciate the change that has occurred in
Fidel:

Silverio.-No hagas caso, Fidel. No es su madre la que ha
hablado. Y dese prisa, no vaya a tener alguno de ellos un
mal pronto y... se vaya a la comisaría.
Fidel.-(*Repentinamente contento*) ¡Claro que sí! (p.104)

Catherine Elizabeth Dowd describes his transformation as follows:

Al final del drama parece que Fidel ha aceptado los consejos
que le había dado Silverio. Cuando se pone al lado de éste
para conseguir el perdón de los vecinos para doña Balbina,
no solamente se redime a los ojos de Daniela, sino que
también llega a una valoración de sus propias cualidades.[16]

The other neighbours also are changed by Silverio's generous attitude to the swindler. Tomasa, who has been encouraging her son Sabas to beat doña Balbina up, ends up by threatening Nati equally violently: "¡... como denuncie a esa mujer le voy a dejar la cara como un tomate pocho!" (p.107). Manola also changes her mind with regard to the six pesetas that doña Balbina owes her, again through Silverio's example:

> Manola. (...) Por lo menos que me devuelva las seis pesetas.
> Silverio. (*Baja la voz*) Yo se las daré.
> Manola.-Y si no, déjelo... Que no las devuelva. (p.106)

Silverio is able to exert an obviously positive influence on his neighbours because he has got to know them, he has been able to discover what is good in them, and he loves them as they are.

As Doménech says, the relationship between Fernandita and Esquilache is far from simple. However, it seems clear that Fernandita's outlook changes radically because of her friendship with Esquilache, to whom she feels mysteriously attracted. Fernadita represents the "pueblo" in *Un soñador para un pueblo*, and she is encouraged by Esquilache to believe in his dreams. Esquilache has apparently failed, but his ideals, his dreams of a moral as well as material regeneration, are accepted almost immediately by the maid. In this, Doménech says, he resembles Ignacio.[11] Buero expresses Esquilache's victory through Fernandita's final rejection of Bernardo, who, though a member of the "pueblo", identifies himself with the ambitions of the reactionary faction, and thus at the end of the play is ready to celebrate Esquilache's defeat. Rejecting Bernardo, Fernandita expresses her belief in Esquilache's dream of a new Spain. Though she thought herself weak and miserable, she acquires a new strength. Like Esquilache, who, as we have seen, has to face humiliation and insults from the same people whom he is trying to save, Fernandita bravely refuses to go with Bernardo, also suffering his violent insults.

In *Las Meninas* the great painter in the court is influenced by Pedro, a beggar who is nearly blind but who, as we have seen, is able to 'see' and understand Velázquez's painting. After a very long time, the painter still remembers Pedro's teaching. "Un hombre no debe ser esclavo de otro hombre", he tells Juan Pareja, calling him "hijo mío" (p.147). He puts into practice Pedro's teaching and acknowledges that the beggar's words made a great impact on him and caused him to change (p.164). On his return, Pedro's words continue to move the painter. Pedro encourages him to believe in his own work, forgetting his scruples:

> Velázquez.-Me siento en deuda con vos.
> (...)
> Pedro.- ... También vos habéis pintado desde vuestro dolor, y vuestra pintura muestra que aún en Palacio se puede abrir los ojos, si se quiere. (p.182)

Velázquez also puts into practice the last piece of advice Pedro gives him before his death: "Sed digno, pero sed hábil" (p.210). The painter strives to defend his painting during his trial, in spite of the sorrow that the betrayal of others causes him.

In his turn, Velázquez exerts a certain influence on the Infanta. Others notice that she has been seeking the painter's company. "La señora infanta doña María Teresa sí frecuenta ahora el obrador. (...) Hablan. Ya sabéis que a la señora infanta le place hablar ... y pensar..." (p.122). The infanta acknowledges that she has a thirst for knowledge which only the painter can assuage: "¡Yo quiero saber! Y recurro a vos" (p.151); "¡Me ahogo en la Corte y sólo confío en vos!" (p.153). Velázquez gives her the example of his honesty, teaches her that one needs to keep one's eyes open. He tells the king honestly and bravely his opinion about the corruption in the Court. The Infanta too dares to confront her own father courageously.

David too exerts a powerful influence on some of the characters surrounding him. From the beginning we see his determination to tell everyone that the blind must not resign themselves, that they must develop their abilities. Donato believes in him, even though he will betray him out of fear. David is like a father to him; he inspires him with confidence. But Donato is not able to remain by David's side; he is too weak and he loses his faith.

Even though at first she does not understand him, Adriana immediately feels attracted by David, and tries to help him, imploring Valindin to allow him to keep his violin, and trying to help him in every possible way.

David does not waver in his faith, in spite of his colleagues' mistrust and of Donato's betrayal: "¡Pero lo que yo quería puede hacerse! ¡Los ciegos leerán, los ciegos aprenderán a tocar los más bellos conciertos!" (p.121). David also has the strong will to which Ortega referred in his *Meditaciones*, a "querer" which initiates the tragic process:

> La volición libérrima inicia y engendra el proceso trágico.
> Y este "querer", creador de un nuevo ámbito de realidades
> que sólo por él son -el orden trágico-, es, naturalmente,
> una ficción para quien no existe más querer que el de la
> necesidad natural, la cual se contenta con sólo lo que es.
> (p.127)

The hero is not happy with the present state of affairs, "anticipa el porvenir y a él apela. Sus ademanes tienen una significación utópica" (p.130). David foresees the realization of his ideal. Though he is not understood, his powerful will also exerts a strong influence on some of those who come to know him. He tries to convince the others that it is all a matter of really wanting to do something. "Hay que poner en esto todo nuestro empeño ... Podremos leer" (p.27). The other blind men will not be able to achieve things because they do not really want to. "¡Hay que querer!", David tells them (p.28). He gives an example of how a strong will can achieve things which would seem extremely hard or nearly impossible: "Me empeñé en que mi garrote llegaría a ser para mí como un ojo. Y lo he logrado. ¡Hermanos, empeñémonos todos en que nuestros violines canten juntos y lo lograremos! ¡Todo es querer!" (pp.28-9).[12] If one believes it possible, it can and must be done.

David does not lack the will to achieve his ideal. Even though he does
not have the time to see his dream accomplished, he has proved that his
determination is real and his faith is unshakeable. It is his faith and
determination which, according to Johnston, remind us of Don Quixote:

> Once again, it is the figure of Don Quijote which springs to
> mind. And although David is given no overt quixotic
> symbolism, unlike others among Buero's canon of visionary
> characters, there can be no doubt that his capacity to
> pursue an ideal in the face of widespread disbelief and
> abuse is a virtue that Buero believes to be the spiritual
> mainspring of Don Quijote.

David also becomes a Christlike figure. "His emphasis on the conquering
of a new world through faith and power of will, and the injection of these
spiritual values into a world lurching into a materialistic stagnation, are
essential of the Christology Buero has embodied in David." Adriana
is ready to give up everything she possesses for a man who has very
little more than dreams and the determination to make them come true.
"Without question" -says Johnston - "it is David who stimulates Adriana
into the realization of the possibility of a form of personal plenitude
beyond the self-interest which defines her relationship with
Valindin."[13] Sancho too was ready to give up whatever little he had
in order to follow a determined dreamer. Despite his betrayal, Donato,
like Carlos, inherits David's anguish. Valentín Haüy refers to him at
the end of the play as

> otro ciego, ya viejo, que toca desde hace años el violín por
> las esquinas. ... Tiene la cara destrozada por la viruela;
> parece medio imbécil y ya es mayor para entrar en mi
> colegio... Nunca toca otra cosa que ese adagio de Corelli.
> Y siempre va solo. (pp.125-6)

Perhaps he has inherited David's faith as he has inherited the music
which symbolized it. As we have already seen, David's dreams do not
vanish; they indeed live on in the people who meet him.[14]

Silvano's ambitions are well defined. He acknowledges his own cowardice, but struggles against and overcomes it. He openly expresses his opinion about the situation of the country, about the dictator. He does not hesitate to speak with the authority of someone who knows, in spite of having discovered that Alejandro is in fact Goldmann, the dictator. He thus attracts Carlos, who had previously obeyed the dictator blindly. He addresses him with firm conviction: "No: usted ha luchado por Goldmann, para que él y su camarilla siguiesen tiranizando al país a costa de los insensatos como usted... que prefieren luchar a pensar" (p.145). Silvano has just met Carlos but is not afraid to talk to him clearly. This security, the authority in his judgements, also attract Ana, who has been subject to Alejandro's power. A weak, fearful woman, bound to the authority of so hateful a being, whose vileness she had not dared to reproach him with because she was living off him, is transformed by Silvano's firm words, which fill her with confidence and calm. Silvano, the intellectual who considers himself spiritless and cowardly, by his audacity wins over the irresolute Ana, and she is now strong, bold, and able to face death.

Sancho came to trust his master's courage, but only after a profound transformation had taken place in him. The Sancho who described himself as "pacífico y enemigo de meterme en ruidos ni pendencias" (I,8), and who had shivered in Part I, Chapter 20 ("Mas era tanto el miedo que había entrado en su corazón, que no osaba apartarse un negro de uña de su amo"), is the same who exclaims in Part II, Chapter 47: "..., y denme a mí de comer; que yo me avendré de cuantas espías y matadores y encantadores viniesen sobre mí y sobre mi ínsula."

Without meaning to be influential, or to transmit his ideas to anyone, el Padre in *El tragaluz* obviously manages to make his son Mario the spokesman for his ideas. Mario strives to make sense of his father's questions and apparently silly remarks. Mockingly, Vicente compares his role to that of the prophet of a ridiculous god:

Estás en peligro: actúas como si fueses el profeta de un dios ridículo... De una religión que tiene ya sus ritos: las

postales, el tragaluz, los monigotes de papel... ¡Reacciona!
(p.78)[15]

Mario's life with his father, with the madman, has transformed him, whereas the mother has not tried to make sense of her husband's words or actions, and has not become his disciple. Mario is able to recognize the "mente lúcida" to which the Investigadores refer. He not only makes an effort to understand the Father's words but also imitates his behaviour. The Father refused to go back to work when he was given a chance after the war. Mario has adopted the same approach to life: he prefers not to get involved with society, he has chosen to remain in the basement, and has adopted the same occupation as his father: watching people. What the Father does with his postcards, Mario does with the people he sees through his "tragaluz". He understands the importance of asking the great question, and he has obviously learnt this from his father.

Eloy, in *Mito*, offers the most evident parallel to Don Quixote. In both, their nerve and courage are due to a profound conviction of their own strength. Simón resembles doubtful, cowardly Sancho, confident only by reason of his master's strength. He doubts the existence of the "visitantes", considers Eloy a madman; but, like Sancho, he trusts his friend and takes refuge in him. On the other hand, he wants to secure a good position for himself when those "visitantes" grant Eloy favours and privileges: "De esta ciudad podrida y despreciable/ Me conformo con ser burgomaestre" (p.156). In the same fashion, Sancho seeks to attain possession of his island or countship, or whatever his master deigns to give him. In Part I, 35, he thoroughly looks for the head of the giant that Don Quixote thinks he has killed, because this will earn him the favours of the person they think is Princess Micomicona: "Sólo sé que vendré a ser tan desdichado que, por no hallar esta cabeza se me ha de deshacer mi condado como la sal en el agua." Likewise, he protects his pack-saddle explaining: "... en buena guerra ganó mi señor don Quijote estos despojos" (I,44).

Simón refers to Eloy's madness in his unpolished language: "A usted y a mí nos faltan los tornillos/ de la sesera y escuchamos músicas/ lo mismo que viajamos en platillos" (p.222). The Sancho of *Mito* considers himself mad, as he compares himself to Eloy. So did Sancho, who considered himself a madman by choice. In Part II, Chapter 10, he reasons in the following terms: "Éste, mi amo, por mis señales he visto que es un loco de atar, y aún también yo no lo quedo en zaga, pues soy más mentecato que él, pues le sigo y le sirvo, si es verdadero el refrán que dice: 'Dime con quién andas, decirte he quién eres'." Other characters think he is even worse than his master: "Perecía de risa la duquesa en oyendo hablar a Sancho, y en su opinión le tenía por más loco que su amo; y muchos hubo en aquel tiempo que fueron deste mismo parecer" (II,32). The duchess herself confesses her thoughts to the squire in the following Chapter:

> Me anda brincando un escrúpulo en el alma, y un cierto susurro llega a mis oídos que me dice: Pues don Quijote de la Mancha es loco, menguado y mentecato, y Sancho Panza su escudero lo conoce, y, con todo eso, le sirve y le sigue, y va atenido a las vanas promesas suyas, sin duda alguna debe de ser él más loco y tonto que su amo. (II,33)

Simón's faith, however, wavers like Sancho's: "¡Su forma es de bacía de barbero!", he insists (p.158). Later on he will pride himself on his friendship with Eloy: "... porque sé que **el que a buen árbol se arrima**..." (p.183), also using a proverb of which Sancho was very fond. The squire too was proud of working for his master:

> ... soy quien júntate a los buenos y serás uno de ellos..., **yo me he arrimado a buen señor** y ha muchos meses que ando en su compañía y he de ser otro como él, Dios queriendo" (II,32).

At the arrival of the second "visitantes", Eloy does not fear. Simón seems to have been instilled with Eloy's serenity (*"Simón se levantó también bruscamente sereno"*, p.195). But when they hear the voices of the fake Martians, "*Eloy se arrodilla conmovido. Simón titubea, se acerca y se arrodilla detrás de él*" (p.196). As we have already seen, the moment of betrayal comes too when Simón hesitates and denies his friendship with Eloy. In spite of this, Simón continues to believe in Eloy as his only protection. When the third group of "visitantes" arrive, Simón screams, "*asustado*": "¡Eloy, visitantes!", while he hides behind him ("*se guarece tras él buscando amparo*", p.228).

The cowardly Simón brings the dying Eloy what he calls "su remedio". After Eloy's death the basin no longer sounds like brass: "*Repentinamente, comienza a sonar la extraña sucesión de notas que Eloy oía en ella y que pronto gana intensidad*" (p.241). Simón and Marta hear the "invasora catarata". The "Electricista", "el Regidor", Salustio, and "Mozas de partido", find themselves stopping to look at the barber's basin, which somehow attracts their attention, though they do not exactly know why.[16] Of course, the spectator or reader is also invited by Buero to believe in Eloy's marvellous world.

Eloy dies struggling, filled with faith, and Simón undoubtedly learns, but continues to lean on Eloy's faith. Simón puts the basin on Eloy's head to try to encourage him. We have seen, however, that Simón does not sound as sincere as Sancho, who also tried to console his master with words that he had obviously learnt from him:

> Levántese desa cama, y vámonos al campo vestidos de pastores, como tenemos concertado: quizá tras de alguna mata hallemos a la señora Dulcinea desencantada, que no haya más que ver. (II,74)

In *La Fundación*, both Lino and Tomás undergo a profound transformation due to the powerful influence of Asel. When Asel confides to them his plan for escaping from the prison, they think it is impossible: "¿Te has vuelto loco?", Lino exclaims (p.235). Tomás says to Asel: "A Tulio y a mí nos confiaste ese proyecto. Pero ahora, explicado a fondo..., lo veo imposible ... ¡Es absurdo, Asel! ... Es

increíble. Una ilusión. ... ¡Nos oirán, nos sorprenderán¡ ... (*Débil.*)
Ni siquiera lograremos que nos trasladen... Si tú pudieras venir con
nosotros..." (pp.236 & 237). Tomás does not consider himself capable
of attempting to carry out the project, unless Asel is with him. "Contigo
al lado me atreveré a todo", he says to Asel (p.241). However, Tomás
learns from Asel and, in a very short period of time, inherits his
courage. After Asel's death, Tomás's determination increases, though
he initially thought that he would be able to do nothing without Asel's
support.

> Tomás.- (...) Si a nosotros nos ha llegado la hora, poco
> importa. (*Se vuelve y lo mira.*) Lino, la afrontaremos como
> Asel. Con valor. Porque Asel no ha sido cobarde. (p.254)

Lino admitted that he was not ready to trust anyone: "Yo nunca me he
fiado de nadie" - he said to Asel. "Ni de ti" (p.234). He also thinks that
the project was impossible. "¿No estás fantaseando?", he asks Tomás,
who has now acquired a new strength and is ready to carry out the
arduous task. But soon Lino too is prepared to run the risk: "¡Oye!...
Me gustaría" (p.255). Asel tried to make Lino see that violence is
useless: "No más violencia" (p.247). Having learnt them himself, Tomás
tries to remind Lino of Asel's teachings:

> Aunque la más justa indignación nos encienda la sangre,
> hemos de aprender a dominarla. Si no acertamos a separar
> la violencia de la crueldad, seremos aplastados. Asel tenía
> razón, Lino. Sabía más que nosotros... Y yo nunca
> olvidaré sus palabras. (pp.255-6)

Asel tried to teach Lino that it is necessary to reflect before acting:

> Lino.-¡Déjame pensar!
>
> Asel.-Piénsalo... Pero bien. (p.239)

First Asel's words, and then Tomás's, make him change:

Lino.-Sí, todo lo he podido echar a perder. Aún tengo que
aprender a pensar...
Tomás.-Y yo... (p.256).

Tomás realizes that a deep transformation is taking place, even inside
themselves: "Ya está cambiando. Incluso dentro de nosotros." They
both know that the cause for such radical change has been Asel's
example:

> Tomás.-Yo no enloqueceré ya por esa ilusión, ni por
> ninguna otra. Si hay que morir, no temblaré. (...) Esa
> fuerza también se la debemos a Asel. Y yo le doy las
> gracias... con fervor. (p.255)

Doubtful and hesitant before, they are now ready to face death if it
comes. Asel has provided them with the strength they needed to trust
themselves.

In *Caimán* one finds Rosa completely absorbed in her firm conviction
that her daughter Carmela is still alive. Her confidence is complete.
Her faith attracts Dionisio; from the beginning he tries to understand
her. Néstor, her husband, attempts to make her forget her obsession.
As early as the beginning of Parte Primera, Néstor remarks: "No hay
que acometer empresas en que sólo se ganen palos." Dionisio replies:
"Entonces, ninguna" (p.21).

Dionisio's faith, nevertheless, is more insecure, more hesitant than
Rosa's. She believes that her little daughter is now in a garden that she
found after she fell into a pit. "¿Cómo puedes tú, ni nadie, decidir lo
que es posible y lo que no puede serlo?", she challenges Néstor (p.46).
Her conviction is so strong that she does not allow anybody to make her
doubt, and the incredulity of the others does not weaken her faith.

Dionisio is the one who interprets Rosa's attitude most lucidly, but
he does not commit himself to it fully. He explains to Néstor:

> Yo... he querido decirte que es en las esperanzas que
> parecen improbables en las que hay que creer, no en las
> que parecen alcanzables y que tantas veces no se cumplen.

Que ella espera lo que cree y debe esperar. Algo a tu parecer irrealizable y quizá más cierto que toda tu palabrería. (p.52)

• Rosa is much more categorical in her statements: "Lo imposible es lo que se cumple", she affirms (p.100). Rosa's illusions stir up Dionisio's old hopes, the hopes of a man who, "con más de cincuenta años, ¡si será necio!, sigue soñando con esa mujer imposible" (p.57). Néstor calls him mad, as he does Rosa: "¿Estás loco?"; "¡Tal vez!", Dionisio replies (p.59). Rosa had been more confident when her husband asked her "¿Estás loca?"; "¡Sí!", she declared (p.98). Dionisio does not make up his mind to support Rosa entirely. When Néstor inquires of him whether he has ever believed that the girl is alive ("¿Has llegado a creer ni un solo momento que la niña está viva?"), he does not answer openly:

Prefiero no contestarte. Si te digo que no, le irías con el cuento a Rosa, y yo creo que es peligroso desilusionarla. Y si te digo que sí vas a reírte ... claro que eso, al Patachula, le importa ya muy poco. (pp.103-4)

"La Dama" refers to Dionisio as "el hombre que quiso amar a Rosa y sólo sabía amarse a sí mismo" (p.108). Maybe this is the reason why he was not able to identify himself fully with Rosa's faith, and tried to understand her only because he wanted her for himself. We do not know what became of Dionisio after Rosa disappeared. Most probably he was not strong enough to inherit Rosa's determination, much less to try to find Rosa and Carmela in the marvellous garden.

Some of the characters I have referred to above are distinguished, therefore, by their firm and mature faith, by a quixotic confidence in their own ideal. It has already been pointed out that their convictions lead them to act, and that they are not deterred by isolation. It is precisely their determination to realize their ideals, to remain strong in their faith, that attracts others and ends up transforming them. Some of the characters' encounters with those mentioned, bring about a radical, definitive change in their lives. That is certainly the case with

Carlos, Ana, Fidel, Daniela, Pilar. Some others are initially changed, but the faith that begins to grow in them has not taken deep enough root, and dies before reaching maturity. That is the case of some of the inmates in *En la ardiente oscuridad*, and of Dionisio. We do not know what became of the faith of some of those we have seen vacillate, like Donato, Simón or Leticia. Any reader or spectator may choose to side with one of these groups. But it would be very difficult not to share in Ignacio's, and also Carlos's, anguish (A spectator who was on Carlos's side at the beginning might find himself eventually on Ignacio's, like Carlos himself). The audience are thus led by Buero to participate, as by the *"lento apagón"* in *En la ardiente oscuridad*; they too hear the mysterious notes that come from the barber's basin, see Riquet change into a handsome prince; witness the transformation of the neighbours in *Hoy es fiesta*; see Ana change into a heroically brave character who dies for her cause. It is up to the spectators or readers to decide which side they want to opt for. But, in any case, they will find it difficult to escape the influence of some of these characters and will possibly undergo a similarly deep transformation. Indeed, Ignacio, Riquet, Silverio, David, Silvano, the Father, Eloy and Asel, possess the quixotic "propiedad de volver locos y mentecatos" those who surround them, to turn them into disciples of an absorbing faith. The same may be said of the dramatist himself.

NOTES TO CHAPTER IV

1.   Carlos Suárez, unpublished lecture "The comic side to Don Quixote", University College, Galway (17 April 1991).

2.   José Ortega y Gasset, *Meditaciones del Quijote e Ideas sobre la novela* (Madrid: Revista de Occidente, S.A., 1960), p. 124.

3.   J.L. Aranguren, *Estudios Literarios* (Madrid: Ed. Gredos, S.A., 1976), p. 101.

4.   Aranguren, *Estudios Literarios*, p.107.

5.   Knud Togeby, *La estructura del Quijote*, translated and edited by Antonio Rodríguez Almodóvar (Secretariado de Publicaciones de la Universidad de Sevilla, 1991), p.28.

6.   J.B. Avalle-Arce y E.C. Riley, eds, *Suma Cervantina* (London: Tamesis Books Limited, 1973), p.59.

7.   Knud Togeby argues, however, that both Don Quixote and Sancho were mad from the beginning of the novel, though they suffered from a different sort of insanity.   In his introduction to Togeby's *La estructura del Quijote* Antonio Rodríguez Almodóvar explains: "De ahí también la necesidad de la Segunda parte, que Togeby, usando terminología francesa, califica de "roman d'education", pues en ella tiende a corregirse el abismo que separa a los dos personajes, que no es el abismo [repetimos] entre un loco y un cuerdo, sino entre dos locos de distinta condición".   According to Togeby, the second part of the novel describes parallel processes of the cure of both Sancho and Don Quixote. "La Primera es el libro de la locura y la Segunda el libro de la curación". (*La estructura del Quijote*, pp. 26 & 24.)

8.   According to Carmen González-Cobos Dávila, Buero's tragic heroes have the duty of transmitting their ideal to others, even if this brings about extreme suffering: "...el hombre deberá luchar y vivir en este mundo, tratando de afirmar su verdad, a pesar del constante forcejeo a que será sometido.   Un vivir desviviéndose será pues el resultado de esa lucha, y así el angustioso vivir será el desarrollo característico del personaje.   El dramaturgo no propugna un ascetismo alejándose del mundo para continuar afirmando y defendiendo su propia libertad, sino un estar dentro de él, pese a las dificultades y al dolor de sobrevivir no en uno mismo, sino en los demás.   Y ha de hacerlo contagiando a los que nos rodean de sus angustias y deseos, de sus anhelos y constantes desvelos por esclarecer la verdad y defender la libertad humana, tratando de lograr, así, la supervivencia en la humanidad."

Buero's heroes who have found their own truth have a mission in the world, which consists in making their truth known to others. "El hombre que posee su verdad, por trágica o dolorosa que sea, debe proyectarla sobre los demás, sacarla a la luz para que éstos puedan contagiarse de su luminosidad y puedan salir de su error" (*Antonio Buero Vallejo: el hombre y su obra*, pp.57 & 58).

9. Ignacio hopes even for a miracle. "Porque Ignacio, el realista, el que se sabe ciego, es capaz de esperar, de esperar 'desde el descubrimiento científico..., hasta el milagro' " (Carmen Díaz Castañón, 'De la Residencia a la Fundación', *Estudios sobre Buero Vallejo*, p.275). Enrique Pajón Mecloy, however, has expressed the view that Ignacio does not have any faith. I do not think that Ignacio's words could lead us to believe that "Ignacio asume su limitación valientemente, pero sin fe, sin esperanza alguna de triunfar, sin proponérselo siquiera, hundiéndose en una estéril desesperación" ('¿Ciegos o símbolos?', Ibid., p.241).

10. Catherine Elizabeth Dowd, *Realismo trascendente en cuatro tragedias sociales de Antonio Buero Vallejo*, Estudios de Hispanófila no.29 (University of North Carolina, Department of Romance Languages, 1974), p.74.

11. "En este Esquilache españolizado -mejor aún: *quijotizado*- reaparece algo muy sustancial al protagonista de *En la ardiente oscuridad* y otros personajes afines. ... Como Ignacio, Esquilache trata de llevar su sueño a los otros: a un pueblo que ama como propio, y cuyas necesidades conoce bien, porque él mismo es hijo del pueblo. Como Ignacio, fracasa de una forma inmediata, pero, como el atormentado protagonista de *En la ardiente oscuridad*, su sacrificio no ha sido estéril: otros -en este caso, y en primer lugar, Fernandita- heredarán su sueño, podrán 'salvarse' merced a él" (Doménech, *El teatro de Buero Vallejo*, pp.141-2).

12. According to Johnston, "David becomes typified by his insistence that 'todo es querer' and this is the most important character trait that he shares with Valentin Haüy. For David, 'querer' is the bridge between the audacious world of his imagination and the world of practical achievement" (*Antonio Buero Vallejo. El concierto de San Ovidio*, p.73).

Victor Dixon thinks that, in his emphasis on will power, David is different from - and at the same time resembles - Haüy: "Cuando Haüy se dice que 'el hombre más oscuro de la tierra puede mover montañas, si lo quiere', recordamos las palabras de Jesucristo sobre la fe; recordamos que las citó, en *La señal que se espera*, el filósofo Julián: 'La fe mueve montañas y produce las señales. Por su poder vivimos'; observamos ahora una nueva insistencia en la voluntad, en el querer" ('*Pero todo partió de allí...: El concierto de San Ovidio* a través del prisma de su epílogo').

13. Johnston, *El concierto de San Ovidio*, pp.74 & 76.

14. "David's dreams, nevertheless, like Ignacio's, live on in the people whom he has influenced: in Adriana, in Donato, who years later walks alone through the streets playing only Corelli's 'Adagio', and specially in Valentin Haüy, the inventor of braille, who, moved by the sad spectacle of the beggars' grotesque concert, devotes his life to devising systems to enable the blind to read and who appears as an old man in the last scene of the tragedy and reminisces about the concert and its results. David's dreams have thus come true. The events depicted in this 'tragedia optimista' have resulted in man's triumph over one of his limitations" (Halsey, 'The Dreamer...', p.56).

15. See Doménech, *El teatro de Buero Vallejo* (pp.121-122) for a study of the Father as God figure. After pointing out some reasons why the Father could be considered a symbol for God, he says: "Hay una premeditada ambigüedad en este personaje, que permite encontrar en él, no sólo un viejo demente, sino algo mucho más hondo y misterioso. Ninguno de los rasgos observados nos permitiría decir resueltamente que es un símbolo de Dios; mas, ante ellos, tampoco nos atreveríamos a afirmar resueltamente lo contrario. Es una figura equívoca, extraña, fascinante, como el Godot beckettiano. Con una diferencia, eso sí, y de suma importancia: este Godot sí ha llegado, además, para castigar."

16. According to Magda Ruggeri, this is Eloy's and Don Quixote's victory. "Quando finisce la burla ed Eloy cade nello sconforto, '(*todos evitan su mirada*)'. Alla fine quando è già morto e tutto torna alla normalità come se non fosse successo niente e si ricomincia la rappresentazione teatrale quotidiana, la vista del catino per terra turba tutti: nei loro cinici cuori si è insinuata un'inquietudine. È questa la vittoria: Eloy e Don Quijote l'hanno ottenuta" (*Il teatro di...*, pp.139-140).

Chapter V
ETHICS
The virtues of the quixotic spirit

"A bueno es a lo que nadie te ha ganado, a sencillamente bueno. Y
por eso tienes un altar en el corazón de todos los buenos que no en tu
locura sino en tu bondad paran su vista" (Unamuno, *Vida*).[1]

Unamuno does not deny the fact that Don Quixote is mad. But,
regardless of his insanity, one could consider Don Quixote as simply
"good". One would not go as far as Unamuno in saying that the knight
is a saint, but undoubtedly Don Quixote is usually considered a good
person. Anthony Close says that the novel

> finds room, in the unlikely combination of a romance-
> besotted madman and a vulgar simpleton, and in their
> dealings with most of those whom they meet, including
> shepherds and prostitutes and convicts, for qualities of
> loyalty, compassion, generosity, civility, and
> seriousness.[2]

He also talks about the "widespread and just recognition of the qualities
of humanity, charity and goodness in the character of Cervantes' hero.
Fielding's scattered comments on *Don Quixote* testify to this recognition;
more practically, so does his portrayal of the quixotic Parson Adams in
Joseph Andrews".[3] The eighteenth-century view of the character
might well have prepared the ground for the Romantic approach to the
novel. True, it has been maintained that Don Quixote's humiliations are

only a fair punishment for his vanity.[4] But Don Quixote is too lovable to be rejected. One could hardly pay excessive attention to his vanity, but indeed would tend to overlook it, because it is due to his simplicity and innocence and not to his pride. In fact, in spite of Don Quixote's abundant proud remarks in Part I, the knight considers himself the last amongst knight-errants: "...mas el trabajo, la inquietud y las armas sólo se inventaron e hicieron para aquellos que el mundo llama caballeros andantes, de los cuales yo, aunque indigno, soy el menor de todos" (I,13). The knight knows the importance of humility, of knowing one's miseries and weaknesses:

> Has de poner los ojos en quien eres, procurando conocerte a ti mismo, que es el más difícil conocimiento que puede imaginarse. Del conocerte saldrá el no hincharte como la rana que quiso igualarse con el buey. (II,42)[5]

Henry Fielding suggested that whoever reads Cervantes (and four other writers), "must either have a very bad head, or a very bad heart, if he doth not become both a wiser and a better man."[6] His quixotic Parson Adams, he says in his preface to *Joseph Andrews*, "is designed a character of perfect simplicity" and "the goodness of his heart will recommend him to the good-natured".[7] Don Quixote's goodness of heart recommend him also to the good-natured, who are ready to forgive what could be seen as vanity, mainly in Part I of the novel. Goodness is indeed seen in the novel as an essential aspect of his nature, when Don Quixote is sane (and is called "el Bueno"), but also during his madness:

> ...porque verdaderamente, como alguna vez se ha dicho, en tanto que don Quijote fue Alonso Quijano el Bueno, a secas, y en tanto que fue don Quijote de la Mancha, fue siempre de apacible condición y de agradable trato, y por esto no sólo era bien querido de los de su casa, sino de todos cuantos le conocían. (II,74)

Once Don Quixote's goodness has been established, we need to look at his code of behaviour and his most outstanding virtues. We will have to rely first of all on his own words, as he stated "Yo sé quien soy". Of course, Sancho's opinion should also be borne in mind, since he knows the hero better than any character in the novel. Don Quixote says of himself in I, 50: "De mí sé decir que después de ser caballero andante soy valiente, comedido, liberal, biencriado, generoso, cortés, atrevido, blando, paciente, sufridor de trabajos, de prisiones, de encantos." And Sancho remarks about his master: "No tiene nada de bellaco; antes tiene un alma como un cántaro: no sabe hacer mal a nadie, sino bien a todos, ni tiene malicia alguna" (II,13).

The knight also says that the knight-errant has to be "mantenedor de la verdad aunque le cueste la vida el defenderla" (II,18). Don Quixote himself enumerates the virtues that befit a good knight, but those qualities do not constitute a merely theoretical set of values. Luis Rosales stresses that Don Quixote's behaviour might not be logical but it is ethical: "La lógica de don Quijote no es pura lógica, sino ética. No atiende a realidades, sino a valores."[8] Almost all the characters who have dealings with him recognize his discretion and good nature. For example, in II, 21, we read that, after the episode of Camacho's wedding, Basilio and Quiteria "lleváronse consigo a don Quijote, estimándole por hombre de valor y de pelo en pecho ... y al par de la valentía le graduaron la discreción, teniéndole por un Cid en las armas y por un Cicerón en la elocuencia."

Cide Hamete himself, even though he hesitates to believe the adventures in the Cave of Montesinos, does not dare to doubt the veracity of the knight, referring to him in the following terms: "Pero pensar yo que don Quijote mintiese, siendo el más verdadero hidalgo y el más noble caballero de sus tiempos, no es posible; que no dijera una mentira si le asaetearan" (II,24). Cide Hamete does not accept the story as truthful, but does not doubt the good intentions of Don Quixote. He would never purposely lie. The knight encourages the others to be truthful and seeks to be truthful himself. In Part I of the novel he believes he possesses the truth about himself, about his perception of reality. In Part II his interest in finding the truth is more obvious precisely because he is not so sure of himself, of his own perception of the world surrounding him. As I have already mentioned when referring to Don Quixote's dreams, after the episode in the Cave, he is worried that the story he is telling Sancho might just be a concoction. He who believes that a knight must be "mantenedor de la verdad" seriously doubts that he is speaking the truth himself. This concern worsens after the Clavileño episode, when the knight says what he has seen, and Sancho lies. The realization that Sancho could either be lying or dreaming worries the knight: "...o Sancho miente o Sancho sueña" (II,41). The doubt is sown in his mind and he does not tire of searching. Prompted by Sancho, he asks Master Peter's ape "si ciertas cosas que había pasado en la cueva de Montesinos habían sido soñadas o verdaderas" (II,25). Not having obtained a satisfactory answer, he asks the enchanted head in Barcelona: "¿fue verdad o fue sueño lo que yo cuento que me pasó en la cueva de Montesinos?" (II,62) Don Quixote not only has a truthful nature, and advises others to be truthful; he sets Sancho a good example by seeking the truth. Comparing Don Quixote and Tomás Rodaja, Luis Rosales refers to the truthful nature of their behaviour, which, according to him, is the root of their madness: "...la locura de ambos consiste en ser únicamente verdaderos" (pp.109-110). Don Quixote has his own truth: "Don Quijote entiende la verdad como coincidencia del hombre consigo mismo y no como conformidad del pensamiento con las cosas" (p.453). He does not proclaim the truth in absolute terms, but what he thinks to be the truth, showing a predominantly truthful nature.[9]

In Chapter 26, after the adventure of the puppet show, Sancho consoles Master Peter with laudatory words for his master: "No llores, maese Pedro, ni te lamentes, que me quiebras el corazón; porque te hago saber que es mi señor don Quijote tan católico y escrupuloso cristiano, que si él cae en la cuenta de que te ha hecho algún agravio, te lo sabrá y te lo querrá pagar y satisfacer con muchas ventajas." And Master Peter himself will later on have to acknowledge the truthfulness of Sancho's words: "No esperaba yo menos de la inaudita cristiandad del valeroso don Quijote de la Mancha, verdadero socorredor y amparo de todos los menesterosos y necesitados vagamundos". Cervantes himself adds: "En resolución, la borrasca del retablo se acabó y todos cenaron en paz y buena compañía, a costa de don Quijote, que era liberal en todo extremo." Cervantes confirms that the knight is "tan cortés y tan amigo de dar gusto a todos" (II,16). Don Quixote has a real aim: justice tempered by mercy. His task is the service of his neighbour; that is the reason for his being on earth. He himself states: "...soy católico cristiano y amigo de hacer bien a todo el mundo; que para esto tomé la orden de la caballería andante que profeso, cuyo ejercicio aún hasta hacer bien a las ánimas del purgatorio se estiende" (II,48). There is no human being to whom Don Quixote does not want to lend the strength of his arm. He is detached from any material concerns. He lives on scarcely any food and spends many nights wide awake. "'Tened las cosas como si no las tuviésedes', decía Cervantes recordando a San Pablo (1 Cor.,31)" (Rosales, p.873). As he is a generous, self-denying knight, the service of his neighbour consititutes his food, his nourishment.[10] He lives with the most extreme sobriety, and yet he is ready to give away all he owns. His refined courtesy, on the other hand, shows his profound respect for the dignity of every human being.

For her part, the duchess remarks: "...según se me ha traslucido, la que más campea entre sus virtudes es la de la honestidad" (II,44). And, of course, like a good knight, he is able to keep his word: "...y aunque perdí la honra, no perdí, ni puedo perder, la virtud de cumplir mi palabra" (II,66).

We also see Don Quixote suffer unbearably cruel humiliations. He really is "sufridor de dolores". In Chapter 59 he remarks: "...cuando esperaba palmas, triunfos y coronas, granjeadas y merecidas por mis valerosas hazañas, me he visto esta mañana pisado, y acoceado, y molido, de los pies de animales inmundos y soeces." This capacity to suffer is also part of his virtue. When referring to quixotic heroism, Luis Rosales speaks of his capacity to suffer humiliations and his struggle against the environment: "La humillación es el supuesto previo del heroísmo ... El heroísmo no consiste en derrotar ejércitos y enamorar doncellas (éste sería más bien el heroísmo de Amadís o de Don Galaor), sino en la intencionalidad de sus hazañas y en la manera de conllevar la repetida humillación de sus fracasos" (pp.429 & 429). His heroism is not like that of Amadís, does not consist of triumphs, but springs from failure, from constant humiliation. "No sólo la derrota, sino la humillación son necesarias para que nuestro héroe se vaya revelando íntegramente. El amor al prójimo nos hace humildes y lleva a Don Quijote a límites extremos de renunciación" (pp.434-5). There would be no heroism, or indeed we could not talk of quixotic heroism, if triumph and victory constantly accompanied his actions. Don Quixote, and some of Buero's characters, reveal themselves as heroes only as a result of their arduous struggle against their environment:

> La lucha con el medio ambiente es un supuesto previo del heroísmo quijotesco, y por tanto, todos los personajes de la novela han de cumplir esta función y evidenciarla con palo, escarnio y risa. ...la burla es justamente la aureola de su espiritualidad, y en arrostrarla estriba la mejor parte de su heroísmo. (Rosales, p.428)

Nevertheless, Don Quixote is heroic above all in his virtues. There is no mediocrity in his behaviour. The virtues he is blessed with are not only heroic but multiple. And, according to don Antonio Moreno, "la virtud se ha de honrar donde quiera que se hallare" (II,62). Besides trying to put all the virtues into practice, on several occasions Don Quixote expounds clearly and methodically the basis of what he considers good behaviour. It would suffice to examine closely the pieces of advice that the knight gives his squire when the latter is about to head off for his "ínsula". For his part Ernest A. Siciliano enumerates among the "natural virtues" the knight is endowed with, the following: "Affability, goodbreeding, courtesy, civility, diligence, generosity, valiancy, patience, defense of the truth, sacredness of keeping one's word".[11] Ricardo Aguilera remarks on the knight's generosity: "Don Quijote se sublimiza en la generosidad extremada, en el desinterés personal llevado a sus últimas consecuencias."[12] Finally, Mauro

Olmeda attributes to Don Quixote the virtues of a modern man; "...frente al código de los supuestos formales del honor en que cifraba su alcurnia el caballero medioeval, don Quijote encarna en el tipo de caballero andante las mejores calidades representativas del hombre moderno" (p.262). He stresses Don Quixote's nobility, generosity, resilience, and optimism, and laments the fact that Cervantists have often failed to recognize those quixotic virtues in Sancho; he praises above all Sancho's loyalty and faith.[13]

Other critics have stressed Don Quixote's concern for liberty. "Non bene pro toto libertas venditur auro", Cervantes quotes in the prologue to the novel. Cervantes expresses through his hero the supreme value of individual freedom. The knight proclaims and teaches his squire its immense value. On the other hand, as J.B. Avalle-Arce has argued, "el hacerse caballero andante ... es la cabal expresión de su absoluta libertad de escoger."[14] In fact, many of Cervantes' characters speak readily of freedom, and certainly the narrator misses no opportunity to remark on the free will of the individual, a concept which is emphasized by many Golden Age writers. In El licenciado Vidriera, for example, Cervantes remarks almost by the way: "...como si hubiese en el mundo yerbas, encantos ni palabras suficientes a forzar el libre albedrío".[15] Again, in El celoso extremeño, he writes of "este suceso, ejemplo y espejo de lo poco que hay que fiar de llaves, tornos y paredes cuando queda la voluntad libre".[16]

In Don Quixote the knight appears as the upholder of the freedom of all mankind, of every creature. The episode of the liberation of the galley slaves is well known:

> En resolución -replicó don Quijote-, como quiera que ello sea, esa gente, aunque los llevan, van de por fuerza, y no de su voluntad ... Aunque bien sé que no hay hechizos en el mundo que puedan mover y forzar la voluntad ... Porque me parece duro caso hacer esclavos a los que Dios y naturaleza hizo libres. (I,22)

It is clear that Don Quixote is reflecting Cervantes' ideas on freedom, the ideas of a man who suffered imprisonment and knows that individual free will cannot be curtailed by chains. Don Quixote sympathizes immediately with these prisoners, even if they are chained for the right reasons, and for the good of other members of society. He is also quick to stop those who try to pursue Marcela in spite of her desire to remain free (I,14). Luis Rosales goes so far as to say that "la libertad es la clave decisiva del pensamiento cervantino. Para Cervantes ser sí mismo es, ante todo y sobre todo, ser libre". "La obra de Cervantes es un esfuerzo inteligible, tenaz y denodado, para reedificar la libertad, poniendo al descubierto sus raíces" (pp.161 & 25). Many of Cervantes's characters want to choose their own future; only by being free can they find their real selves. They make an effort to be free of their own past, though at times it is not feasible. It is not possible for them to start all over again.

> Los personajes cervantinos quieren desarraigarse no solamente de su mundo, sino también de su pasado. No peregrinan: huyen de la vida social. Sueñan con vivir sin atadura alguna, y casi todos, igual que don Quijote, el hermano mayor, no pertenecen a su tiempo, sino a su libertad. (Rosales, pp.36-7)

Buero considers it essential to have an "ética quijotesca": "Considero indispensable la persistencia de un fondo quijotesco -de una ética- en el hombre, que se armonice con su acción práctica". He is interested in the individual, in man, in whom he is aware that there is something mysterious. It is also clear that Buero is an ethical writer.[17] He makes his audience face their own flaws. "Buero Vallejo ha sido considerado y aceptado como un escritor crítico, como un fustigador de lacras sociales y morales, y ello pese a cualesquiera reservas e incluso a veces ataques muy duros de los más opuestos sectores ideológicos." He tries to address the conscience of the individual, and Doménech maintained in 1973 that no other Spanish author in the previous three decades had managed to do it in such depth: "...ningún otro autor español de las últimas tres décadas ha calado tan profundamente en la conciencia de sus contemporáneos."[18]   Critics, and Buero himself, have stressed his concern for the moral regeneration of the individual rather than, though in addition to, social and political reform of the community, aware that only a deep moral regeneration of the individual can bring about the desired change in society. This is what he tries to provoke in his spectators, freeing them "from the destructive nexus of forces imposed from within and without ('la ceguera'), by awakening them to the clear-sighted realization that moral re-examination and correction can challenge what has been consistently presented as a static and ineluctable destiny".[19]   Buero does not consider himself one of those writers whom he calls "acomodaticios"; he is among the "escritores que quieren poner en su obra lo que podríamos llamaɪ ɪa responsabilidad humana" (Interview).[20]   Buero's interest in Don Quixote is closely related therefore to his interest in human ethics and values. In words I have quoted in the Introduction, he states: "Me atrae el hallazgo 'ético' que representa el hidalgo manchego".   Let us now consider to what extent we can say that Buero's characters behave according to ethical values that could be described as "quixotic". I propose to examine some of their most outstanding virtues: passion for truth, generosity and compassion, heroic courage and love of liberty.

Buero considers Rosales's view of quixotic truth very accurate, "porque la verdad externa a nosotros, la verdad de las cosas, es una verdad cambiante"[21] (Interview).   Ruiz Ramón also speaks of this passion for truth in Buero's theatre. Again, he does not think Buero is looking for the Truth, but for individual truths: "Es esa pasión por la verdad, la de cada uno y la de todos, y no Verdad alguna con mayúscula y en abstracto, la que convierte el teatro de Buero Vallejo, por amargo y oscuro que a veces parezca, en un teatro de salvación, de salvación radical del hombre muy por encima de todo optimismo y de todo pesimismo."[22]

One of the characters who make the greatest effort to pursue the truth is Amalia. Her determination is so firm that she overcomes all the obstacles in her way, draws strength from weakness. She plays with the feelings of the painter's ambitious family, disguising her own sorrow after Mauricio's death. The discovery of the truth is vital for Amalia. In the first act, Sabina tells the nurse that Amalia is about to change her dress in order to welcome her "amigos". The nurse is surprised, and she explains: "La he visto tan deshecha por la muerte del señor... No la hubiera creído capaz de pensar en eso." Sabina replies: "La señora es capaz de eso y de mucho más" (pp.9-10). Amalia is capable of anything in order to find out the truth. The information that Amalia is trying to discover is not the only truth that is revealed that night. We hear about the humiliating and pitiful situation in which Mónica and Leonor found themselves before Mauricio's death, having to beg for money, treated like "pordioseras y esclavas" by Dámaso. We also come to realize the truth about Dámaso's false dignity. His own wife reproaches him: "¡Él es un caballero condecorado! ¡La compraste [la medalla] en el rastro! ¡Te la pusiste por primera vez hace quince años, cuando el amigo que te recomendó te dijo que te la habían denegado!" (p.52). Dámaso also discovers that night that his wife had been hiding from him the money they managed to get out of Mauricio. And finally, we learn the truth that Amalia yearned to find. It is Leandro who eventually admits: "¡Me propuso sacarte dinero si te lograba. ¡Y por negarme... nos calumnió a los dos, ante Mauricio, aquella tarde!" (p.73). Lorenzo completes the truth with his confession: "Después me negó el dinero... Me disgustó la negativa y le hablé de vosotros dos; sí... Y me contestó: 'Estáis muy insidiosos hoy el padre y el hijo. Leandro acaba de aconsejarme que tenga cuidado con Amalia'" (pp.73-74).

Amalia has struggled earnestly to find the truth. Her in-laws' tears and resistance, her own exhaustion, do not weaken her determination. All of them are humiliated, and she triumphs: the truth has been found after two long hours. Amalia is now happy to have recovered Mauricio forever. Her effort also brings about a radical change in her husband's relatives, who may have been helped to lead a more truthful existence. As Ruiz Ramón says about the inquiry that she carries out on that unforgettable night: "Esa finalidad de la investigación es el descubrimiento de una verdad que puede destruir o salvar a Amalia, pero que es necesaria para dar sentido y autenticidad a su existencia personal."[23]

Silvano also strives to be rid of his weariness and struggles to the end. He considers himself weak, cowardly; when Alejandro and Ana arrive, the professor is physically exhausted, not having eaten for two days. He has six months of intense suffering behind him: he was expelled from his professorial chair by the Government, and the professor himself says: "Mis propios alumnos apedrearon mi casa" (p.129). The reason for his disgrace was that he had written the truth in a pamphlet that Alejandro considered defeatist ("derrotista") but that actually turned out to be truthful, as defeat followed: "Eran verdades inoportunas, peligrosas" (p.144).

With his acute historical outlook, Silvano examines the facts objectively:

> Carlos.-¡Esos canallas nos han destrozado así a muchas mujeres!
> Silvano.-Sí. Ellos decían lo mismo el siglo pasado, cuando les invadimos nosotros. (p.141)

In spite of his genuine sorrow at Isabel's ill fortune, he does not fail to look at the facts with the detachment of an honest historian, who seeks the truth and pays no heed to fanatics. He does not hesitate to speak up and state his opinions even though he is "medio trastornado por la debilidad" (p.144). Neither is he afraid to tell Goldmann that he recognized him the first night: "Buenas noches, Goldmann ... Yo no le confundo con nadie. Usted es Goldmann" (p.166).

Used to scientific investigation, it is Silvano who, in his miserable state of hunger and exhaustion, encourages the others to find out who was Isabel's killer. And he then insists that they have the obligation to clarify what happened: "Si pudiéramos, deberíamos aclarar esto". Georgina, Alejandro and the sergeant repeat: "Al tren, al tren" (p.194), while Silvano reiterates: "Quedan veinte minutos para que venga el sargento. Intentémoslo" (p.197). And very soon he states: "Yo ya sé quién es" (p.199). Though he already knew who was guilty, and time is short, he patiently shows that Carlos's confession is only the account of a nightmare.

Not even the closeness of the threat of death undermines the professor's veracity. He does not consent to saving his life with a lie, and refuses to confess to having been the murderer of Goldmann, which might have gained him the respect of the invaders. Ana understands that victory is in the truth, even if this means total sacrifice. Silvano also dies totally convinced of his victory. This sort of behaviour is very much in accordance with the wise piece of advice that Don Quixote gave his squire as a norm of good management: "Procura descubrir la verdad por entre las promesas y dádivas del rico como por entre los sollozos e importunidades del pobre" (II,42). It is necessary to discover the truth even if it requires a great effort. And if the promises and gifts of the rich or the sobs and pestering of the poor cannot excuse anybody from seeking it, neither can Silvano's weakness or the frivolous apathy of some of the characters in *Aventura* prevent him from seeking and so finding the truth.

Mary Barnes also makes a great effort to discover the truth in *La doble historia*. When, through her old pupil Lucila, she realizes that she had always been unaware of the true nature of her husband's job, nothing will prevent her from finding out about it: "Dime la verdad", she begs Daniel (p.79). After receiving the book *Breve historia de la tortura*, she reads the whole of it in a café, and believes that "es veraz" (p.87). She even slapped Lucila when she told her of the torture her husband was suffering. Nevertheless, once she has discovered that Lucila's story is true, she fights on Lucila's side. She is not content with knowing the facts, but intends to apply them to her own life, to suffer in her own flesh the consequences of the facts of which she was unaware.

Mario, in *El tragaluz*, struggles in a similar fashion to clarify the truth about his father's illness, the truth of a story that others do not dare to uncover. Vicente and his mother had both learned to live a lie. The Father ended up losing his mind, in a certain sense like Mary Barnes, by suffering the terrible consequences of the discovery of a terrible truth. Mario brings up the old story in spite of the opposition of his mother and of Vicente, who first feigns innocence and eventually makes excuses for his past actions. Mario tells his brother: "Porque yo sé". He in fact knows the truth but is not content with that: he thinks it is time that the others recognized it too: "Antes de Encarna ya has destrozado a otros... Seguro que lo has pensado ... Que nuestro padre puede estar loco por tu culpa" (p.288). This is only the beginning of the search which is going to cause great sorrow both to the family and to Encarna, one of Vicente's victims. The mother guesses what will happen and prefers to stop Mario; she is afraid of facing the truth which she pretends not to know: "Hoy no, hijos... Otro día, más tranquilos" (p.296), "Otro día..."; "Pero no hoy... Ahora estáis disgustados..." (p.297); "¿Por qué esto, hijo?" She tries to postpone the suffering, and Mario knows that it is going to be painful for her: "Madre, perdónanos el dolor que vamos a causarte" (p.298).

The moment comes to talk about the train, the dangerous topic, and she still tries to stop them: "¡No, hijos! Hay que olvidar aquello" (p.302). It is made clear that the Father went mad because of Vicente's disloyalty, "porque él no era un hombre al uso. Él era de la madera de los que nunca se reponen de la deslealtad ajena" (p.303). The Father is made of the same stuff as Mary Barnes. He does not recover because he knows the truth in all its depth. In his madness he is still searching for it, wondering about the identity of the figures he cuts out of magazines and postcards.

The whole truth about the past has emerged. After so many years spent trying to forget the facts, Vicente makes a confession of his guilt. Encarna tries to console Mario after his brother's death: "El quería seguir engañándose... Acuérdate. Y tú querías salvarlo" (p.310). Vicente tried to deceive himself all those years but his younger brother reveals a truth which is hard and brings punishment with it. Vicente pays for a death for which he had not confessed himself responsible before. As he admits his guilt, he pays with his own life.

We have already seen that Julio finds in his dreams part of the truth about his father, his past, Margot, Artemio, Matilde, etc., . He has to face the opposition of all, even of little Nuria; she does not want to accept the awful reality that Julio presents her with. When he reveals what he knows about Felipe and Matilde's affair, she calls him a "sucio mentiroso". They all refuse to admit the truth that they are aware of. This hypocrisy irritates Julio, but he is determined to tell the truth despite the reluctance he encounters. When he openly tells them that he knows that Nuria is Felipe's daughter, what really matters to Artemio, Felipe and Matilde is the fact that Julio "ha reconocido que era una broma" (p.321). What worries them is that somebody else might be aware of their corruption. Hearing the truth openly told by Julio awakens Felipe's remorse. After his son's accusations he begins to feel "cansado, fatigado" (p.326), and will soon die. "Estás demacrado, padre", Julio notices when he recovers his sight for a short while (p.331). Felipe pays for his past crimes. Julio, like Mario, will feel responsible for his death, for having made him confess his guilt. Felipe has felt pangs of remorse for his crimes, as Vicente has for his. But neither is saved from the punishment. Thus, it is necessary to follow Don Quixote's advice and seek the truth always.

Larra is another example of a character who takes risks for the sake of the truth. He expresses this by saying that he refuses to wear a mask: "Aunque los demás crean vérmela intentaré no llevarla. Mi careta será mi risa. Pero no ocultaré nada al que sepa leer" (p.47). His wife reproaches him that he endangers the security of the family, and she advises him to write "como Mesonero", without running any risk of getting into trouble. "Mi deber es decir verdades", Larra replies to her complaint (p.87).

He also suffers the opposition of the censors and of his friends. As happens with Vicente, Daniel and Felipe, the acknowledgement of the truth brings about death. However, this time it is Larra himself who, not being able to cope with bitter reality, takes his own life. The knowledge of a sad truth, and the cowardly reluctance of the others to accept it and do something about it, was impossible to bear.

With a different nuance, the theme reappears in *Jueces en la noche*. Both Julia and Cristina are determined to find out the truth. Cristina realizes that the only reason why Julia has called her instead of her doctor is that she is keen to investigate the past. Juan Luis and Julia's marriage was founded on a terrible lie. The discovery of that falsehood causes, once more, remorse on Juan Luis's part, and atrocious suffering on Julia's; she prefers to die rather than go mad. Cristina plays a similar role to that of Lucila in La doble historia.[24] She reveals to Julia everything that her husband's job involves. Julia also learns from Cristina that Fermín had not betrayed her, that he had been beaten to death in prison but refused to name anyone. Finally, she finds out also that Juan Luis and Ginés had known each other from college. Once again, the truth turns out to be too cruel to be borne, so much so that its discovery can change a whole life. But no effort has been spared in order to reveal it.

It is necesary to be truthful at all costs and at the right time. Otherwise life becomes a ridiculous farce. The characters who strive to find the truth and to live in accord with it are those who are victorious in Buero's plays. As Magda Ruggeri Marchetti writes, "todo el teatro de Buero es una búsqueda constante de la verdad y cada personaje triunfa en la medida en que consigue alcanzarla o, al menos, en que se esfuerza en ello".[25] This search for the truth by our characters becomes all the more arduous and therefore more heroic in so far as for Buero there is no static truth that one can easily find:

> A la verdad uno se acerca por medio del ensayo y del error, lo mismo que en el terreno de la ciencia. . . . ¿cuál es la verdad, la verdad definitiva? No la hay; o, si la hay, la hay en un plano suprafísico que..., hoy por hoy, está fuera de nuestro alcance. Esto acentúa el papel de búsqueda de la verdad. (Interview)

We have seen too that Don Quixote prides himself on being "liberal, biencriado, generoso, cortés" (I,50). In *Aventura en lo gris*, we see Ana and Silvano giving themselves continually, moved to compassion by the other characters' needs. On seeing Silvano, Ana immediately realizes his weakness and hunger, and suggests to Alejandro that they give him some of the food they have. But Alejandro prefers to hide it, to avoid the moral duty of sharing it with the others:

> Ana.-Oye... Ese hombre está muy débil...
> Alejandro.-¿Y qué?
> Ana.-¿No deberíamos darle algo de comer? (p.135)

Again, when she sees Isabel's starving baby, she tries to convince Alejandro to let her give Isabel some food, so that the baby can be properly breast-fed. Alejandro refuses to consider it, but Ana insists:

> Ana.-Alejandro, ella ha intentado darle el pecho al niño...
> pero la criatura apenas saca nada, y ese poco será como
> agua. Si se pudiese encontrar para ella algo de comer.
> (pp.149-50)

When she has realized that it is impossible to convince him, we learn from Isabel that Ana gives her a sandwich against Alejandro's will. "Ella me ha dado ya algo de lo suyo", Isabel says to Silvano (p.172). Ana also shares her food with Silvano:

> Ana.-Le traigo esto. Cómalo y sosténgase.
> Silvano.-Usted... es muy bondadosa. (p.168)

If Ana's generosity is extraordinary, Silvano's verges on the heroic. After all, Ana claims that she is not hungry, as she has eaten something shortly before they arrived at the shelter. By contrast, Silvano had not taken any food for days, only hot water to warm himself up. When he is offered the sandwich, he just takes a bite and smells it. In spite of his weakness, he decides to give it to Isabel so that she can feed the baby. "Venga y cómase esto", he whispers. Isabel thinks she should only eat half. The professor insists: "¿La mitad de esto? Dar la mitad no es dar nada" (p.172). He wants to give the little he has, everything. His generosity knows no bounds.[26]

As they all notice, the professor can hardly remain upright. Nevertheless, in very gentlemanly fashion, he stands up and tries to carry Ana's larger case. "*Ana va a coger las maletas. Silvano se adelanta instintivamente a coger la mayor. No puede con ella y desfallece*" (p.130). Despite the resistance of the fanatical Carlos, Silvano offers to heat water for the baby and to prepare its bottle: "Habrá que hervirlos. Traiga ... Traiga, hombre. Cerillas aún me quedan ... Es para esa pobre criatura" (p.146). Silvano, like Don Quixote, is ready to use the last bit of strength he has left. Don Quixote also offered all his energy when aware that he was running out of it:

> Si vuestras cuitas, angustiada señora, se pueden prometer
> alguna esperanza de remedio por algún valor o fuerzas de
> algún andante caballero, aquí están las mías que, aunque
> flacas y breves, todas se emplearán en vuestro servicio.
> (II,38)

Both Ana and Silvano draw strength from weakness because they are generous, because they know how to give themselves to others. Like Don Quixote, they deprive themselves of nourishment in order to feed the weakest. That is why they are able to give their lives when the moment comes for a total sacrifice, which Don Quixote would have made for anyone in need.

We could perhaps apply to Ana and Silvano the words that J.J. Allen uses of the knight, who, though he "began as a figure... inferior to his environment, the anti-type of Amadís, moves through a process of self-purification to a position of superiority through humility and self-knowledge."[27] They both know their cowardice, their weakness, but both overcome it with total generosity.

We have already seen how powerfully influential is Silverio's generosity. He is another one of those characters who are dedicated to achieving the happiness of others: Fidel's, Daniela's, his wife's, and that of all the other neighbours. When they all think they have won a prize in the lottery, he is the last to say that he also expected to win fifteen thousand pesetas, because to him "lo importante es que les haya tocado a muchos que lo necesitaban de veras" (p.97). Like Silvano, Silverio wants to give everything. He has also lost something valuable himself. He will have to suffer "una semana de estrechez por el aparatito que he tenido que romper" (p.104). The other neighbours have not lost much because they possessed very little before doña Balbina played the trick on them. But Silverio, in order to defend one of the neighbours from being beaten, has to destroy the little contraption that was going to keep him going for a few days. He told Elías in the first act: "Hoy lo termino y mañana lo cobro ... Con esto tiraré hasta la semana próxima, que inauguran la verbena" (p.44). But he does not hesitate to break it the same day, only to prevent Sabas from hitting doña Balbina, who, after all, is a swindler: "*Sin pensarlo, toma su aparato de latón, lo empuña y sacude a Sabas...*" (p.100). He does not hesitate to give all he has. He behaves like a good knight; like the one from La Mancha he has to be "caritativo con los menesterosos" (II,18).

He does not base his judgements on the evil he finds in his neighbours. He admires what is good in them: "Son de oro", he says (p.108); he looks at reality with hopeful eyes. Likewise, Don Quixote not only refuses to concentrate on the negative side of the other characters, but does not even see that bad side. As Luis Rosales points out,

> Don Quijote despersonaliza generalmente a sus ofensores. Su bondad es ilimitada y no concibe una intención aviesa en las personas que le rodean (...)
> Don Quijote es invidente para la maldad. Su mirada es un acto de fe. Todo aquello que existe, y es real, y cae bajo sus ojos, se encuentra limpio de pecado. (...) En su historia, la maldad es cosa de encantadores y no de hombres. (p.459)

In the play we witness what doña Balbina calls "la comedia del perdón" (p.110). The knight from La Mancha was known for his forgiveness. He cannot hold grudges against anyone. In Part I, Chapter 30, when Sancho "blasphemed" against Dulcinea, Don Quixote "le dio tales dos palos que dio con él en tierra." Once forgiven by his master, Sancho begged him not to be so vengeful. Don Quixote replied: "Ya te perdoné entonces, y bien sabes tú que suele decirse: 'A pecado nuevo, penitencia nueva'." He highlights that virtue in one of the pieces of advice that he gives his squire, "...que fue que cuando la justicia estuviese en duda, me decantase y acogiese a la misericordia" (II,51).

Silverio shows a clearly merciful nature, not only forgiving the swindler himself, but inviting the rest of the neighbours, who were furiously disappointed, to have mercy on her too. When they all rush into the fray, Silverio tries to hold them back. And when they try to denounce her to the police, Silverio begs them "que no la denuncien"; "¡Espere!", he implores Tomasa (p.102). "¡Calma! Fidel, ¿quiere pedir a todos los vecinos, en mi nombre y... en el de estas dos pobres mujeres, que perdonen a doña Balbina y que devuelvan las papeletas?" (p.104). Doña Nieves points out that "...eso es un delito y que hay que pagarlo." "No lo olvido", replies Silverio. "Pero, como no ha habido perjuicios, es preferible la piedad. ¡Todas ustedes son pobres! ¿Y no van a tener compasión de la más pobre de todas?" (p.105). This episode reminds us of another in which Don Quixote acts as a peace-maker. In Chapter 40 we read: "Ya a esta sazón estaban en paz los huéspedes con el ventero, pues por persuasión y buenas razones de don Quijote, más que por amenazas, le habían pagado todo lo que quiso." Don Quixote, who thought himself exempt from paying in the inns because of his being a knight-errant, now convinces with "buenas razones" two guests who wanted to leave the inn without paying, taking advantage of the racket caused by the whole story of the Judge, doña Clara, don Luis and his father's servants. Like the knight, Silverio manages to convince and calm his furious neighbours with his own "buenas razones". After the

humiliating confession and the neighbours' forgiveness Nati says to
Silverio: "Muy bonito, señor Quijote" (p.107). Doña Balbina had also
spoken of "las palabras de ese Quijote" (p.110). Even though some of
his neighbours call him "Quijote" mockingly, Silverio is really like the
knight, moved to compassion by his neighbours' misfortune.

Pilar too prefers to forgive. During the row on the stairs she is hit
on her head, but she refuses to reveal the name of the person who did
it:

> Elías: Ha sido Sabas, ¿verdad? (*Pilar lo mira. Él le toca*
> *la cabeza.*) ¿Sabas?
> Pilar: No sé qué dice.
> Elías: (*Suspira*) Nunca lo dirá. (p.109)

Both Silverio and Pilar seem to have listened to Don Quixote's
advice. Doña Balbina, nevertheless, does not humble herself, does not
bow before the neighbours' generous forgiveness and is not grateful for
Silverio's action: "Bien perdidas estamos de todos modos. Hoy, por lo
pronto, cenaremos aire, a causa de esa hermosa comedia del perdón, en
la que también he tenido yo que echar mis lagrimitas" (p.110). But the
greatest irony is that the one who has forgiven and encouraged the
others to forgive, has not been able to find the forgiveness he himself
needed.

David also forgives, like Pilar, the one who will be the cause of his
death. Donato betrays him to the police mainly out of jealousy. David
had already noticed that Donato had begun to envy him. He asked him
"Hace tiempo que me odias, ¿verdad?" "No", Donato answers, "*débil*".
When David announces that he is leaving the next day, Donato begs:
"Pero, ¿solo? Te irás solo, ¿eh? ¡Solo, David, solo!" (p.108). David
suffers to think that he is going to hurt his friend by leaving with
Adriana: "¡Adriana, Donato va a sufrir!" (p.118); however, it is Donato
who betrays David, and the latter forgives him without hesitation: "¡Dile
al pequeño que le perdono!" are his last words in the play (p.123).

David does not spare Valindin's life because he laughed contemptuously at the blind musicians, did not scruple to abuse the dignity of the poor, of the weak. He forgives Donato's treason, even though it will cost him his life, because Donato is only a miserable blind man who has begun to glimpse a bit of happiness. He has been weak. Valindin was one of the strong who laughed at the unfortunate and deserved punishment, but David also shows regret and compassion after killing him.

In *Lázaro en el Laberinto*, we find in the protagonist another character who tries to give himself without measure. His sister Fina constantly reminds him that he has given everything for his family, not being in justice obliged to do so: "¡Qué bueno has sido! ... Tú no estabas obligado a nada con nosotros... y tenías que cuidar de tu negocio." Lázaro replies: "Y de vosotros" (p.79). He feels that he is in duty bound to look after Fina, Mariano and Coral, who try to respond to his generosity in their own way. "He ayudado a mis sobrinos como si fueran mis hijos", he says. He does indeed care for them as if they were his children, and is bent on their having all the time possible to give to their studies. His generosity extends to everyone, not only his family. "Tú siempre ayudas", Amparo tells him (p.115). Many of Buero's characters are always willing to help. They set no conditions. The atmosphere of some of the scenes in *Lázaro*, as in *Hoy es fiesta*, or *Aventura*, reminds us of that of the great novel: "Vibra en el aire de la novela una emoción de fraternidad caritativa y contagiosa" (Rosales, p.841). The real knight must always be ready to give himself, to help, and so is Lázaro. Nevertheless, he has not been able to overcome himself, to acknowledge his past cowardice. However, there is hope for him in the future, as he seems to have taken the first steps and he now knows his weakness. He is on what Don Quixote considers the right road for self-knowledge and humility: that of love and generosity.

We have seen that Don Quixote's virtue bordered on heroism. His courage can indeed be considered heroic. Some of Buero's characters also behave in a remarkably courageous fashion. For example, Prince

Riquet in *Casi un cuento de hadas* appears as a hero ready for anything: "¡Oriana! Aquí me tienes dispuesto a luchar." He is not afraid of the difficulties he has to face in the palace. Oriana assures: "Vencerás" (p.71). The idea of triumph, of victory, is present in Riquet's mind. He is not intimidated when confronted with danger: "No me resignaré: él y yo nos encontraremos. Lucharé por ella..." (p.118). The ugly Riquet defies Armando in very knightly fashion: "Va contra las normas de nuestro siglo ¿verdad? ¡Sacad vuestro espadín de corte!"; "¡Que nadie se interponga!" (pp.124 & 125). The freak, the fright, the "engendro", kills the handsome Armando, thus gaining the hand of his beloved Leticia.

We can also refer to Silverio as "heroic". He saves a life: "¡Ya estás viva, Daniela! La vida siempre dice sí" (p.112). Even before this, Daniela had told her mother: "¡Nos ha salvado!" (p.110). What is most courageous in Silverio is that he manages to help all his neighbours generously even though his own soul is anguished by his sorrow, his perhaps exaggerated guilt complex. He nevertheless manages to put himself out to look after the others' needs. Likewise, Don Quixote emits heart-rending sighs of sorrow and sadness, calls himself "el caballero de la Triste Figura", not because of his untidy looks, as Sancho suggests, but because of his profound sorrow. The miserable, pensive Don Quixote, does not hesitate to forget about his own misery in order to relieve the needs of the helpless; as he himself says:

> Caballero soy de la profesión que decís, y aunque en mi alma tienen su propio asiento las tristezas, las desgracias y las desventuras, no por ello se ha ahuyentado della la compasión que tengo de las ajenas desdichas. (II,12)

Precisely because of this, his adventures are more heroic. Silverio does not solve his problem, but tries at all costs to help his neighbours with theirs. He failed to save the life of Pilar's child and has also to contemplate, helplessly, the death of his wife. He is nevertheless a hero.

Silvano and Ana can also be considered heroic. They had been insecure. Ana had come to accept her life with Goldmann out of sheer fear of poverty, in spite of the fact that he was a person of no scruples. On his part, Silvano admits: "... no valgo nada. Nunca he sabido vivir, ni luchar. Si supiese luchar me habría ido a las montañas con las guerrillas..." (p.221). However, both of them decide to struggle and sacrifice themselves; that is why they prove to be real heroes.

In contrast, Goldmann, who had led the crowds, who knew how to command, escapes in a cowardly way when the time for sacrifice comes. He prefers to save his life. Silvano and Ana risk and lose their lives for the innocent baby, Isabel's son. It is difficult to believe that the same Ana who had submitted to the dictator, can dare to accuse Alejandro openly. "¡Tú lo hiciste!", she screams (p.206), and from this moment she will not look back. "Tú la mataste: es tu estilo". She dares to stand up to so unscrupulous a murderer. Her abusive accusations and insults surpass Silvano's in ferocity: "Estoy harta de ti. Pisoteabas mi cariño una y otra vez con mujerzuelas. Te reías de lo que llamabas mis sensiblerías y mis prejuicios... Te has reído de todo y lo has manchado todo en nombre de la eficacia" (p.207). She makes up her mind to face solitude and poverty: "¡Ya no iré contigo!" (p.210). When the moment of departure comes, she is completely terrified, but understands that she has to save the baby's life and risks everything she has: her uncertain future, her freedom, her own life. Everyone tries to convince her to leave, to try to save her life; even Silvano does. But her reply is: "No puedo... No puedo irme ... Me quedo también" (p.218).

In *Aventura en lo gris*, both Silvano and Ana are victorious heroes. As Silvano says, "hay otras maneras de vencer" (p.221). One can win even shaking with fear at the approaching danger. Facing the enemy soldiers, Ana's courage seems incredible. At their initial refusal to take the baby to safety, she cries:

> No puedes ¿eh? Primero los engendráis y luego..., que se
> mueran. ¡Canallas! ... Después volveréis a vuestras casas
> y besaréis a vuestras mujeres y a vuestros hijos, sin
> acordaros de la pobre criatura que habéis dejado morir.

¿Sabes si acaso es tuyo? ¿Estuviste tú en Valderol? ¿Y tú?
¡No importa! ¡Ametralladle también! ¡Quién sabe si
ametralláis a vuestro hijo! (p.224)

Ana and Silvano's courage saves the life of a baby. Ready to be executed, they become aware of their complete victory: "¿Es esto vencer?", Ana exclaims. "¡Sí! ¡Esto es vencer!", Silvano replies (p.225). Both accomplish a noble task and die for it without hesitation. Their victory is very quixotic. On arriving at their village Sancho exclaimed: "Abre los brazos y recibe también a tu hijo don Quijote, que si viene vencido de los brazos ajenos, viene vencedor de sí mismo; que según él me ha dicho, es el mayor vencimiento que desearse puede" (II,73). Silvano and Ana achieve the victory that Lázaro did not because he lacked the courage to win his battle. They were two characters who considered themselves weak and cowardly; "No me desanime, Ana... Yo no soy un hombre valeroso" (p.217); "Silvano, no me hables así... Yo tampoco soy una mujer valerosa" (p.218). Their will to save a life and maybe their own dignity has turned a cowardly man and a weak woman into two heroes. Their attitude reminds us of the entertaining conversation between master and squire in the well-known Chapter 8 of the second part of the novel. Don Quixote teaches Sancho about the rectitude of intention that must always guide the hard and heroic life of a knight-errant:

...que los cristianos, católicos y andantes caballeros más habemos de atender a la gloria de los siglos venideros, que es eterna en las regiones etéreas y celestes, que a la vanidad de la fama que en este presente y acabable siglo se alcanza.

In a moment of weakness, Ana suggests to Silvano that they could try to save their lives by making the soldiers believe that they killed Goldmann, their enemy. Similarly, Don Quixote had his moments of weakness.

Don Quijote, que los vió puestos en tan gallardo
escuadrón, los brazos levantados con ademán de despedir
poderosamente las piedras, detuvo las riendas a Rocinante
y púsose a pensar de qué modo los acometería con menos
peligro de su persona. (II,11)

It is only human for Ana to try to carry out her task with the least
danger. But both Ana and Silvano become quixotic heroes. They die,
then, undertaking a great task, that of saving a life.

Larra does not behave in a cowardly way either. He is not afraid to
speak the truth. Mesonero acknowledges: "¿No me va a perdonar mi
miedo? Todos no podemos ser héroes, Larra" (p.62). The hero can feel
his weakness; he fears, and doubts, but he always strives to forget
himself. His determination to go ahead in spite of opposition, or inner
difficulty, makes the hero more exceptional, more courageous, more
extraordinary. "Te consta que estoy librando una penosa batalla. Y
que tengo miedo. Pero también esperanzas", Larra says (p.88). The
struggle of the hero proves to be arduous, as it is for Silverio, and Don
Quixote, who have to conceal their sorrow, and at times their fear, in
order to serve others with extraordinary courage and daring. "Sólo una
fraternidad indestructible puede hacer soportable la existencia de los
hombres. Sólo así cobra sentido el heroísmo: 'El hombre sacrificado por
la redención de los demás', en palabras de Roa Bastos."[28]

As we have seen, love of liberty is another trait of Don Quixote's
character. In Buero's plays many characters are eager to choose their
own future.[29] Their desire for freedom no doubt constitutes an
expression of a metaphysical yearning to transcend their own limitations,
to achieve not just their own self-determination but a fuller freedom for
themselves and for others. *Historia de una escalera* is the tragedy of
characters who yearn in vain to be free. Fernando resolves to "dejar
toda esta sordidez en que vivimos" (p.46), but he fails; he can only
hope that the young will do better. And what is the highest ambition,
the desire of Adela in *Las cartas boca abajo*, but to "volar"?: "Me parecía
que también yo, cuando fuera mayor, sería como ellos, libre y alegre.
... Míralos. No son como nosotros: vuelan. Luchan por sus hijos; a

veces caen bajo la garra de sus enemigos... pero vuelan" (p.134). That is the terrible tragedy of Adela's life. Adela does not manage to achieve her freedom, whereas Cervantes' characters assert theirs. They uproot themselves from their society and go away in search of their own selves with a cheerful sense of freedom. The essence of their liberty is that they have also managed to free themselves from slavery to their own passions, to fill themselves with the desire to serve; that is how they find their real freedom, in being generous. Adela hears other characters talking of flying and listens to them sadly. Mauro says that he was made to fly, to be free. He prides himself on having flown, though Adela knows that he has not succeeded in achieving real freedom:

> Mauro.-Nuestro padre se llevó un disgusto tremendo, ¿te acuerdas? Pero yo estaba hecho para volar...
> Adela.-(*Melancólica*.) Volar...
> Mauro.-Y he volado lo mío, ¿eh? ¡Y aún me quedan alas!
> (p.119)

One of the characters who has managed to fly is Carlos Ferrer. "Ha volado" - Adela says -, "mientras nosotras envejecemos aquí oscuramente" (p.152). Juanito wants to try to imitate him; he needs to breathe new air:

> Juanito.-Tienes que ayudarme, mamá. No quiero retrasarme definitivamente, como le ocurrió a él. Todos los días piden el pasaporte cientos de muchachos. Necesitan respirar, como yo. Volar...
> Adela.-(*Melancólica*.) Volar...
> Mauro.-Yo también lo quise a su edad... Es lógico...
> (p.128)

Adela has to resign herself to seeing others flying; she has clipped her own wings by living for herself. Now she is not free, and she will never be, because she did not know how to give, how to live for others.

This metaphor of flight becomes almost allegorical in some of the plays. Eloy, in *Mito*, dreams of his "visitantes", who will fly to the earth from far planets. It is necessary to fly in order to escape from the sordid world in which he lives. His flight, however, is not merely a way of escaping or of attaining certain ambitions, but of overcoming human limitations. He dreams of "otro cielo y otros astros/ la humanidad que aquí hemos violado" (p.219). And to reach that new planet, to attain his freedom, he needs to fly very high. Eloy has managed to achieve the freedom he dreamt of. He did not know that he did not need to fly to a different planet. The only way he had to achieve his freedom was by making up his mind to help others. Once he has discovered this, Eloy is free. His death is not a failure, as Don Quixote's death is not a failure: "La verdad de la vida sólo se nos define ante la muerte" (Rosales, p.852). Don Quixote's death does not need to be justified. In order to live heroically one needs to dare to make mistakes, to fail drastically:

> Cervantes nos enseña que el fracaso es inherente a la existencia humana. Si vivimos en peligro fracasaremos heroicamente. Si vivimos sin afrontar el riesgo, fracasaremos totalmente. No hay opción. Hay que atreverse a vivir. Hay que atreverse a ser hombre. (Rosales, p.851)

Failure is part and parcel of human existence. Don Quixote considers his life on his deathbed, finds himself there. Ana and Silvano become really free just before death, and so does Eloy.

Francisco de Goya also dreams of flying. The flying creatures he draws seem to symbolize freedom. Those he imagines are winged creatures, but not angels: "¡No estoy soñando con ángeles!" (p.137). As we have seen in the chapter on dreams, the "hombres-pájaros" Goya imagines could help if they wanted to. They could save mankind. Asmodea can also save men by taking them to her mountain: "Asmodea se lo lleva a él, que todavía tiembla por lo que se ve abajo. Desde la montaña lo seguirá viendo, pero los seres que allí viven le calmarán. Es una montaña muy escarpada. Sólo se puede subir volando" (p.134).

David too is crying for freedom when tears run down his face on the day of the first concert. In trying to protect themselves from external limitations to their freedom, Larra and Velázquez defend a fuller freedom of mankind. Larra actually fights for it, because for him "la libertad es nuestra única dignidad" (p.102). Don Quixote had expressed that thought in a similar way:

> La libertad es uno de los más preciosos dones que a los hombres dieron los cielos; con ella no pueden igualarse los tesoros que encierra la tierra ni el mar encubre: por la libertad, así como por la honra, se puede y debe aventurar la vida; y, por el contrario, el cautiverio es el mayor mal que puede venir a los hombres. (II,58)

With regard to human dignity, Américo Castro points out that the concept "no pende de las circunstancias externas (fama, opinión, galardones), sino de la intimidad de la virtud individual. El honor es atributo de la virtud; pero ésta existe y vale, no obstante la virtud que los demás observen."[30] The dignity of man lies, then, in his individual freedom on the one hand, and in his individual virtue, on the other. What are the virtues that a quixotic character must practise? What do the quixotic ethics that Buero considers necessary consist of? Undoubtedly, it must be a mixture of contemplation and action. A contemplation that comprises the brave search for truth and freedom, the daring to entertain dreams, ideals, that the world might consider utterly unattainable, a magnanimity and courage that are inward dispositions of the soul, an unshakable faith, a profound sense of justice; and an action that consists of not being dismayed by the struggle, of defending the truth even if that defence costs one's life, of an unselfish and noble self-giving that has no limits, that is totally generous, not only in helping the needy, but also in attacking evil, and which is the consequence of total respect for the dignity of man.[31] As Buero says, "la ética quijotesca no es solamente la de la conducta recta y la defensa de los débiles; es también la del improperio de la maldad, o ante lo que a él le parece la maldad" (Interview).

These are the values of a quixotic spirit, which are found in many of the characters of Buero's plays. At times, some of them have to be helped to behave according to those values. Verónica and Cristina, for instance, provide Julio and Julia with their constant support and encouragement and so help them to pursue their search of the truth to the end. The same could be said of Amparo and Lucila with regard to Lázaro and Mary Barnes. Some of the purely "positive" characters stand on their own feet: The Father, Mario, Silverio, Pilar, Silvano, David, Riquet, Goya, Velázquez, Larra. Some others go through moments of weakness, when they need the help of another quixotic character, not to be "unethical". Ana, for example, needs Silvano's "lessons", but learns quickly to put into practice the quixotic values which were already in her soul.

We recognize, then, in many of those characters a whole series of values which constitute an ethic in itself. They appear in different degrees in those characters. As Buero says, he would prefer neither Mario nor Vicente but a mixture of both: "El tipo ideal para una conducta equilibrada hubiera sido un hombre intermedio entre los dos hermanos, una simbiosis de ambos, un 70% del menor y un 30% del mayor. Del hermano menor no me gusta su resentimiento fraternal... Del hermano mayor no me gusta su forma de tomar el tren y viajar en el tren, en ese tren que hay que tomar."[32] Buero, therefore, singles out Mario's contemplation, his courageous struggle to find the truth, his sense of justice, though he would wish it free of resentment; and finds that a certain measure of Vicente's readiness to act would make Mario more daring, more enterprising. What would come from such a mixture but the most quixotic character that we can imagine?

NOTES TO CHAPTER V

1. Unamuno, *Vida*, p.166.

2. Anthony Close, *The Romantic Approach to Don Quixote* (Cambridge University Press, 1978), p.17.

3. Close, *The Romantic Approach*, p.12.

4. "The examination of Cervantes' maintenance of the balance of justice in the novel through the equilibrium of pride and punishment, and the alteration in Part II of this balance by a series of 'undeserved' defeats and humiliations corroborates the perceptive comments of Alexander Parker: 'The essence of it is that his boastful vanity corrupts his ideal and weakens and destroys it in practice... In order that the innate goodness of Don Quixote become the measure of his actions, his ideal must be purified of all egotism. He must renounce his arrogant ambition, he must humble himself to the point where he recognizes the reality of things and of himself'." ('El concepto de la verdad en el *Quijote*', quoted in John J. Allen, *Don Quixote. Hero or Fool? A Study in Narrative Technique* (Gainesville: University of Florida Press, 1969), p.51)

5. Buero himself seems to practise this virtue as well: "Ninguna, o muy pocas veces, se ha citado a Cervantes con motivo mío. Yo me creo un hijo muy directo de él, aunque modestísimo" (Medardo Fraile, 'Charla con Antonio Buero Vallejo', *Cuadernos de Agora*, 79-82 (mayo-agosto 1963), p.8).

6. G.E. Jensen, ed., Covent Garden Journal no.10 (4 Feb 1752), vol.I, 1915, quoted in *Henry Fielding*, edited by Claude Rawson (Harmondsworth: Penguin Education, 1973), p.125.

7. Henry Fielding, *The Adventures of Joseph Andrews* (London: George Routledge and Sons, 1857), p.VIII.

8. Luis Rosales, *Cervantes y la libertad* (Madrid: Ediciones de Cultura Hispánica, Instituto de Cooperación Iberoamericana, 1985), p.64. (Further references are given after quotations in the text.)

9. Américo Castro attributes this truthfulness to both Don Quixote and Sancho. Commenting on Part II, 3, he states: "Don Quijote hablará en nombre de la verdad universal y verosímil; Sancho defenderá la verdad sensible y particular. La oposición, como es natural y cervantino, no se resuelve, sino que queda patente, como problema abierto" (*El pensamiento de Cervantes*, p.33).

10. Aubrey F.G. Bell emphasizes the spirit of true service in Cervantes's character: "Far from 'smiling Spain's chivalry away' or 'casting scorn upon the holiest principles of humanity', as Byron and Ruskin would have had us believe, he incorporated in *Don Quixote* the true spirit of chivalry, the renunciation of self in the service of others" ('Cervantes and the Renaissance', *Hispanic Review* 2 (1934), 89-101, p.92).

11. Ernest A. Siciliano, 'Virtue in the Quixote', in *Cervantes. Su obra y su mundo* (Madrid: EDI-6, 1981), p.603.

12. Ricardo Aguilera, *Intención y silencio en el Quijote* (Madrid: Editorial Ayuso, 1972), pp.76-7.

13. Olmeda finds that the traditional approach to the novel emphasizes Sancho's defects to such an extent that it seems to be describing Avellaneda's, not Cervantes' Sancho. Madariaga - he says - was right in emphasizing the parallelism between the knight and the squire. Most quixotic virtues are found in Sancho, though expressed in a more rudimentary fashion:
"La lectura detenida y reiterada del Quijote con la atención concentrada en la compleja figura de Sancho -no menos compleja que la del mismo hidalgo ingenioso- pone al descubierto en el fondo de un natural inculto y elemental, un acervo de virtudes que se hermanan con las universalmente reconocidas en don Quijote, si bien en el personaje principal con el resplandor de su natural cortés, refinado y culto" (*El ingenio de Cervantes y la locura de don Quijote*, p.270). "Lo cierto es que en Sancho se manifiestan desde el primer momento en formas rudimentarias, pero bien acusadas, como expresión definida de su carácter, las mismas virtudes redentoras que todos reconocen en el señor don Quijote" (p.271).

14. J.B. Avalle-Arce, *Nuevos deslindes cervantinos* (Esplugues de Llobregat: Ed. Ariel, 1975), p.343.

15. M. de Cervantes, *El licenciado Vidriera*, in *Novelas Ejemplares* (Madrid: Castalia, 1982), Vol.II, p.116.

16. *El celoso extremeño*, p.220.

17. "Muchos críticos han subrayado con razón el carácter ético de la obra de Buero Vallejo: su afirmación fundamental es la necesidad de vencer el egoísmo, en sus múltiples formas. En su teatro, adquiere importancia absoluta la primacía del don de sí sobre cualquier otra actitud humana" (Jean Paul Borel, 'Buero Vallejo: Teatro y política', in *Estudios sobre Buero Vallejo*, p.40).

18. Doménech, *El teatro de Buero Vallejo*, pp.24 & 25.

19. Johnston, *Antonio Buero Vallejo. El concierto de San Ovidio*, p.21.

20. Iglesias Feijoo very accurately discusses the suitability of tragedy to perform this task: "...la expresión teatral más adecuada para abordar la problemática humana en toda su hondura resultará así la tragedia" (*La trayectoria*, p.3). He also emphasizes that the role of Buero's tragedy would not be to provoke action directly but to transform man from within: "...función social del teatro, que no se dirige a promover la acción, sino a transformar al hombre en su interior, elevándolo a un plano ético superior" (p.4).

21. He indeed puts this into practice in his own work. Carmen González-Cobos describes the search of the truth that Buero's characters carry out as follows: "El conocimiento de la verdad propia es, por lo tanto, el primer paso necesario para llegar a obtener la libertad. Y al poseer cada uno su verdad, podrá conocer la verdad de la realidad que le rodea ... La primera responsabilidad está, por lo tanto, en el hombre y no en la sociedad. Cualquiera que sea el papel de ésta en el desarrollo vital del individuo, hay en cada uno de los hombres una primera responsabilidad para la búsqueda de la verdad íntima. Encontrarla puede ser que nos resulte trágica y dolorosa, pero sólo asumiéndola valientemente hay posibilidad de vencer y de salvarse, superando todas las dificultades externas" (*Antonio Buero Vallejo: el hombre y su obra*, pp.57-8).

22. Ruiz Ramón, *Historia del teatro español*, p.338.

For her part, Martha Halsey also states: "From the time of the ancient Greeks to that of contemporary dramatists, tragedy is often viewed as man's search for truth or understanding about himself and the universe; and it is in this way that the tragic theater of Buero Vallejo may perhaps be understood" (*Antonio Buero Vallejo*, p.149).

23. Ruiz Ramón, *Historia del teatro español*, p.353.

24. Magda Ruggeri remarks on the parallel between Cristina and Lucila: "Si noti el parallelismo tra Cristina e Lucila (*La doble historia del doctor Valmy*). Anche se quest'ultima ha una minor rilevanza nell'economia del dramma, è il personaggio che incita Mary a cercare la verità." Julia is also compared to Amalia and Mary: "Per questo Julia è il personaggio esemplare dell'opera, quello che, come Amalia (*Madrugada*) o come Mary (*La doble historia del doctor Valmy*), incarna la volontà di raggiungere la verità come unica salvezza personale possibile" (*Il teatro di...*, p.86).

25. Magda Ruggeri Marchetti, 'La mujer en el teatro de Antonio Buero Vallejo', *Anthropos*, p.37.

26. It is not easy to accept Jean Paul Borel's statement that: "No se puede decir que Silvano se conduzca de una manera, en sí, moral: no deja de sorprendernos el que este gran revolucionario acepte unirse con la que fue querida del dictador" ('Buero Vallejo: Teatro y política', p.40). Silvano is an example of someone who gives himself fully, which, as we have seen, Borel considers the essence of Buero's ethics.

27. John J. Allen, 'Don Quixote and the Origins of the Novel', in *Cervantes and the Renaissance*, edited by Michael McGaha (Easton: Juan de la Cuesta, 1980), p.130.

28. Pedro L. López Algora, 'Augusto Roa Bastos, premio Cervantes. La creación de una lengua mestiza', *Aceprensa*, S.A., Servicio 37/90 (Madrid, 14 de marzo 1990), p.2.

29. Carmen González-Cobos speaks of a "búsqueda trágica de la libertad". She says that "los personajes dramáticos de Buero buscan ansiosamente su libertad y esto ocurre en dos vertientes: en el plano metafísico y en el plano social" (*Antonio Buero Vallejo: el hombre y su obra*, p.59).

30. Américo Castro, *El pensamiento de Cervantes*, p.355.

31. Ramón de Garciasol says that respect for human dignity constitutes an essential quality of the knight: "El caballero se distingue por tener un fino sentido de la responsabilidad y una elevada estima de la dignidad humana, considerando al hombre, como pedía Séneca, 'cosa sagrada para el hombre'... No se es hombre hasta que no se tiene sentimiento de la dignidad humana y se es capaz de arriesgar la vida por defenderla" (*Claves de España: Cervantes y el "Quijote"*, pp.183 & 203).

32. Ángel Fernández Santos, 'Una entrevista con Buero Vallejo sobre *El tragaluz*', *Primer Acto*, no.90 (1967), p.14.
     Ortega y Gasset also spoke of the need for a balance between contemplation and action: "la situación prácticamente óptima para conocer -es decir, para absorber el mayor número y la mejor calidad de elementos objetivos- es intermediaria entre la pura contemplación y el urgente interés. Hace falta que algún interés vital, no demasiado premioso y angosto, organice nuestra contemplación, la confine, limite y articule, poniedo en ella una perspectiva de atención" (J. Ortega y Gasset, *Meditaciones del Quijote e Ideas sobre la novela* (Madrid: Revista de Occidente, 1960), p.171).
     Buero also sees the need for a balance: "...para Buero la inactividad completa no es buena, ni es suficiente poseer una ética o una moral individual, sin proyectarla al entorno social. No basta ser bueno, hay que luchar dentro del mundo para que nuestra verdad no quede al margen" (Carmen González-Cobos Dávila, *Antonio Buero Vallejo: el hombre y su obra*, p.65).

Chapter VI
FALSE QUIXOTES
The simulated quixotism of the "activos"

We have already considered how Don Quixote sees only what is good in others: he attributes evil-doing to the enchanters. This outlook on the part of the knight, his good intention, exposes the false virtues of other characters, who pretend to be virtuous but in fact take advantage of others for their own enjoyment; their actions are not motivated by generous intentions. In contrast with Don Quixote's virtues, Cervantes exhibits others' selfishness and falsehood. A clear example of this is the behaviour of Sansón Carrasco. He initially looks for Don Quixote in order to cure him, but he then seeks dishonest revenge. He says to his squire that he has no intention of going back to his village until he defeats Don Quixote:

> ...porque pensar que yo he de volver a la mía hasta haber
> molido a palos a don Quijote, es pensar en lo excusado, y no
> me llevará ahora a buscarle el deseo de que cobre el juicio,
> sino el de la venganza, que el dolor grande de mis costillas
> no me deja hacer más piadosos discursos. ... Tomé Cecial
> se volvió y le dejó, y él quedó imaginando su venganza.
> (II,15)

He first pretends to be a knight-errant in order to save his friend. Later, however, he continues to pretend in order to defeat him. His squire, Tomé Cecial, knows well, and so he tells Sancho, that his master is "más bellaco que tonto y que valiente" (II,13), and that Sansón

Carrasco convinced him to go with him with "embustes y enredos" (II,14). Cervantes has already provided a description of the *bachiller* in Chapter 3: "...carirredondo, de nariz chata y de boca grande, señales todas de ser de condición maliciosa." Tomé is convinced that his master is a fool, as he says to Sancho in Chapter 13: "mi amo es de aquellos que dicen: Cuidados ajenos matan al asno, pues porque cobre otro caballero el juicio que ha perdido, se hace él loco"; and to Sansón in Chapter 15: "Sepamos, pues, ahora cuál es más loco, ¿el que lo es por no poder menos, o el que lo es por su voluntad?". Don Quixote, however, cannot believe that the knight whom he defeats is his friend Sansón, in spite of the fact that he "vio, dice la historia, el rostro mismo, la misma figura, el mismo aspecto, la misma fisonomía, la misma efigie, la perspectiva misma del bachiller Sansón Carrasco" (II,14). "Advierte" - he says to Sancho - "lo que puede la magia, lo que pueden los hechiceros y encantadores". He does not doubt his friend's honesty:

> ¿En qué consideración puede caber que el bachiller Sansón Carrasco viniese como caballero andante armado de armas ofensivas y defensivas a pelear conmigo? ¿he sido yo su enemigo por ventura? ¿hele dado yo jamás ocasión para tenerme ojeriza? ¿soy yo su rival, o hace él profesión de las armas para tener envidia a la fama que yo por ellas he ganado? ... Todo es artificio y traza... de los malignos magos que me persiguen, los cuales, anteviendo que yo había de quedar vencedor en la contienda, se previnieron de que el caballero vencido mostrase el rostro de mi amigo el bachiller, porque la amistad que le tengo se pusiese entre los filos de mi espada y el rigor de mi brazo, y templase la justa ira de mi corazón. (II,16)

His good intentions, his true love for his friend, expose Sansón Carrasco's ill-will and pride, which move him to pretend to be a knight-errant.

Cervantes also censures the lack of scruples of the supposedly noble Duke and Duchess. A priest warns the Duke that he has the moral responsibility of looking after the knight properly:

El eclesiástico que oyó decir de gigantes, de follones y encantos, cayó en la cuenta de que aquel debía de ser don Quijote de la Mancha, cuya historia leía el duque de ordinario, y él se lo había reprendido muchas veces, diciéndole que era disparate leer tantos disparates; y enterándose ser verdad lo que sospechaba, con mucha cólera, hablando con el duque, le dijo: Vuestra excelencia, señor mío, tiene que dar cuenta a nuestro Señor de lo que hace este buen hombre. Este don Quijote, o don Tonto, o como se llama, imagino yo que no debe de ser tan mentecato como vuestra excelencia quiere que sea, dándole ocasiones a la mano para que lleve adelante sus sandeces y vaciedades. (II,31)

Like Sansón Carrasco, the Duke is accused of being a fool: "Por el hábito que tengo, que estoy por decir que es tan sandio vuestra excelencia como estos pecadores: mirad si no han de ser ellos locos, pues los cuerdos canonizan sus locuras" (II,32). Cide Hamete agrees with the priest's view: "Y dice más Cide Hamete, que tiene para sí ser tan locos los burladores como los burlados, y que no estaban los duques dos dedos de parecer tontos" (II,70). The Duke and Duchess seek their own pleasure and enjoyment selfishly. Don Quixote's disposition offers a sharp contrast with theirs: "¿Por ventura es asunto vano, o es tiempo malgastado el que se gasta en vagar por el mundo, no buscando los regalos dél, sino las asperezas por donde los buenos suben al asiento de la inmortalidad?" (II,32). Don Quixote has made himself mad for the sake of others, to offer his generous help. The Duke and Duchess, on the contrary, seek their own enjoyment and pleasure at the expense of others. Don Quixote and Sancho provide entertainment for everyone in their house. The servants learn "la intención que tenían de hacerles algunas burlas" and play jokes on the knight and the squire on their own initiative. Don Quixote does not approve of their making fun of his friend: "Perecida de risa estaba la duquesa, viendo la cólera y oyendo las razones de Sancho; pero no dio mucho gusto a don Quijote verle tan mal adeliñado" (II,32). He, however, does not realize that he has been the victim of the same joke a few minutes before. He always presumes a good intention in those who deal with him, and this exposes the cruelty of those who do not hesitate to take advantage of his innocence. The Duke and Duchess go too far in their jokes:

> Y queriendo dar remate a la extraña y bien fabricada aventura, por la cola de Clavileño le pegaron fuego con unas estopas, y al punto, por estar el caballo lleno de cohetes tronadores, voló por los aires con extraño ruido, y dio con don Quijote y con Sancho Panza en el suelo medio chamuscados. (II,41)

> Quedó don Quijote acribillado el rostro, y no muy sanas las narices... Aquella aventura le costó cinco días de encerramiento y de cama. (II,46)

Cervantes criticizes their wickedness less explicitly when referring to Antonio Moreno, "caballero rico y discreto, y amigo de holgarse a lo honesto y afable, el cual, viendo en su casa a don Quijote, andaba buscando modos cómo sin su perjuicio sacase a plaza sus locuras, porque no son burlas las que duelen, ni hay pasatiempos que valgan si son con daño de tercero" (II,72). Don Quixote does not realize that he is being laughed at. The Duke and Duchess make use of both knight and squire, while pretending to be noble and generous. More than Don Quixote's innocence, Cervantes exhibits the pretenders' ill-will and hypocrisy. The knight's simplicity shows up other characters' duplicity. His generosity exposes their self-interest.

The example of pretence which Cervantes criticizes most harshly, however, is Avellaneda's Quixote, who is mentioned in the novel as one more character, "el que ha querido usurpar vuestro nombre y aniquilar vuestras hazañas" (II,59). Cervantes abhors the imitation and attacks it very strongly, pinpointing Avellaneda's errors and inconsistencies: "Yerra y desvía de la verdad en lo más principal de la historia" (II,59). The hero explains that the false Quixote has very little to do with himself, and complains that, with that distorted picture given, he has been ill-treated: "Retráteme el que quisiere, dijo don Quijote, pero no me maltrate". He rejects falsehood as if it was an obscene image: "Pues de las cosas obscenas y torpes, los pensamientos se han de apartar, cuanto más los ojos." As if this open rejection was not sufficient, in

Chapter 72 Cervantes introduces don Álvaro Tarfe, whose role is to confirm that the two Quixotes are extremely different, as well as the two Sanchos: "Y dígame vuesa merced, señor don Álvaro, ¿parezco yo en algo a ese tal don Quijote que vuesa merced me dice? No por ciero, respondió el huésped, en ninguna manera." "Y ese Sancho que vuesa merced dice, señor gentilhombre, debe de ser algún grandísimo bellaco, frión y ladrón juntamente." Don Álvaro is supposed to have met the imitation and Cervantes makes him confess that he must have been under the influence of the enchanters, because the new Quixote is completely different from the one he remembers: "Osaré yo jurar que le dejo metido en la casa del Nuncio, en Toledo, para que le curen, y ahora remanece aquí otro don Quijote, aunque bien diferente del mío". Don Álvaro speaks of "dos tan contrarios Quijotes". In his introduction to Avellaneda's *Quijote*, Fernando García Salinero calls him "Quijote contrahecho", "tontiloco don Quijote", "Quijote de alfeñique"[1]; Avellaneda calls him "locazo mentecato" in Chapter 31 of his *Quijote*. Cervantes makes it clear that his Quixote is authentic. "Yo, dijo don Quijote, no sé si soy bueno; pero sé decir que no soy el malo" (II,72). Avellaneda's Quixote certainly served the purpose of making Cervantes express once more his horror of duplicity and falsehood.

In Buero's works one can easily find characters who boast falsely of being altruistic, of leading a life of sacrifice for the sake of others. Through their external appearance, their speech, their gestures, one might even be led to think that they are generous souls. In almost all these fake Quixotes, we find vanity, self-love: they all praise themselves, proclaim themselves as examples of detachment from all personal interest, of a readiness to do their duty towards their neighbours. But behind their verbosity there hides a hateful selfishness, a despicable sense of superiority, neither of which can be considered quixotic values. It is true that Don Quixote at times praises himself, boasts that he leads a sacrificial life, and so on, but in his case, it is true: his abstention from sleep, from food and material advantage, is real.

None of these characters can be called quixotic, because they live for themselves, using others as stepping stones to their own success, no matter how much others may suffer at their expense. They have very little idealism left, if indeed they ever had any; that is why most of them do not know how to dream. They naturally laugh at those who do have any sort of ideals, they despise the "dreamers". These "activos" need to appear immaculate, since they also want to be admired. But their virtues are false, put on. False Quixotes are normally deceitful. They need to appear charitable and good-hearted. They try to conceal their selfish intentions under the guise of philanthropy. Even the love that they may claim (genuinely, perhaps, in some cases) to feel for other characters is vitiated by an essential selfishness; they love people only in their own interest, and that is why they fail to communicate effectively. None of these features befits a quixotic hero. That is why "activos" are usually punished for their selfishness, for their abuses. That punishment is often a deep sense of loneliness. As we have seen in Chapter Three, one of the characteristics of truly quixotic characters is an isolation from others which they are only rarely spared. Ironically, the false Quixotes invariably impose upon themselves a different, more definitive isolation.

In *En la ardiente oscuridad* Carlos, for example, behaves from the beginning of the play as a model, an example for the other students: in his appearance, in his behaviour and manners, in his diligence in his studies. Buero gives us a clear picture of his looks:

> *Es un muchacho fuerte y sanguíneo, de agradable y enérgica expresión. Atildado indumento en color claro, cuello duro.* (p.12)

The contrast with Ignacio, the dreamer, is obvious:

> *Es un muchacho delgaducho, serio y reconcentrado, con cierto desaliño en su persona: el cuello de la camisa desabrochado, la corbata floja, el cabello peinado con*

ligereza. Viste de negro, intemporalmente, durante toda la
obra. (p.15)

Carlos is don Pablo's right hand. However, when difficulties or some
sort of opposition to his plans arise, he is unable to admit defeat: he
ends up killing. He is too concerned about his own image, his privileged
position in the school, even though he might have thought that his main
concern was the good of the other inmates and of the institution. Doña
Pepita, who had referred to him as a "caballero andante" (p.28), will
have to admonish him at the end of the play: "A veces, Carlos, creemos
hacer un bien y cometemos un gran error" (p.84). Carlos perhaps
wants to believe that he is acting for the good of the institution. But he
kills in order to recover his own peace, his role as an example to be
followed by everyone else, his reputation, and, of course, Juana. He
is not a real knight, an authentic Quixote, because he is moved also by
selfish interests. He appears to be a Quixote but turns out to be a
murderer. There is, however, a redeeming factor, what Buero calls "un
altruismo final" which "envuelve a su pesar a los protagonistas. ...
Envuelve a Carlos, que ama con fatídica irreversibilidad al hombre que
acaba de asesinar hasta el extremo de hacer suyas sus palabras."[2] We
would be mistaken to think that Carlos is a pure "activo". He undergoes
a gradual evolution. He actually planned to help Ignacio, offering him
his friendship at the beginning of the play; but he obviously failed.
Later, he plans to defy him; but, as Iglesias remarks, "el reto que se va
a producir estará viciado en su origen, porque Carlos no admite la
posibilidad de ser vencido por su contrario; él se sitúa en posesión
indiscutible de la verdad y no la cuestiona: 'La razón no puede fracasar
y nosotros la tenemos'."[3] But Carlos will end up reincarnating Ignacio.
If Carlos inherits Ignacio's anguish it is because he had somehow a
disposition to accept Ignacio's truth. His concern in the second act is
due not only to the fact that Juana has left him but to the agony which
is beginning to pierce his soul. Ignacio's victory is approaching.
Carlos is already beginning to understand Ignacio's point of view, even
before Ignacio's death.

> D. Pablo.-Que cómo es posible que Ignacio se baste y se
> sobre para desalentar a tantos invidentes remotos. ¿Qué
> saben ellos de la luz?
> Carlos.-(*Grave*) Acaso porque la ignoran les preocupe.
> D. Pablo.-Eso es muy sutil, hijo mío. (p.74)

He is an "activo" in that he kills to his own advantage. He can be quite
sarcastic, and he talks to doña Pepita coldly and scornfully because she
knows the truth, that he has not won: "... el insobornable contrincante
de Carlos obra sobre él como un Cid que ganase su batalla después de
perder la de la vida" ('Comentario', p.93). But his soul has suffered a
complete transformation. He is now open to the light.

We can establish a parallel between Carlos's evolution and that of Don
Quixote. In the first place, both lose the confidence in themselves that
they showed at first. Carlos appeared to be very confident in his own
ability; he did not need to use a walking stick, he knew the rooms very
well. He had told Ignacio:

> ¡Lo que te hace tropezar es el miedo, el desánimo! Llevarás
> el bastón toda tu vida y tropezarás toda tu vida. ¡Atrévete
> a ser como nosotros! ¡Nosotros no tropezamos!

But when Ignacio places an obstacle in his way, Carlos is put on the spot
in front of all the other inmates; he is lost because he fears:

> Ignacio.-Muy seguro estás de ti mismo. Tal vez algún día
> tropieces y te hagas mucho daño... (*Ha cogido por su tallo
> el velador y marcha, marcando bien los golpes del bastón,
> al centro de la escena. Allí lo coloca suavemente, sin el
> menor ruido.*) (p.48)

> (*Carlos da unos pasos rápidos, pero, de pronto, la
> desconfianza crispa su cara y disminuye la marcha,
> extendiendo los brazos. No tarda en palpar el velador y
> una expresión de odio brutal le invade.*)
> Ignacio.-Vienes muy despacio. (pp.49-50)

For the first time, Carlos vacillates. His self-confidence is beginning to collapse. By the end of the play, once Ignacio has died, or has been born again in him, Carlos is surprised, shocked by his own clumsiness.

> *Luego, se levanta, vacilante. Al hacerlo, derriba involun-*
> *tariamente con la manga las fichas del tablero, que ponen*
> *con su discordante ruido una nota agria y brutal en el*
> *momento. Se detiene un segundo, asustado por el*
> *percance, y palpa con tristeza las fichas. Después avanza*
> *hacia el cadáver. (p.87)*

Although in a different way, Don Quixote is also put on the spot by Sancho. He has to give in when he is questioned by his squire "¿cuál es más: resucitar a un muerto o matar a un gigante?". Sancho actually makes the knight confess that being a saint is more important than being a knight-errant, which Don Quixote would have not been so willing to do in Part I:

> Cogido le tengo -dijo Sancho-. Luego la fama del que
> resucita muertos, da vista a los ciegos, endereza a los cojos
> y da salud a los enfermos, y delante de sus sepulturas
> arden lámparas, y están llenas sus capillas de gentes
> devotas que de rodillas adoran sus reliquias, mejor fama
> será, para este y para el otro siglo, de la que dejaron y
> dejaren cuantos emperadores gentiles y caballeros andantes
> ha habido en el mundo. (II,8)

To that compromising question Don Quixote could only answer: "También confieso esa verdad." Once again in Chapter 58 Don Quixote sadly compares himself to the saints whose images he has seen:

> Por buen agüero he tenido, hermanos, haber visto lo que he
> visto, porque estos santos y caballeros profesaron lo que
> yo profeso, que es el ejercicio de las armas; sino que la
> diferencia que hay entre mí y ellos es que ellos fueron
> santos y pelearon a lo divino, y yo soy pecador y peleo a lo
> humano. Ellos conquistaron el cielo a fuerza de brazos,
> porque el cielo padece fuerza, y yo hasta agora no sé lo que
> conquisto a fuerza de mis trabajos.

The knight has begun to understand that his mind might be deceived:

> ...así como vi este carro imaginé que alguna grande
> aventura se me ofrecía; y ahora digo que es menester tocar
> las apariencias con la mano para dar lugar al desengaño.
> (II,21)

This had not happened to him before. He used to project on reality the adventure in his mind. Now, reality disappoints him. Likewise, the little table in the middle of the room takes away Carlos's confidence. He was indeed an "activo", but he is now open to light. Buero says in his 'Comentario' to the play:

> El propio Carlos, al comprender que no mató sólo porque le
> quitaban su fe en la Institución, sino también por Juana,
> oye a su conciencia que le grita la falta, y el camino de su
> oscurecida vocación hacia la luz queda ahora en tinieblas,
> pero no oscuro: por fin abierto. (p.92)

He is not a Valindin, a Ulises, or a Goldmann, because he is able to change his mind. And he was always partly right, even before he inherited Ignacio's contemplative spirit. Buero speaks of "dos parciales verdades" and "dos sombras parciales" (p.91). They both have part of the truth.

Don Pablo seems to be the benefactor, almost the father of the students. He calls them "hijos" (p.21). At first, he gives an impression of self-sufficiency, security and efficiency. Nevertheless, when the time for battle comes, he lets Carlos fight it by himself. He is not as self-confident as he appears at the beginning:

> Don Pablo.-(...) Pero un accidente puede ocurrirle a
> cualquiera, y nosotros podemos demostrar que el tobogán
> y los otros juegos responden a una adecuada pedagogía.
> ¿Verdad, Pepita?
> Doña Pepita.-Sí, anda. No te preocupes por eso. Yo me
> quedaré aquí. (p.81)

He is basically interested in maintaining peace and order in the school for the sake of his own reputation: "Si Ignacio se marchase todo se arreglaría. Podríamos echarlo, pero... eso sería terrible para el prestigio del Centro" (p.75). He considers Ignacio's death a "complication" for the school. He refers to it with a surprising detachment:

> Don Pablo.-(*A moro muerto, gran lanzada.*) En vez de aprender cuando se le indicaba, nos busca ahora esta complicación por su mala cabeza. Espero que esto sirva de lección a todos.
> (...)
> Menos mal. La hipótesis del suicidio era muy desagradable. No hubiera compaginado con la moral de nuestro Centro. (p.81)

Another typically active character is Ulises. A reputed hero, he has not managed to fulfill his duties as a husband. He is proud, possessive, dominant, revengeful. But he sees himself as a king devoted to the good of his people. "No he venido a matarte" - he tells Penélope. "He vuelto para cuidar de mi país y de mi mujer. He venido a evitar muchas cosas, no a desencadenarlas" (p.195). He considers himself a hero who is going to solve the problems of his country. But he does it in the same way as Carlos: killing, murdering even the one who did not deserve death. By killing Anfino, he recovers his role, his image. That is what he mainly seeks, more than the good of his country or his wife's love. Penélope will never see her husband as the hero of her dreams.[4]

Pisandro refers to Ulises as a tyrant: "...otro tirano, como lo fue Ulises. No queremos más tiranos" (p.129). Buero's Ulises has no illusions, does not dream, like all the other "activos". Penélope tells him clearly: "Yo soñaba entonces; ¡sentía! Lo que tú, mezquino razonador, nunca has sabido hacer" (p.202). He destroys his wife's dreams because he ceased to be part of them years ago. He is the judge of Penélope's dreams and calls her "soñadora". He does not dream, he only acts, as he himself acknowledges: "Mezquino pero verdadero. Yo no sueño" (p.199). He also destroys both the second dreamer of the play, Anfino, whom he calls "iluso", and Penélope's happiness. Ulises does not entertain any dreams, but only desires for revenge. He was once part of Penélope's dreams but cannot be so any more:

> El Ulises con que yo soñé, ahí, los primeros años... ¡Y no
> este astuto patán, hipócrita y temeroso, que se me presenta
> como un viejo ruin para acabar de destruirme toda ilusión
> posible! (p.202)

Ulises' fear, hypocrisy and cunning are indeed the opposite of true quixotism.

Ulises appears to have the loyalty of Telémaco and Filetio and Emeo, but his triumph is a lonely one. He has lost his wife's love forever because Anfino has gained her affection. The latter was brave but Ulises has behaved in a cowardly way; he is no longer a hero. There is nothing left in him of the husband Penélope once loved.

> Y ahora te queda tu mujer, sí, a los ojos de todos; pero
> teniéndome no tienes ya nada, ¿me oyes? ¡Nada! Porque él
> se lo ha llevado todo para siempre. Una apariencia; una
> risible... cáscara de matrimonio te queda. ¡Tú eres el
> culpable! Tú, por no hablar a tiempo, por no haber sido
> valiente nunca. Te detesto. (p.203)

Doménech sums up Ulises' miserable situation as follows:

> Ulises -como tantos otros "activos"- se verá condenado a la
> más completa soledad. Ha derrotado a Anfino por la razón
> de la fuerza, pero Anfino, más allá de su muerte, ha
> derrotado a Ulises -como Ignacio a Carlos- por la razón del
> espíritu.[5]

Leandro ironically poses as a true knight also. He tries to act as Amalia's protector when he arrives in the house: "¡...no toleraré que se la insulte ni se la humille!" Leonor is quick to penetrate his pose and calls him "caballero andante": "¡Digo! Si ella no salía porque esperaba a su defensor... El caballero andante, que la recogerá después, en su pobreza. ¿A que no?" (p.24). Leandro turns out to be a liar. When the truth of his betrayal, of his calumny, is discovered, and he therefore loses his hope of getting Amalia for himself, he tries to recover Paula, who, of course, punishes him by her refusing to accept him. He is again a completely false Quixote, who is not blessed with any of the quixotic virtues, and who ends up abandoned by those he appears to love.

Dimas is another "activo". He boasts that he looks after his family, that he is making an effort to give them all he can, that he is sheltering his daughter-in-law: "...un hombre como yo, que alimenta, y viste, y da techo, no ya a la familia sino a extraños que no lo ganan" (p.136). But in fact Irene is like a slave whom everyone can use when they need to. Dimas is extremely rude to her, calling her "esa simple" and all sorts of other insults. Aurelia, his daughter, also reproaches him for the fact that she has not been allowed to study. Dimas is partially reponsible too for his own son's death, because he did not want to supply the money for the medicines his son needed: "¿Y nuestro pobre hijo, Dimas? ¿También pensaba en despilfarrar cuando necesitaba las medicinas?".

Dimas makes life unbearable for the family because of his extreme meanness, but he does not allow anybody to judge him: "¡No consiento que se juzguen mis actos!" (p.157). He wants to appear efficient and to be successful in his business, but fails to make his family happy. He is not interested in people, but in his own success. He is, of course, a thief, as his name implies. He is clearly one of those who do not dream, and he too fails to communicate effectively with those around him.

The title "Las cartas boca abajo" clearly indicates a failure - often voluntary - to communicate. In the play Adela finds it extremely difficult to reveal her feelings, her true motives; indeed she is not unlike Silverio in this regard. Buero makes it clear that she isolates herself. Her ambitions cannot easily be shared by other members of the family because these ambitions are rooted in her selfish desire for freedom. When she talks to Mauro about the birds that she loves to look at and listen to, he falls asleep; and Anita leaves the room, not making the slightest effort to listen to her younger sister:

*Retrocede un paso para apoyarse en la mesa sin dejar de
mirarlos con ojos extasiados. Hace tiempo que Mauro no la
escucha: ha vuelto a rendirle el sueño. El sonoro escándalo
de gorjeos invade la habitación durante unos segundos.*

She is left with the birds which are challenging her to try to be like
them. Anita "*vuelve a mirar a su hermana, recoge el periódico y va
hacia el chaflán con expresión impenetrable, desapareciendo tras la
cortina...*" (p.134).

Obviously, Adela does not make an effort to communicate with her
husband either. She fulfils her domestic tasks and looks after him,
makes coffee to facilitate his study, but does not give him the real
affection that he desperately needs. Juan describes the situation for
her: "Nos vamos hundiendo en el silencio y acabamos por pensar mal los
unos de los otros"; "nuestra unión parece una lucha sorda", a struggle
without words (pp.138 & 139). Adela refuses to put her feelings into
words, does not dare to acknowledge her incapacity to love her husband
because he has not succeeded in life.

Adela tries to communicate to her sister Anita when her remorse is
too overpowering; but Anita also insists on remaining silent; "un silencio
premeditado, porque tú no estás loca", Adela tells her (p.142). Not
even her confession makes Anita react; she neither accuses Adela nor
defends herself. Adela struggles desperately to be understood, to
provoke some sort of reaction but she cannot get one word out of Anita:

> Adela.-(...) Ya sé que hice mal. (*Vuelve.*) Pero alguna
> razón tenía ¿no? (*La sacude con brusquedad.*) Vamos,
> ¡defiéndete! (*Anita la mira sobresaltada y angustiada.*) O
> acúsame ¡pero habla! (*La deja, defraudada, y va a sentarse
> al sofá. Con el cuerpo encorvado, habla cansadamente.*)
> (p.156)

She continues to beg for a word, but her pleas remain unanswered:

Adela.- ..., dime una palabra, una sola palabra de
perdón... (*Le toma de la mano.*) ¿No? ¿Es que no te lo he
confesado todo?... (*Ante la severa mirada de Anita.*) ¿Pues
qué puedo decirte aún? Ayúdame tú... (*Se deja caer sobre
una silla, con los ojos arrasados.*) Yo ya no veo más... Yo
estoy ciega... (p.157)

Her husband sadly resigns himself to accepting their situation; Anita
had always known her sister's motives, and now Juanito also begins to
sympathize with his father, admires him and gradually separates himself
from his mother. Juanito is now going to "fly", to be free, which she
never managed to do. Adela feels that her son has also abandoned her:

Juanito.-Si me esperas, salgo contigo, padre.
(*Adela, sin volverse, cierra los puños.*)(p.193)

When father and son leave the house, their departure seems to be
definitive. Adela has condemned herself to absolute solitude.

Adela.-Adiós. (*Salen padre e hijo por la izquierda del
foro. Anita cierra los ojos, dolorida. Después va a sentarse
a la mesa, frente a su libro, que mira distraídamente.*) Es
como si se hubiese ido para siempre. Volverá esta noche,
pero será lo mismo; yo ya estaré sola. Sola contigo,
definitivamente. (pp.196-7)

Though there is a certain degree of self-isolation in other characters,
especially Juan and Anita, Juan at least tries to overcome it and
succeeds with Juanito, and Adela knows that her sister loves both
Juanito and Juan. At the end of the play she is first left on stage with
Anita, who refuses to communicate, and then completely alone. She has
to suffer the torture of talking without getting an answer, of confessing
her sins without being absolved. She has to bear the weight of what
Buero calls "un horror sin nombre". Anita, the only person she has,
refuses to give in. Once again Adela is left with the noise of the birds,

which is now deafening, and no longer reminds her of their freedom but
of their fear of death.

> ¡Hermana! (*Anita se vuelve desde el chaflán.*) ¿Todavía no
> me has castigado bastante? ¿Es que va a ser así toda la
> vida? (*Anita desaparece tras la cortina. Adela llega junto
> a ella. En un alarido.*) ¡Anita! ¿Me entiendes siquiera?
> (*Una pausa. Adela retrocede unos pasos, con los ojos muy
> abiertos, fijos en la cortina. Luego se vuelve lentamente y
> mira al balcón, espantada. Al fin, humilla la cabeza bajo el
> peso de un horror sin nombre. La algarabía de los pájaros
> ha llegado a su mayor estridencia y parece invadir la casa
> entera.*) (p.197)

Adela has been offered a chance to prove that she can still love, but she
refuses to accept it. Her selfishness condemns her to isolation, an
isolation which is not quixotic.

Ensenada is another man of action who, as he himself tells
Esquilache, has already lost his ideals: "No irás lejos con esas ilusiones.
Yo las perdí hace veinte años" (p.111). The contrast is very clear
between the man of ideals, who wants to serve the Spanish people, at the
risk of being misunderstood, and Ensenada, who pursues his personal
ambitions. He is completely jealous of Esquilache; he even compromises
with the enemy in order to pull him down.

Ensenada lives for himself, not for the good of his people.
Esquilache clearly understands this and tells him: "¡El hombre más
insignificante es más grande que tú si vive para algo que no sea él
mismo! Desde hace veinte años tú ya no crees en nada. Y estás
perdido" (p.201). In order to recover his power, Ensenada has
conspired "para encender el infierno en todo España" (p.202).
Esquilache would also like to have his power back, but only because,
with it, he would be able to protect the poor, the weak; to punish
crimes:

¡Y no poder vengarte! (*Crispa una de sus manos*) En esta
mano estaba el poder de España y ahora está vacía... ¡Dios
mío, dame el Poder de nuevo! (p.190)

Ensenada seeks only to satisfy his hunger for power; he lives for
himself. That is why he does not spare any effort, any violence.
Esquilache's ambition is service, and therefore he prefers to sacrifice
his own position. That is something a man of action would never
understand.

Of course, Ensenada criticizes Esquilache's dreams; the latter sees
that the solution to the corruption of those in power is to dream that
such corruption does not exist, that instead there is uprightness, an
eagerness to serve the country and its people, the desire to be useful;
to dream that everyone is moved by the same ideals. Those who avail of
their position to their own advantage know nothing about dreams.
Ensenada therefore accuses Esquilache: "¡Deliras! ¡Sueñas!" "Tal vez.
Pero ahora sé una cosa: que ningún gobernante puede dejar de
corromperse si no sueña ese sueño" (p.203). Those who have power and
do not dream of serving, of giving themselves, of dedicating their lives
to the welfare of their country, very easily become corrupt.

Valindin is the prototype of the active character, who wants to seem
a Quixote. It is obvious that he is interested only in his own benefit,
but he tries to appear a charitable soul, concerned for the suffering and
problems of his neighbour. He is completely rude and disrespectful
towards those who surround him. He tries to cover up his ambition with
a feigned charitable purpose:

Yo tengo buen corazón y soy filántropo.   ¡Pero la
filantropía es también la fuente de la riqueza...!   Esos
ciegos nos darán dinero. ¡Y yo los redimo, los enseño a
vivir! (...) ¡Ah! ¡Hacer el bien es bello! (p.33)
No todos quieren entender la belleza de una sana
filantropía. (p.42)

He wants to be seen as a redeemer. But he is not saving anybody, he
is not freeing them from their misery, because he is taking advantage of

them; he is denigrating, humiliating them, disregarding their human dignity.

He also gives the appearance of being efficient, like all the "activos". He tells Adriana: "Soy duro porque soy eficaz. También dices que soy duro para ti. Pero te salvo, como a ellos" (p.45). He also thinks he is saving Adriana but is in fact using her.

At the beginning of the play he tries to pretend that he really sympathizes with the blind, in order to convince the Reverend Mother that he is interested in their spiritual welfare:

> (*Da unos pasos hacia ella con los ojos húmedos; parece realmente conmovido.*) Palabras muy bellas y muy ciertas, madre... (*Se enjuga una lágrima*). Perdonad. Peco de sensible... Pero lo que habéis dicho me llega al corazón. Vos sabéis que la idea que he tenido el honor de exponeros posee su cara espiritual, y os empeño mi palabra de que no es para mí la menos importante. Si la llevamos a cabo, no sólo me depararéis la alegría de ayudar con mi bolsa al sostén de esta santa casa de Dios, sino el consuelo de esas oraciones que los cieguecitos rezarán cada año por mi alma pecadora. (p.17)

The man who pronounces these words is unbelievably the same one who tells Adriana laughingly: "Tiempo de hambre, tiempo de negocios" (p.33). He wants to make money out of the unfortunate. This feature of his personality, what Doménech calls his "capacidad de simulación"[6], perfectly befits an "activo". We cannot imagine Don Quixote trying to pretend; he is always genuine, guileless.

Valindin's words sound ironic when he talks about himself, about his good intentions: "Sólo desea uno dar trabajo a la pobre gente que lo ha menester ... ¡Decidle vos a este asno cómo se porta Valindin con la pobre gente! ... Decidle lo que habría sido de vos y de los vuestros sin Valindin"; "Y además, hijo, quiero dignificar vuestro trabajo: que ganéis vuestra vida sin pedir limosna" (pp.42-43).

He, who calls Adriana "galga" and beats her up, who dares to hit a blind man, who treats all the poor blind men cruelly and makes others laugh at them, at their ridiculous costumes and silly songs in what he calls "el espectáculo más filantrópico de todo París" (p.77), does not really know anything about dignity. His arrogance is punished because he laughs at the poor, as Don Quixote would never dare to do. Don Quixote, and any good quixote, gives himself, renders a service without expecting anything for himself. Valindin only gives something when he is planning to get something out of it. That is why his ethics are not quixotic: his altruism is false. As Iglesias says, the society around him is also responsible, but Valindin must be condemned as well:

> Valindin ha asimilado los valores de la sociedad y sabe explotarlos en beneficio propio; ... Sin embargo, en este punto surge el gran problema de la responsabilidad individual, constante en Buero. Ante un mundo envilecido, la aceptación implica culpabilidad y Valindin resulta por ello culpable. Valindin es, por lo tanto, un hombre complejo, lleno, como todos, de ambigüedades, que parece amar verdaderamente a Adriana, aunque quizás ella no sea en el fondo más que otra cosa de su propiedad, y suspira porque le dé un hijo; pero, situado en un mundo insolidario y cruel, se acomoda a él y extrae su provecho, utilizando todos los recursos que le brinda.

Valindin seems to think that he loves Adriana but the relationship between the two is not very clear. Adriana reproaches him that he used to spend whole nights on his own:

> Adriana.-Te pasabas los días y las noches en la barraca.
> Valindin.-(*Deja la copa apurada.*) ¡Era mi barraca!
> Adriana.-Este año harás lo mismo, ¿no? Te estarás allí hasta la madrugada, en tus juergas solitarias.
> Valindin.-Naturalmente. (p.31)

Valindin wants to be with what is his, in his "barraca". He wants to befriend influential people in his own interest. But they do not seem to be at home for him. He sends Catalina repeatedly to invite the Barón de la Tournelle, but he is never there. And later on, when the ignominious concert is about to start, he is sorry to have to say that his distinguished guest has not been able to come:

Valindin.-Si me hacéis la merced de entrar, Adriana os
acomodará en la mejor mesa. Estaba guardada para el señor
barón de la Tournelle, que ha sentido tanto no poder
venir... (p.76)

The prioress of the asylum also sees through his honeyed and emotional
words. She will have no time for Valindin in the future either: "Sor
Andrea, si ese caballero vuelve algún día a esta casa, yo no estaré para
él" (p.86). He is gradually abandoned by those who get to know him.
When he discovers Adriana's betrayal, he learns that he cannot count on
her either. Their relationship seems to be based on self-interest.
Before his death, Valindin decides to spend the night on his own again.
Dubois warns him that the night is dark and offers him company, but
Valindin prefers to be alone.

Dubois.-Veníos hoy al retén.
Valindin.-Prefiero mi barraca.
(...)
Dubois.-Volveos a casa. Yo estoy aquí para vigilar toda
esta hilera.
Valindin.-(Deniega.) Quiero sentirme entre lo mío.
Dubois.-¡Nada hay más propio que la cama propia! ¡En la
mía quisiera yo verme ahora!
Valindin.-Esto es más mío que mi cama. ¡Ya puede arder mi
cama y el piso entero! Aquí es donde yo celebro mis
alegrías... y donde paso mis penas. No hay nada como
estar solo. (p.109)

On his last night, Valindin sees himself abandoned. He cannot trust
Adriana, he has nobody he can possibly rely on. Wine is all he has:

¡Al diablo todas la perras del mundo! (Termina de quitarse
la casaca, que deja en una silla; aparta otra y se sienta
pesadamente. Atrapa la botella, destapona y bebe un largo
trago. Se pasa la mano por los ojos.) No te vas a
enternecer, Valindin. Tienes vino y ya no eres joven. ¡Al
diablo! (p.110)

Adriana reveals that Valindin's agony is not so different from David's. Valindin too cried at times, even before he was abandoned by everyone that night: "...él, ...también llora a veces... el muy cerdo" (p.89). In *Aventura en lo gris* Ana looks back on the fifteen years she spent with Goldmann as a hell, and she is ready to abandon him. From the beginning of the play, the very first conversation, one can notice that the relationship between them is tense, and somewhat cold. It does not show real affection. They seem to be together out of mere convenience.

> Alejandro.-(...) Esto no parece muy cómodo.
> Ana.-Desde luego, menos que tu palacio de la capital.
> Alejandro.-¿Quieres callarte ya, con mi palacio? Me parece que era tan tuyo como mío.
> Ana.-Yo nunca he tenido nada mío. (p.210)

Ana's complaint is similar to Adriana's:

> Valindin.- La galga no volverá a salir corriendo... Ahora tiene su casa y su barraca.
> Adriana.- ¿Mías? (p.32)

Neither Adriana nor Ana feels that they can share everything with the men they live with. They do not think they possess anything; they feel like part of someone else's belongings. There is a distance between Ana and Alejandro in spite of the many years they spent together. Alejandro has not managed to communicate. He is too interested in power, in wealth, and that interest she cannot share with Alejandro. Like Valindin, he is abandoned. Ana can understand and share her ideals and intimate desires with Silvano only after a few hours. But Alejandro made it impossible for her. He has also isolated himself through selfishness and vile ambition.

It seems very clear that lack of love and excessive activity lead to isolation. Paulus, another active character, says himself that he has had to learn to live alone, without any company. He once hoped to find strong men like himself, who would remain "sane". But the cruelty of his job separates him radically from other human beings, as it has begun

218

to affect Daniel. His contact with people remains at a cold professional level. He himself acknowledges his isolation.

> El mundo es el mismo ahí fuera que aquí dentro. Por eso es un iluso el que crea que, para hacer nuestro trabajo, se pueden encontrar hombres diferentes o forjarlos aquí. Mírame: yo he sido ese iluso. Cada uno de tus compañeros ha sido para mí una desilusión y tú has sido la última... Porque en ti confiaba; tú eras distinto. Como yo. ¡Tú hubieras debido mantenerte sano! Bien. Actuarás de todos modos. Enfermo, como ellos. Hace muchos años que he aprendido a estar solo, hijo mío. (p.120)

As in Valindin's case, we learn that other people who have been in contact with Paulus rejected him before, for example Daniel's mother.

> Daniel.-(...) ¿Le es imposible olvidar hasta ese punto que ella le rechazó?
> Paulus.-(*Lo mira con asombro y se levanta.*) Cállate.
> Daniel.-He llegado a sospechar que usted era mi verdadero padre. Todavía hace un momento me ha llamado hijo. ¡No vuelva a llamármelo! Ahora le comprendo a fondo. ¡Usted nunca ha dejado de odiar al hombre que fue mi padre! (p.121)

"Activos" do not forgive, do not forget, and this is the source of the hatred that separates them from others and prevents them from having any real affection or even communication with anyone.

Vicente is again an "activo" ("es un espíritu eminentemente práctico, un activo como era Carlos"[8]). His brother Mario refers to such men in the following terms: "¡Veo a mi alrededor muchos activos, pero están dormidos! ¡Llegan a creerse tanto más irreprochables cuanto más se encanallan!" (p.58). That is the case with many of Buero's "activos": they consider themselves faultless. Like Valindin, who asks Bernier to explain to the blind musicians how good he was to him when he needed help, Vicente asks one of his victims, Encarna, to convince Mario that he has done nothing to be reproached for: "¿Verdad, Encarna? Porque tú no tienes nada que reprocharme. Eso se queda para los ilusos que miran por los tragaluces y ven gigantes donde deberían ver molinos" (pp.82-3). He is obviously accusing his brother of being a Quixote, using again this concept in a negative sense: Mario is in fact one of those who does very little about the world that he contemplates. Vicente is using the concept of quixotism in that way because he lacks precisely that aspect of quixotism: contemplation.

He is using Encarna as Valindin was using Adriana, and he also adduces generous intentions: "Y me gusta ayudar a la gente, si puedo hacerlo. Eso también lo sabes tú" (p.83). He likes helping people, but he does not in fact help Beltrán, ruining his career as a writer, when his own position in the company is at stake. Even the financial help he gives his family serves him to quieten his conscience, which reminds him constantly of the evil he did to them before. The little things he does for others contribute to his belief that he is above reproach. But in fact Vicente does not use his privileged position to do justice. He only helps as long as his reputation and his job are safe. He can afford to offer Mario a job, but he does not hesitate to betray Beltrán.

Like most of the other "activos", he dresses impeccably: "*Es hombre apuesto y de risueña fisonomía. Viste cuidada y buena ropa de diario. En su mano izquierda, un grueso anillo de oro*" (p.16).

The ambition of those "activos" is generally selfish. There may be a trace of selfishness also in Mario's isolation, but Vicente is worse because he uses others to his own advantage. As Iglesias points out,

> Vicente es un activo que reúne mucho de lo visto anteriormente en Goldmann, Valindin y Paulus. Como el primero[9] desprecia al contemplativo y tiene una secretaria-amante.

Vicente can be as rude as Goldmann is to Ana. Like him, he is not willing to marry his mistress, only to use her, as one more victim: "Además, que, si no la amparas, se queda en la calle con un mes de sueldo", Vicente warns his brother (p.85). That is one of the main features of the "activos": they use people, even when they are helping them. They take advantage of those who have very little to give, who serve them only as a way to satisfy their pleasures or to silence their consciences.

Vicente keeps coming back to the basement; he is feeling remorse for what he did and he actually confesses to his father, as Adela did to Anita and Silverio to Pilar. He would like to be forgiven. However, the recognition of his past faults is not enough to make him change because he is too weak and he is not ready to stop making victims: "Dentro de un momento me iré ... a seguir haciendo víctimas", he confesses to his father (p.103). Vicente is not different from the Vicentito who refused to get off the train: "Es Vicente, padre. Vicentito", Mario says to his father (p.27). There has been no change and there will be none in the future either.

Juan Luis also behaves like an "activo". Years ago he appeared to Julia to be a real Quixote. He acted the brave man who prevented her being arrested. Ginés, the policeman who was in fact his accomplice, compared his attitude to that of Don Quixote: "Es usted muy joven. Le aconsejo que no haga el Quijote. Poner obstáculos a la actuación policial puede costarle caro" (p.48). He was acting the Quixote, trying to make Julia believe that he was like a heroic knight, saving her from being arrested through his brave action. We learn that Juan Luis is not as courageous as that in real life. He does not dare to do something to prevent a murder that he suspects is going to be committed, even though Father Anselmo advises him to warn the police.

Juan Luis tries to make excuses to avoid having to face difficulties. His own security, his reputation, are more important for him than a life which can be saved. He refuses to risk anything. Father Anselmo warns him that one should always try to avoid a probable death. But Juan Luis seeks to be understood, to be spared the sacrifice; he wants the priest to absolve him of his cowardice: "Tenga presente que quizá me equivoco y ese hombre no tiene tales intenciones. Es solamente una sospecha, aunque fundada" (p.108). He is actually responsible for the murder. That is why he is accused even before it takes place. The general is indeed Juan Luis's victim, as Ginés suggests ("Es la tuya"), even though he has not pulled the trigger (p.103). His judges, his own conscience, keep trying to make him denounce Ginés but he refuses: "No puedo" (p.127). Eventually, not only General Ruiz Aldán but also three men of his escort, his driver and an innocent woman who was just passing with her child, are killed. Juan Luis has murdered, like Ginés, because he did not and will not inform on him: "Tú has matado conmigo porque no avisaste y porque no hablarás" (p.143).

Juan Luis is not brave enough. He wants to believe that he is no longer the young man who shot somebody, that he has changed. But he is not different from the Juan Luis who did not oppose the unjust execution of Eladio González, as the cellist reminds him: "Usted votó mi muerte en el consejo de ministros" (p.125). Eladio's death did not matter much to Juan Luis at the time. As the violinist tells the cellist, Juan Luis only saw a photograph, and now he cannot even remember Eladio's face. Juan Luis's victims return to let him know that he has not changed. Don Jorge makes him understand at the end of the play that, even though he wants to persuade himself that he has left his past behind, he is the man he always was, because he has not notified the police. Once more, he does not prevent the killing of innocent victims.

At the beginning of the play Juan Luis imagines the departure of the guests from his supposed wedding anniversary party. In the first part Cristina leaves, and so does the general, while Juan Luis asks them: "¡No se vayan todavía!" (p.43). He hears the voices saying laughingly "Decididamente hay que irse", and "Juan Luis está acabado".

Voces.-Vámonos... Vámonos.. (*Sólo los músicos, que miran a Juan Luis fijamente, y la viola solitaria siguen iluminados. De cara al proscenio, Juan Luis muestra su turbado rostro. Un vivo foco lo destaca...*) (p.44)

Juan Luis is left alone on stage. His marriage has not worked out as he expected. His wife Julia never really loved him, but he continues to struggle to deserve her love. Julia refuses to get any closer to him. This is, again, the solitude of two beings who live together without any real communication. And Juan Luis has to suffer his dreadful remorse on his own, without being forgiven or understood.

> J. Luis.-(*Tras ella.*) Estás perdiendo la fe. Y así tu
> soledad es aún mayor que la mía.
> Julia.-¿Tú te sientes solo?
> J. Luis.-Sabes que sí. (p.77)

Both feel lonely, but Julia at least has Cristina. Juan Luis has only his thoughts, and he constantly attempts to approach his wife, who openly despises him.

> J. Luis.-Pues os invito a donde queráis...
> Julia.-No, gracias. Vete tú a casa. (*Se levanta y saca un
> billete, que deja sobre la mesa.*) ¡Vámonos, Tina! (*Cristina
> se levanta despacio. Julia da un paso hacia el lateral*).
> J. Luis.-(*La toma del brazo.*) Pero, Julia...
> Julia.-(*Levanta la voz.*) ¡Suéltame! (*Se desase.*)

He is again left alone. Julia does not make the slightest effort to understand or to forgive Juan Luis's weakness. She refuses to listen or to let him explain, humiliating him in front of witnesses:

> Julia.-(...) ¿Quieres que baje la voz? Serás complacido.
> (*Susurra.*) No tengo ganas de hablar contigo. ¿Y sabes
> por qué? Pues porque eres un necio.
> J. Luis.-¡Julia! (p.93)

Juan Luis cannot trust anyone. He was not able to open up to Padre Anselmo, he wanted his consolation and absolution without confessing everything; with Don Jorge, he has to pretend. In her depression, Julia can trust Cristina. Juan Luis is also depressed, but he needs to hide it:

> J. Luis.-Sí. Tomo las píldoras sin que lo sepa Julia.
> Prefiero que se crea ella sola la enferma... Sí. El
> protagonista está muy deprimido... ¿Cómo voy a decirte
> que no soy yo? (p.95)

The greatest agony that he has to suffer, one very similar to Lázaro's, is that of having to judge himself, as the violinist tells him: "Nadie te juzga, salvo tú mismo" (p.127). Julia does not accept his sincere desire to make amends, to begin again. She abandons him forever, leaves him with nothing. "A la doncella la despidió esta tarde y ella se ha ido escupiéndole su desprecio. Ahora está solo" (p.159). After Julia's suicide, the imaginary party starts again but they all one by one leave Juan Luis alone. He asks himself a question that nobody can answer: "¿Es que no puede un hombre rectificar sinceramente? ¡Contestadme!" (p.162). All he can do is to call Julia, though no longer expecting an answer: "¡Julia! (*Nadie repara en él. La música se expande.*) ¡Julia!" (p.165).

Juan Luis does not succeed in communicating, in achieving forgiveness from the only person he cares about, his wife. The idea of isolation is clearly perceived by the audience from the very beginning of the play. Buero's notes on the stage props are very specific:

> *Adosado al de la izquierda, viejo diván de café suficiente para dos personas y, ante él, mesa en la que descansan una copa de licor, una taza y un periódico. Junto a la mesa, una silla.* (p.33)

The audience do in fact see Cristina and Julia occupying that sofa, while Juan Luis is left on his own. In the first dream that the spectators witness, Juan Luis seems to live happily with his wife:

> *Julia y Juan Luis se miran tiernamente.* (p.37)
>
> *Se estrecha contra él, mimosa.* (p.41)
>
> *Se besan y abrazan. Cristina y el General aplauden.* (p.42)

The audience, nevertheless, soon realize that Juan Luis fails even to approach his wife without being rejected. The spectator can clearly see this on the encounter of the couple after the first nightmare: "*Va luego hacia su esposa e insinúa levemente la intención de besarla. También muy levemente, ella aparta la cabeza*" (pp.59-60). It is then that Juan Luis leaves and occupies the chair that was reserved for him: "*...baja el peldaño del salón y se sienta en el diván del café. Allí se engolfa en la lectura de un periódico que había sobre la mesa y bebe de vez en cuando de su taza*" (p.60). In the second scene Juan Luis is again found on his own, now with a glass of whisky in his hand: "*Con un vaso de whisky en la mano, Juan Luis mira al frente*" (p.69). By the end of the play, not even the Julia Juan Luis imagines pays any attention to him. She cannot look at his eyes any more. "*Mientras tocan, Julia y el violinista se contemplan con honda ternura. A los pocos segundos Juan Luis se deja caer de rodillas, de espaldas al mirador*" (p.165). There is no tenderness for Juan Luis, there never was. She has her eyes fixed on somebody else.

Juan Luis has been alone for years, because he never truly possessed Julia. But when, partly forced by circumstances, he wants to make up for his mistakes, his solitude becomes even more bitter, because no one wants to listen, no one wants to forgive.

In *Diálogo secreto*, Fabio is also unable to communicate fully because he has something to hide.[10] He holds his secret conversations with the Braulio he invents for himself. His father, however, is not aware of the responsibility that Fabio attributes to him at the beginning of the play. Fabio is alone with his guilt, with his remorse. Like Juan Luis, he recognizes his fault only when it is discovered by someone else. And like Silverio, he does not dare to talk to those who could help him to clarify his position; to say what he feels to his father, to accuse him of having launched him into a career for which he was not fitted.

Fabio.-¡Buena manera de disuadirme, la de inclinarme a ser lo que soy ahora! (*Breve pausa.*) ¿Por qué? (*No hay *respuesta.*) Un día te sentaré ahí y tendrás que explicarte. Algún día me atreveré.(p.40)

He is also afraid of not achieving his wife's forgiveness, so that here too there is a lack of communication, even though, like Pilar, Teresa knows more than he suspects. As soon as Teresa leaves the room, he goes back to what obsesses him, to his secret dialogue with Braulio, who does not really listen. "No sé para qué hablo contigo", Fabio says (p.52). He does not want to stay alone, to be tormented by the thought of his real responsibility for the death of Samuel Cosme. "¿Qué prisa tenéis? Quedaos un rato conmigo", he asks Braulio and Gaspar (p.68). But once more, as soon as they both and Teresa leave, his dialogue begins again, not with Velázquez but with his Braulio. "*La figura de Braulio reaparece... por el primer término derecho y se sienta en el diván. La luz lo destaca y Fabio clava en él sus ojos*" (p.75). Fabio needs to share the burden of his terrible responsibility with somebody else.

The figure of Braulio appears again immediately after Aurora's open accusation. She leaves her father alone to face his terror, shame and cowardice. The ghostly Braulio comes as Fabio's own conscience trying to console him, to calm his fear: "Quizá no diga nada" (p.84). Fabio himself hopes Aurorita will not publicize his defect. Fabio communicates with his own created Braulio because he himself dreams their conversations. But when Fabio attempts to present his thoughts to his father, Braulio is not aware that father and son have anything in particular to say to each other:

Fabio.-(*Con la voz insegura.*) Yo creí... que querías hablar conmigo.
Braulio.-¿De qué?
Fabio.-De nosotros dos.
Braulio.-Ya lo tenemos todo hablado. ¿O tienes tú algo que decirme?
Fabio.-(*Lo mira fijamente.*) No.
Braulio.-(*Va hacia la derecha, murmurando.*) Sí... Todo hablado...
Fabio.-(*Para sí.*) Y todo callado.

Braulio.-(*Se detiene.*) ¿Qué?
Fabio.-Nada. (pp.93-4)

In view of this lack of communication, Fabio returns to the memories of his happy and distant past. It is only at the end of the play that Fabio dares to confess his thoughts openly to his father. However, Braulio does not even admit to the fact that he was ever aware of any optic defect in his son. Fabio is determined to make his father confess that he had always known of his colour blindness: "¡Basta de disimulos, padre!"; "¡Padre! ¡Entre tú y yo se han acabado los fingimientos!" (p.125); but Braulio's absolute denial is followed by more isolation. Now, Fabio cannot even entertain the thought of a shared guilt: he is the only one to blame for the deceit. He is absolutely alone with his responsibility. The imagined Braulio has vanished and Fabio thinks he cannot go on. The only thing that saves him is the discovery that Teresa had always known his agony and had tried to suffer it with him silently.

Another character who strikes one as an "activo" is Germán. At the beginning of *Lázaro en el Laberinto* he appears to be the most willing to help Lázaro, the quickest to make up his mind to do something about his supposed madness. While Amparo suggests thinking about it first, he feels urged to act: "Pues mientras vosotros lo pensáis, yo actuaré" (p.70). He is another false Quixote, who is eager to act without stopping to think first. We hear him again: "¡Hay que actuar! ¿No te parece, Amparo?" (p.113). But Germán does not really provide any help. He finds the information he was looking for but has not the tact to communicate it to Lázaro at the right moment. On the other hand, he wants to appear idealistic, someone who exerts all his effort in the service of the ideals he preaches. Nevertheless, he gives himself away. When the moment comes to get a job, a good position for himself, he does not scruple to betray his friend Mariano, or the ideals that he has so vehemently preached. He tries to explain his behaviour: "Cuando se pone la vida al servicio de la revolución que el mundo necesita, se miente si es preciso" (p.138). Amparo knows that he is not one of those who can give their life for an ideal; she is disappointed: "Creí que pertenecías al ejército de los luchadores insobornables. Me había equivocado" (p.139). She feels sorry for Lázaro, because he is not yet able to face the tragedy of his own cowardice, but she has no hope for Germán at all: "Pobre Germán. Tú ni siquiera oyes un timbre" (p.140). He cannot even hear the bell which would make him think, because he is too concerned with his personal ambitions.

In his last play, Buero shows once more how excessive and selfish action, lack of love, lead to isolation. Adolfo is presented as a man of action who has lived for himself. He did not even marry the woman he loved. He comes back to live with his daughter Sandra in an attempt to recover her company and Isolina's love. "El hombre de acción que ha aprendido que el precio de su forma de actuar es la soledad, ha vuelto a casa a recuperar lo mejor de su pasado, el sueño del amor que todavía lleva dentro" (p.38). Buero, however, makes it clear that his previous lack of love, his living only for himself, has raised a barrier between him and others. When Adolfo chooses to diminish his level of activity and involvement in his business, and leaves it to his son Javier, another clear and frightening example of an active character, love and company are denied to him. His daughter makes up her mind to buy her own flat and leave him, and then she is killed. Lorenza leaves the house immediately, because she was one of Adolfo's victims. Adolfo begs René to stay and run his "fundación cultural", but he also leaves. Even though Adolfo makes an attempt to abandon part of his activities, he decides to isolate himself in a room in order to play a game which consists of watching himself. His own action has been the cause of his isolation. In his introduction to the play, David Johnston says that Buero "intenta demostrar,..., cómo las últimas consecuencias de nuestras acciones pueden convertirse en cárceles que imposibilitan la misma libertad que anhelamos" (p.27). These words in reference to Adolfo could well be applied to Adela, and to most of the active characters who are punished with isolation. Though Adolfo tries to start a new life, Buero makes it clear that it is too late. Sandra, Lorenza, René, abandon him. Even his hopeful dream of an Isolina who awaits him and remains youthful and beautiful after so many years, vanishes forever. She is seen at the very end of the play and Buero describes her appearance:

> *Muy avejentada para su edad, muestra las bolsas del cansancio bajo sus ojos, el rictus endurecido por los años de su boca, el cabello casi blanco y peinado con desaliño.* (p.147)

The last word of the play pronounced by Adolfo, "Isolina", is only the memory of a lost dream. "*Con brusco ademán y sonoro golpe, la señorita cierra su ventana.*" Buero calls Isolina "*la mujer marchita*", making it clear that the man of action is left completely alone. The video that Adolfo constantly watches becomes the symbol of his isolation. "Siga solo ante su vídeo, páselo mil veces. No verá más que su propio horror", René told him before leaving him forever (p.147). All he has now is the horror of a sterile past, and the terrible responsibility for the consequences of his actions.

The solitude of Ulises, Adela, Goldmann, Valindin, Paulus, Adolfo, is deserved. Theirs is not a quixotic solitude. There is however a redeeming factor in the cases of Juan Luis and Fabio because there is a desire to make amends even if this desire is provoked by their situation.

Apart from their inability to communicate, which is a self-inflicted punishment, the characters who have a tendency to over-activity, who live for themselves, are often judged and sentenced by others.

Carlos does not seem to be punished by anyone, because the person who knows the terrible crime prefers to hide it. But the fatal punishment comes inexorably, as he will have to suffer the excruciating agony that afflicted Ignacio, his victim, who seems to be punishing his murderer even after death.

Of course, Ulises loses Penélope for ever, because she cannot dream of him any more. The deceitful Leandro has to suffer the loss not only of Amalia, whom he expected to gain through his vile swindles, but also Paula.

Dimas is punished by his own wife, whom he had been driving mad with his ridiculous meanness. He did not show any affection for his own family, because he was concerned only about his money. Irene is like a slave or a mad woman as far as he is concerned. And Justina and Aurelia are just a source of expenses. He is therefore confined to a mental asylum, where he himself will be treated as a madman.

Ensenada's punishment, his exile, also comes at the hand of his victim, Esquilache. Esquilache himself has to leave as well, but does not lose anything, because he lived for something other than himself. But Ensenada loses power, all he wanted. Exile is the just punishment. As Esquilache says, it is a full reparation: "¡Reconozco el estilo del rey! El hombre por cuya causa me destierran tiene que sufrir la humillación de ser desterrado por mi mano. Para mí, una reparación completa" (p.200).

Apart from being isolated by his own selfishness, Valindin is killed by the hand of one of those whose dignity he abused. He deserves death because he laughed at the poor; he is killed brutally because he was brutal. Even before he dies he has to bear the thought of Adriana being unfaithful to him precisely with one of the blind men of whom he is taking advantage. We almost feel sorry for him, as we see him terrified, and guess that in his own way he truly loved Adriana.

Alejandro too is outrageously selfish and does not care about anything or anyone but his own welfare. Like Valindin, he is first abandoned by the woman with whom he has chosen to live, and then killed by Carlos, one of the many young men whom Goldmann had managed to deceive with his false image of idealism and eagerness to serve.

Vicente's case differs somewhat from the others, since he is trying to make up for his crimes. He has made victims but is coming back to the basement more and more often, in his desire to be forgiven for what he knows was his crime. Mario notices this and tells his brother: "Estás volviendo al pozo cada vez con más frecuencia..., y eso es lo que prefiero de ti" (p.58). Nevertheless, he is not spared punishment because he has not been able to stop taking the train he once took. The sentence is executed by one of his victims, as in the case of Valindin. Vicente's punishment becomes a sort of liberation. It is similar to Daniel's, in *La doble historia*. Though not a false Quixote, Daniel Barnes is also killed, even though his wife's love and respect are more important to him than his job; he feels remorse for the torture he inflicts and his conscience is in fact torturing him already. But that does not seem to be enough. Moreover, he finds it hard to stop torturing. Though he resolves to stop, Paulus reminds him: "Estás atrapado y no hay escape" (p.118). Mary also understands that he will never be able to abandon his job: "¡Tu jefe lo sabe y tú también lo sabes! ¡Porque quieres volver, quieres volver!" (p.130). "No hay escape", he admits. Death is a kind of merciful release, as it is for Vicente, who wants to change but cannot stop taking the train. Daniel too must to pay a high price for his past crimes. Buero makes it clear that when he is shot, he almost smiles as he falls ("*Daniel cae, casi sonriente*") and still has time to thank his wife: "¡Gracias!". As in Vicente's case, his punishment becomes his only possible liberation.

Juan Luis is punished too. He never had the love of the woman he adored. He wants to keep Julia at all costs, but he loses her for ever, as Adolfo loses Isolina. All are punished, even if they come to realize the need to make up for their mistakes.

Simple, good, charitable, big-hearted Don Quixote would not understand those who pretend to feel a generous interest in others, who conceal their motives with such feigned philanthropy and impeccable external appearance; those who, despite loving only themselves and using others for their own benefit, despite displaying an artificial kindness towards their equals and superiors, but extreme rudeness towards those who are weaker or poorer than themselves (Valindin, Ensenada, Goldmann, Vicente...), consider their own behaviour faultless. This is the worst mistake of such "activos", for which they need to be punished: that they want to appear real Quixotes, but are not endowed with any of Don Quixote's heroic virtues: therefore, their ideals, their interests, do not go beyond themselves.

When referring to the antinomy "activo"-"contemplativo", Doménech says, it is not safe to classify characters in those two categories: "lo frecuente es que, en relación con ello, cada obra adopte un punto de partida distinto y, consecuentemente suministre aspectos nuevos y particulares."[11] Not all the characters that we have been analysing can be easily pigeon-holed. We find a good example of that difficulty precisely in the play in which those terms were used to characterize the antithesis. The actual word "contemplativo" is not used in El tragaluz. We hear about the "activos" and "quienes contemplaban". The word "contemplativo" was used before in Aventura: "Soñar es faena de mujeres... o de contemplativos"; "Usted es un contemplativo inconfundible" (p.157). In that play there is reference to "acción", and not to "activos": "hombre de acción" (p.176) is used by Ana in the dream, and by Silvano, who calls Goldmann "un hombre de acción, que nunca sueña" (p.206). In El tragaluz the two groups are described negatively by one of the Investigadores: "El mundo estaba lleno de injusticia, guerras y miedo. Los activos olvidaban la contemplación; quienes contemplaban no sabían actuar" (p.105).

The "activo" Vicente is right in that he maintains that some action is necessary, even though he himself lacks contemplation, which is also essential:

> Mario, toda acción es impura. Pero no todas son tan egoístas como crees. ¡No harás nada útil si no actúas! Y no conocerás a los hombres sin tratarlos, ni a ti mismo, si no te mezclas con ellos.

Mario, the "contemplativo", tries to explain what he understands by contemplation; it is obvious that he is also seen negatively, in the sense that he is incapable of sufficent action to make contact with people, to get to know them and himself. He describes his attitude in life as one of "looking", contemplating: "Prefiero mirarlos" (p.57); "Me conformo por eso con observar las cosas, y a las personas, desde ángulos inesperados. ... Los activos casi nunca sabéis mirar" (p.59); "Y es que hay que observar, hermano. Observar y no actuar tanto" (p.60).

Like the Investigadores, we cannot agree with Mario either. "Looking", "contemplating", have to be followed, or accompanied by, "doing". Therefore, Vicente the "activo" is not wholly "wrong", as there is an attempt on his part to rectify his conduct. Mario says: "Yo no soy bueno; mi hermano no era malo. A su modo, quiso pagar" (p.107). Like Juan Luis, he would have liked to rectify; but also like him, he needs to be punished. We sympathize with their remorseful consciences, with their desire to make up for the damage they had done. They are not totally without scruples.

Carlos had the potential to become a "contemplativo", and so he does at the end of the play. As for Valindin, David himself hints at the fact that he was not completely selfish in his actions: "La última palabra que dijo fue tu nombre. (...) Te quería, Adriana. Y te golpeó y nos golpeó a todos, porque te quería" (p.118).

On the other hand, David, a "contemplativo", ends as a murderer. Mario's intentions are not clear either: "El quería engañarse... ver claro; yo quería salvarlo... y matarlo" (p.107). And Carlos, in the process of becoming a "contemplativo", also murders.

Buero clearly rejects that pure action which is the result of personal ambition, of selfish interests. Action can only be good when it is the fruit of contemplation.[12] Nobody would accuse Esquilache, Silvano, Ana, Silverio, Velázquez, Eloy, of being "activos", because their action is inspired and moderated by a great deal of contemplation; consequently, that action is quixotic, is inspired by ideals, and seeks to reach and help others.

NOTES TO CHAPTER VI

1. Alonso Fernández de Avellaneda, *El Ingenioso Hidalgo don Quijote de la Mancha* (Madrid: Castalia, 1972), pp.9, 11 & 13.

2. Buero's 'Comentario' to *En la ardiente oscuridad*, p.92.

3. Iglesias Feijoo, *La trayectoria*, p.61.

4. Martha Halsey compares Ulises to Asaf (*Las palabras en la arena*): "Like Asaf, Ulises... leads a life of spiritual blindness and hypocrisy. It is his failure to come to grips with the truth about himself which causes his defeat, just as it causes Asaf's" (*Antonio Buero Vallejo*, pp.45-6).
 The problem of many "activos" is that they do not make an effort to get to know themselves, because they lack the necessary contemplation. Ulises ends up murdering, like Asaf and Carlos, who never thought themselves capable of doing such a thing.

5. Doménech, *El teatro de Buero Vallejo*, p.248.

6. Doménech, *El teatro de Buero Vallejo*, p.211.

7. Iglesias Feijoo, *La trayectoria*, p.307.

8. Doménech, *El teatro de Buero Vallejo*, p.116.

9. Iglesias Feijoo, *La trayectoria*, p.356.

10. Eric Pennington says that *Diálogo secreto* could be interpreted "as a treatise on deception". He affirms that "deception permeates every aspect of Fabio's life". Fabio is isolated by his own deception. However, Fabio is not at ease with his situation. As Pennington points out, "Fabio's discomfort at living a life of pretension" is sensed from the beginning (Eric Pennington, 'Buero Vallejo's *Diálogo secreto*: the masks of mortals', *Hispanófila* 103 (Sept. 1991), 17-32, pp.16, 17 & 20).

11. Doménech, *El teatro de Buero Vallejo*, p.67.

12. We already considered the need for a balance between contemplation and action in the previous chapter (See note 32).

Conclusion

Buero Vallejo firmly believes in the need for moral regeneration of the individual, if this individual is to make any significant impact on his society. Hence the need for heroes that I have stressed throughout this study, for extraordinary individuals, for solitary, heroic beings, for dreamers, for madmen. Don Quixote provides a model for Buero.[1] Quixotic values are positively inspiring. Though Buero himself has said that one can approach *Don Quixote* from multiple and varying angles (according to one's age, or even to a particular work one wants to write), it seems clear that Buero's view of the novel, of quixotism, is always of a Romantic type. In other words, Buero attaches great value to the inspiring power of dreams, of ambitious ideals. The following statement is indicative of his positive idea of quixotism:

> El pensamiento utópico puede ser muy dinamizante, muy operativo, hasta el punto de dejar de ser utópico para convertirse en algo práctico. Una de las maneras de llegar a una práctica positiva es el pensamiento utópico, y, por lo tanto, la ensoñación.
>
> La actitud íntima de un don Quijote frente a la realidad ... lleva dentro más futuro que las innumerables actitudes mal llamadas prácticas. (Interview)

This assertion is indeed revealing of Buero's approach to quixotism. The internal disposition of the knight has great value, "lleva dentro más futuro". Practical approaches to life deal with the present moment, solve the immediate needs, but do not change the world because they do not mean to. The task of transforming the world from inside belongs to heroes. Revolution starts in the individual. David Johnston says that "the history plays of Buero Vallejo, in particular *Un soñador para un pueblo* and *El concierto de San Ovidio*, are concerned to reassert the role of the hero, in the words of Buero 'uno de los motores que elevan a la especie humana como conjunto, y le abren puertas'." The hero thus becomes the cause of radical changes, and also the inspiration for the transformation of other individuals. "The hero in the theatre of Buero Vallejo is, therefore, the embodiment of a speculative hope, the transmission of an image of the struggle for change to an audience chained to an abiding and destructive sense of stagnation and impotence." He quotes Buero's words once again:

> Un pueblo sin héroes, al estilo suizo o sueco, que va progresivamente mejorando sin necesidad de héroes, es más bien reformista que revolucionario, porque la revolución en la cual creía Brecht inevitablemente necesita héroes. Pero también estoy por decir que la vida diaria, aunque no sea de una etapa revolucionaria, también los necesita. Es decir, el heroísmo marca uno de los buenos techos del ser humano.

"Buero" - he says - "clearly considers the figure of the hero to be an integral element in the creation of a revolutionary consciousness ... the hero is the ordinary man who undertakes the creative struggle against circumstances, who asserts himself in the face of injustice and who, in doing so, in the words of Buero, opens the doors of possibility to his companions."[2] The hero's faith and daring therefore constitute the source of the creation of history. This is possible only because the hero looks towards the future, refuses to become stagnant, and thus dreams. The role of "ensoñación", as Buero says, is absolutely essential to cause first of all a deep internal transformation, and then the awakening of the consciousness of other individuals, which may not be immediate, but happens eventually. In keeping with a long-standing tradition, Buero makes it clear that dreaming and madness are often productive, thus showing his view that Don Quixote's madness is not sterile. When Buero says that it is necessary to have and to live according to an "ética

quijotesca", he is obviously stressing the positive aspects of Don
Quixote's behaviour and set of values, the fact that he struggles bravely
to change his surroundings, and to do good, no matter what the results
may be. He talks about his

> personajes, generalmente protagonistas, que llevan dentro
> una pequeña llama quijotesca. Pueden tener sus
> claroscuros, sus imperfecciones, pero en el fondo son
> idealistas frente a una realidad a menudo hostil y
> partidarios por ello de una manera digna y ética de
> entender el comportamiento humano en general y el suyo
> propio en particular. (Interview)

The little quixotic flame burns in the midst of imperfections, personal
mistakes, complex personalities. We have seen that it is not easy to
pigeonhole some of Buero's characters because they have a mixture of
positive and negative features by reason of the psychological depth of
their personality. E.C. Riley has emphasized that in Don Quixote too
there is a combination of virtues and defects as in any other true-to-life
character: "Don Quixote is much more humanly interesting than any
mere paradox of madness and sanity would be. Like any real person, he
combines strengths and weaknesses and tendencies which are divergent
and even contradictory".[3] The hardest struggle to be fought by
heroes is the one against themselves, like Don Quixote's. Dark
moments, tormenting doubts, are clearly part of their hostile
environment. This personal conflict does not exempt them from their
duty. While their struggle takes place, they may not even be aware of
the huge fire that their flame has kindled. They may not even see it
themselves, but dreaming, and a readiness to put dreams into practice,
yields fruit. Madness is fruitful and provides an enlightened vision of
the future. E.C. Riley describes Don Quixote as "an extreme case, an
extension of certain human proclivities. That is one definition of
madness, loosely speaking, and that is what primarily marks out Quixote
from the other characters and from you and me". Don Quixote is thus
a very human character, an idealist who has gone mad enough to be able
to proclaim his ideals, because he is fully convinced of them.[4] It is,

however, clear that his madness does not render his ideals useless, or at least, it seems obvious that Buero does not think so.

At this point it may be useful to go back to some of the opinions that various critics have expressed about Buero himself, which I have mentioned earlier. We have seen that Ramón de Garciasol called him a "príncipe moral y quijoteador". Kronik thinks that he is an "autor que tiene que decirnos algo profundo e importante y que nos atañe a todos, un dramaturgo serio, preocupado y soñador". Ruggeri Marchetti suggests that "solitudine ed allucinazioni sono esperienze personali di Buero Vallejo". When Buero is compared to his quixotic characters in these aspects, it is obviously meant in a laudatory manner.[5] Buero is seen as a person who thinks, who dreams, and who tries to put his dreaming into practice by awakening the consciousness of his audience. This has often meant for him a quixotic struggle, but it is evident that he deems it worthwhile. Buero is one of those who maintain that thinking has to come before acting, and that a personal ethical commitment needs to come before the proclamation of the ideal. The defence of certain ideals without personal commitment to them, easily degenerates into empty dogmatism, as Buero makes clear in the case of Germán. Buero is much more of a Mario than a Vicente, and he is obviously to be considered a dreamer, a contemplative. He wants to make his audience think because he thinks, wishes to encourage them to look for the truth, because he is also searching.

As we have seen, the truth which is being sought by Buero is not "algo que se posee, sino que se conquista constantemente a fuerza de dudas y replanteamientos".[6] In many of his plays Buero deliberately leaves an open question. He avails of the same mixture of fantasy and reality that he admires in Cervantes' novel, "suma de espejo reflectantes en que realidad y fantasía se construyen mutuamente".[7] "Fundir en el mismo plano la realidad y la ficción" - Rosales says - "no es, desde luego, un método científico recomendable, pero constituye el fundamento del quijotismo."[8] By combining fantasy and reality (as in Irene, Caimán, Mito,...), Buero manages to make the audience experience the doubt and the difficulty of searching, but also the need for it. The search often has to turn towards the inner nature of the individual. And self-knowledge also becomes an arduous task because this search is accompanied by doubts and perplexities, as in Don Quixote's case. However, the difficulty of answering the "gran pregunta" to which Buero returns in his latest play, does not entitle anyone to abandon the search, much less to neglect action.[9] By exploring the fantastic and the marvellous, and by intermingling it with reality, by making use of what Castro considers Don Quixote's "novedad extraordinaria" ("que las cosas puedan ser al mismo tiempo yelmo y bacía y que vivan como tales"[10]), Buero opens up new horizons for the audience and invites them to engage themselves in the search that he himself is pursuing.

On the other hand, his positive idea of quixotism is supported by the fact that, as we have seen, those characters who use the term "Quijote" or refer to quixotism negatively, those who do not dream and who laugh at dreamers, are also seen negatively, and condemned by Buero. In his plays, dreaming, madness, also mean serious commitment, responsibility, real and generous concern for others. Don Quixote might have been mad, but he took his knightly life seriously because of the depth of his conviction. False quixotism, pure action, means concern for one's own material profit, and brings about punishment. For Buero, dreams have a purpose, madness is productive, heroes have a role to play and the term "quixotic" has no negative implications. Though he acknowledges the existence of madness, he does not look at it negatively. It is worth being accused of quixotism, Buero seems to think, and indeed show in his plays, where the accusations of quixotism which are made expose the evil intentions of the accusers much more than they denounce the defects of the accused. Quixotism is synonymous with individual integrity and responsibility. It generates trust because it entails simplicity, generosity and living for something other than oneself.

Spain needs quixotic dreamers who risk their lives for an ideal, and Sanchos who believe and preserve the quixotic faith. When Esquilache and the king talk about the dreamers that the country needs, they mean it seriously. Dreamers are essential to any significant change. Spain still needs them now, as Buero says, and not just "soñadores" but "soñadores que sepan de números", he quotes from *Un soñador*. Besides their dreams, the dreamers should have or try to acquire the necessary skills to make their dreams come about and yield fruit. Dreaming alone is not productive. From the historical perspective adopted in some of his plays (*El tragaluz*, *El sueño de la razón*, *El concierto*, ...), whereby he shows the realization of the so-called impossible dreams, Buero implies that dreams come true. He shows that certain dreams were valid, prophetic, and that, therefore, it was worth daring to dream. The victory achieved by Buero is thus similar to Ignacio's; it consists of sowing "inquietud", not merely for the sake of provoking anxiety, but in order to incite the thought of the impossible. "Lo imposible es lo que se cumple", Rosa says in *Caimán*. "¡Si soñamos así saldremos adelante!", Tulio exclaims in *La Fundación*. This sums up, to my view, Buero's positive and inspiring approach to quixotism. His incitement to serious thought has a purpose, is hopeful and quixotic. It does not intend to remain at the level of thought and individual awareness but, on the contrary, it is, like his tragedy, "esperanzado"; it looks forward to a time when one will be able to exclaim, with Tulio:

"Nos atrevimos a imaginarlo y aquí estamos."

NOTES TO CONCLUSION

1. Pilar de la Puente has said that "el tipo soñador de Buero difiere con mucho del personaje cervantino" (see Chapter Three, note 11). This study tries to prove that Buero's dreamers are indeed very close to Cervantes'.

2. David Johnston, *A. Buero Vallejo. El concierto de San Ovidio*, pp.63, 64, 65.

3. E.C. Riley, *Don Quixote*, p.57.

4. One has to be fully absorbed by the ideal before one dares to preach it. In *La doble historia del Doctor Valmy* Daniel says to Paulus that he is "como un loco que quiere tener razón, pero no está lo bastante loco para proclamarla" (p.118).

5. Luis Morales Oliver also compares Cervantes' heroism to that of his Don Quixote; he says that Cervantes "luchó como bueno ... Magnífica simbiosis entre dos heroísmos. El de Cervantes en la batalla naval y el de Don Quijote ante las empresas inesperadas que se presentaban en su camino." He attributes the virtues of gratitude, optimism, capacity to suffer to both character and author. (*La heroicidad del Quijote en Cervantes* (Madrid: Fundación Universitaria Española, 1974), p.15.)

6. Iglesias Feijoo, *La trayectoria*, p.62.

7. Personal letter (27 April 1989).

8. Rosales, *Cervantes y la libertad*, p.445.

9. In *Música cercana* René remarks on the difficulty of finding an answer to that question:

René.- ... Inquirir qué es o qué no es uno es la pregunta más difícil... Ningún hombre sabe a fondo qué es.

Adolfo.-¡Ésa sí que es la gran pregunta! Yo me la hago todos los días. ¿Qué soy yo? ¿Cómo soy?

René.-Y yo, señor. Pero eso no me impide actuar como si lo supiera. (p.73)

10. Américo Castro, *El pensamiento de Cervantes*, p.90.

Appendix

Entrevista a Antonio Buero Vallejo
(21 diciembre 1989)

-Dijo usted en el discurso de recepción del Premio Cervantes que había reconocido rasgos quijotescos en su teatro. ¿Cuáles son esos rasgos que otros han notado y usted ha reconocido?

Hablando muy por encima, diría que, por un lado, en buena parte de mi teatro hay personajes, generalmente protagonistas, que llevan dentro una pequeña llama quijotesca. Pueden tener sus claroscuros, sus imperfecciones, pero en el fondo son idealistas frente a una realidad a menudo hostil, y partidarios por ello de una manera digna y ética de entender el comportamiento humano en general y el suyo propio en particular. Este es uno de los aspectos en los cuales creo que puede haber conexión entre mi teatro y el *Quijote*. Por otro lado, me parece que también puede haber en algunas de mis obras -no en todas pero sí en algunas- derivaciones hacia la imaginación, hacia la irrealidad, que pueden, sin embargo, sustentarse en un sentimiento más profundo de lo que la realidad misma puede ser, y que también, en ese sentido, coinciden más o menos con las lucubraciones de don Quijote en su aventura vital. Esto sucede en unas otras obras mías, pero, por citar un ejemplo concreto, o un par de ejemplos, podría recordar *El tragaluz*, donde hay un loco que, sin embargo, en cierto sentido es más vidente que algunas de las personas cuerdas que lo rodean; y también en este aspecto alguna otra obra mía, por ejemplo *La Fundación*, es obra en la cual realidad e imaginación andan constantemente conectadas de manera en cierto modo similar a la quijotesca, suscitando incluso algunos escapes a la fantasmagoría; cosa que, por un lado, depende sin duda del *Quijote*, y, por otro lado -y lo he dicho en más de una ocasión- también depende de Calderón de la Barca, de *La vida es sueño* concretamente. Pero, naturalmente, fueron dos personajes prácticamente contemporáneos y no tan separados entre sí en cuanto a concepción literaria como pudiera pensarse a primera vista. Además, aunque de manera más bien cómica pero en el fondo patética, en otra de las obras maestras de Calderón, *El alcalde de Zalamea*, como todos sabemos, hay una pareja -se llaman Mendo y Nuño, me parece- que está directamente influida por la lectura del *Quijote*: ...el hidalgo famélico, con su criado acompañante; y esto, claro, corrobora la huella verdaderamente omnipresente de la creación cervantina en nuestras letras ya entonces, y por supuesto mucho después, hasta nuestros días.

-También se ha referido usted al quijotismo de H.G. Wells, en concreto en tres obras suyas: *El padre de Cristina Alberta*, *El país de los ciegos*, y *Mr Blestworthy en la isla Rampole*. ¿En qué sentido son estas tres obras quijotescas? En la primera está claro que tenemos un loco, que también cura de su locura al final de su vida como don Quijote. ¿Se asemeja esa locura a la de sus personajes locos?
No sabría contestar con exactitud por una razón que debo confesar. Yo leí *El padre de Cristina Alberta* cuando era un muchachito, y, aunque conservo muchas otras obras de Wells de las que entonces adquirí, por alguna razón que he olvidado, *El padre de Cristina Alberta* la perdí, o se me extravió, y hace todos esos años que no la he releído. Entonces, conservo de ella un recuerdo, claro, todo lo vívido que me ha permitido rememorar que, efectivamente, había una conexión, para mí indudable, con el tema quijotesco. Ahora bien, cómo termina exactamente *El padre de Cristina Alberta* se me ha borrado, ...completamente. Lo he buscado alguna vez por ahí pero no lo he encontrado, porque, siendo un escritor

que a mí me parece inmenso, está más olvidado de lo que yo pensaba. Sin embargo, creo que es uno de los supremos cradores de mitos de la literatura de nuestros días.

-¿Y recuerda algo de las otras dos obras?

Bueno, en *El país de los ciegos* naturalmente hay relaciones obvias en el sentido de la ceguera misma, claro, aunque no es que lo tuviera yo realmente muy presente cuando escribí mi primera obra de ciegos y después alguna otra, también de ciegos. Pero, aunque no lo tuviera muy presente, estaba muy dentro de mí porque es también una de mis lecturas tempranas; y *El país de los ciegos*, en unión de otros cuentos en mi opinión magistrales, también lo había releído muchas veces. Entonces, claro, el tema de fondo que la obra puede tener, en el sentido de nuestra apreciación de la realidad y cuál es la verdadera según dónde estemos y con quién estemos, ése es un tema de fondo por supuesto de mi obra o de mis obras de ciegos, y es el tema de fondo de *El país de los ciegos*, que es también una pequeña obra maestra. En ella, el protagonista logra al fin evadirse de aquel mundo cerrado en el cual han pensado "caritativamente" en sacarle los ojos, nada menos. Bueno. Este hombre escapa de este destino. Por supuesto, mis ciegos no escapan de su destino de esa manera. Pero, a su modo, cada uno de ellos puede formular la posibilidad de un escape al menos. Bueno, y había otra...

-*Mr Blestworthy en la isla Rampole.*

Sí. Ésa sí la tengo, la conservo. Bueno, ésta ya no es tanto un tema quijotesco como un problema de técnica, de estuctura. La estructura de *Mr Blestworthy*, novelística, es equivalente a la estructura teatral de *La Fundación*. La novela de Wells es una novela en la cual, a partir del segundo o tercer capítulo, muy pronto, al lector se le engaña, y se le engaña muy hábilmente. Mr Blestworthy desembarca en la isla Rampole y vive toda su experiencia en la isla, que es una experiencia que no tiene nada que ver con la experiencia de mi loqueras en *La Fundación*, pero

que es la experiencia de una alucinación continua, y el lector no lo sabe.
El lector no lo sabe, y, para mí, ésa es la gran maestría de la obra. Y
sólo hacia el final de la obra empiezan a asomar en ella ciertos indicios,
ciertos destellos de cosas no muy claras, intrigantes, que poco a poco
nos van llevando, ya en el final de la obra, al descubrimiento de que la
isla Rampole era Nueva York. Bueno, eso es genial desde el punto de
vista de concepción estructural de un relato. Y, evidentemente, eso
influyó en mí al concebir *La Fundación*, en la cual yo también engaño al
espectador, y lo voy desengañando poco a poco hasta que sepa, hasta
que llegue a la convicción, de que no estaban en una fundación, sino que
estaban en una cárcel.

-¿Ve usted en don Quijote al loco idealista, el casi santo unamunesco, o
considera esta tendencia un tanto exagerada?

Mitad y mitad. Yo creo que la lucha del Quijote, vamos, la
confrontación de don Quijote con la realidad inmisericorde, y su
concepción del mundo como un lugar donde la caballería andante sigue
vigente, son dos concepciones opuestas que el genio de Cervantes puede
naturalmente aunar en una sola obra. Pero esas concepciones opuestas
no son incompatibles. La obra misma lo demuestra, que no son
incompatibles. Esto quiere decir que, para la consideración de la novela
quijotesca, inclinarse más hacia uno de los dos aspectos no es
incompatible con inclinarse hacia el otro. Y se puede uno inclinar más
hacia un lado o inclinar más hacia el otro, según incluso la etapa vital en
que se esté viviendo, según la concepción concreta de una obra que uno
quiera escribir. Se puede uno inclinar algo más hacia allá o algo más
hacia acá, porque en realidad no son incompatibles. Y le pasa lo mismo
que a la -una pedantería, pero en fin- que a la ondícula en la física
nuclear. Es decir, este fenómeno detectado, ¿qué es, una partícula o
una onda? Según la lógica macrocósmica de nuestra especie, eso no
puede ser: o es una cosa o es la otra. Y, sin embargo, en la realidad es
las dos cosas a un tiempo. Y no podría ser, pero lo es. Esa apertura,
unificación de conceptos contrapuestos, es otra de las genialidades, en

mi opinión, del *Quijote*, y es uno de los aspectos que resaltan más en la mejor literatura de casi cualquier tiempo, incluido el nuestro.

−Al escribir *Mito*, ¿se basó en la lectura directa del *Quijote*, o tuvo en cuenta la interpretación que de él hacen otros escritores, como Azorín, o el 98 en general,...?

Bueno, no sabría decir. Todas esas cosas las lleva uno dentro, las ha leído y seguramente todas ellas han estado flotando cuando yo escribía *Mito*, pero yo no me atuve a nada concreto en ese sentido. Releí el *Quijote* una vez más, para fijar algunos aspectos más bien argumentales que me interesaba trasladar metafóricamente a esa historia de mi teatro de ópera, y fue la única referencia bibliográfica que en ese momento utilicé, la relectura del libro mismo.

Alguna otra obra −lo recuerdo también, pero seguramente usted lo habrá tenido en cuenta− es en este sentido evidentemente quijotesca..., *Irene o el tesoro*, en la cual hay una enloquecida que ve cosas.

−Sus locos son locos de verdad, quijotescos.

Sí. De hecho están enloquecidos realmente. La psiquiatría los colocaría en el apartado de la locura, en uno de los tipos de locura. Ahora, ¿qué hay dentro de la locura? Habría que estar loco para saberlo. La locura es una situación anímica que miramos desde fuera cuando creemos no estar locos. La miramos desde fuera pero, de hecho, como caso cualquier otro aspecto de la autencticidad humana, es un misterio.

−Muchos de sus personajes se encuentran aislados, incomprendidos. Veo que le atrae la soledad, el aislamiento.

Sí. La soledad es un ingrediente muy frecuente en el ser humano, y puede ser una de las formas de su destino trágico, de modo que por esta razón aparecen solitarios, o solitarios a la fuerza. Esto puede tener relación con el *Quijote*, pero también con muchas otras cosas, no exclusivamente el *Quijote*. La soledad es una vivencia humana frecuentísima, en la vida y en la literatura.

-Ve usted a Silverio en su 'Comentario' como una persona que tiene problemas, un defecto social, aunque a la vez es capaz de comunicarse con todos sus vecinos. Me cuesta entender que Silverio sea un solitario, pues es precisamente el que logra ayudar a todos.

Claro. Silverio fue una persona que cometió un error, y ese error, como es una persona sensible y con un sentido autocrítico pronunciado, le pesa desde que lo cometió. Esto es lo que determina su soledad. Porque ese error que cometió, como es natural, no se atreve a confesárselo a nadie. Es algo que le avergüenza y no se lo confiesa a nadie que le pueda oír y entender, y sólo se lo confiesa a su mujer, que es justamente la que no le puede oír ni entender, cree él, aunque de hecho tal vez ella tenga una cierta intuición, mayor de lo que él supone, en cuanto a la insuficiencia o deficiencia que él puede tener. Pero, claro, eso determina también una soledad radical por parte de Silverio, que tampoco es incompatible con su elevado índice de comunicación con los demás, e incluso de ayuda a los demás. Pero, como creo recordar que incluso en algún momento dice en la obra, él ha cumplido -por decirlo así- ese destino de ayuda y de conexión con los demás como una penitencia.

Bueno, en definitiva, es uno de los casos humanos en los cuales hay un pesar, un remordimiento de conciencia del cual puede salir la rectificación, al menos parcial, de la conducta.

-Unos personajes tienen a otros que les entienden, como Larra y Velázquez. No lo veo tan claro con Eloy y Simón. Simón no llega a entender a Eloy, ni lo quiere...

No con Simón, pero Eloy e Ismael sí pueden tener... Es corto pero, claro, eso es lo insatisfactorio de la vida, pero ahí sí hay una relación de comprensión.

-Sin embargo, cuando Ismael ve a Eloy, lo primero que hace es recriminarlo porque se limita a soñar y no actúa.

Pero luego actúa, y actúa de una manera definitiva. De modo que - aunque con las imperfecciones de la vida- ahí sí hay, potencialmente al menos, una compañía. A lo mejor estaba lejos -no se han visto en años- pero la compañía existe. Al final Eloy, creo recordar, le dice a Ismael algo así como "Triunfará tu acción, también la mía". Triunfarán las dos.

-Tiene usted muchos personajes que se han llamado "contemplativos". En su *Ruta de Don Quijote* Azorín habla de la "vena ensoñadora" que es necesaria para sacar a España del bache. Lo mismo piensa su Esquilache, y el Rey... ¿cree usted que ojos soñadores siguen siendo necesarios en la España de hoy?

"Soñadores que sepan de números", le dice el Rey a Esquilache. Desde luego, los soñadores son necesarios, empleando la palabra "soñador", claro está, en su sentido más amplio; es decir, en el sentido, no de soñar para huir de la realidad, sino de soñar una realidad mejor para intentar conseguirla. Es, por otro lado, lo que se ha solido llamar a veces el pensamiento utópico. Bueno, el pensamiento utópico puede ser muy dinamizante, muy operativo, hasta el punto de dejar de ser utópico para convertirse en algo práctico. Una de las maneras de llegar a una práctica positiva es el pensamiento utópico, y, por lo tanto, la ensoñación.

-También hablaba usted de una "ética quijotesca" que es muy necesaria. ¿Cuáles son los valores o virtudes que componen una ética, un modo de comportarse, quijotescos? ¿En qué medida poseen sus personajes esta ética?

Todo depende de las circustancias con las que uno se enfrenta. Las circunstancias con las que don Quijote se enfrenta son muy variadas, y ciertas ocasiones le llevan incluso a la ira o al improperio. Todo ello puede estar dentro de una ética quijotesca. Porque la ética quijotesca no es solamente la de la conducta recta y la defensa de los débiles; es también la del improperio ante la maldad, o ante lo que a él le parece maldad. Otra cosa es que se equivoque o no en más de una ocasión. Pero no tiene que ver. Subjetivamente la ética quijotesca es ambas cosas. Y, claro, el problema de la ética quijotesca está, como tantas veces se ha dicho -y no lo he discurrido yo- en si estos ingredietes de la ética quijotesca en sí mismos plausibles, no determinarán una forma de conducta recusable, una forma de conducta deplorable por impráctica, o por traducirse en consecuencias negativas, en vez de en consecuencias positivas. Éste es un problema que se puede discutir. Ahora, con toda la discusión que pueda tener, aún equivocándose, la actitud íntima de un don Quijote frente a la realidad, creo yo que lleva dentro más futuro que las innumerables actitudes mal llamadas prácticas.

-Se ha dicho que su teatro es una lucha constante por encontrar la verdad, y que sus personajes triunfadores son aquéllos que en alguna medida encuentran la verdad, o por lo menos se esfuerzan por encontrarla. ¿Ve usted la lucha por la verdad como una parte de esa ética?

Sí. La búsqueda de la verdad puede ser sin duda una de las bases de mi teatro, pero con ello yo no adelanto ni fijo cuál es o cómo es la verdad. La palabra misma lo dice: es una búsqueda de la verdad. Entonces lo que hay es el deseo de acercarse a la verdad, pero no sabiendo en realidad cuál es la verdad, o cuáles son las características que la concretan. Hay un impulso hacia la verdad y un camino hacia ella que puede estar incluso desviado, porque a la verdad uno se acerca por medio del ensayo y del error, lo mismo que en el terreno de la ciencia. En el terreno del arte, las ficticias conductas de los personajes... En algunos de ellos puede presentar una búsqueda de la verdad, pero una búsqueda de la verdad que tiene también sus fallos, sus caídas y sus perplejidades. No es que yo tenga la verdad, y esté metiéndola astutamente en las obras para que el lector, para que el espectador, encuentre la que yo creo que debe, sino para que la busque conmigo.

–Decía Luis Rosales que la verdad para don Quijote era, no la coincidencia del hombre con las cosas, sino la coincidencia del hombre consigo mismo. Supongo, que en ese sentido, también...
Claro, eso es muy exacto. Y es muy exacto además porque la verdad externa a nosotros, la verdad de las cosas, es una verdad cambiante. Si realmente las cosas fueran objetos durísimos, que estuvieran todos ahí y que no cambiasen, y nos acercásemos a ellos y siempre encontráramos lo mismo, sería relativamente fácil llegar a la verdad. Incluso si nos mirásemos a nosotros mismos y nosotros tampoco cambiásemos, y fuésemos también un objeto durísimo, también podríamos autodefinirnos sin gran dificultad. Pero en la realidad, tanto las cosas que están a nuestro alrededor como nosotros mismos, son objetos cambiantes, o sujetos cambiantes en el caso humano. Y son cambiantes, no solamente en el tiempo, porque cambian realmente tanto física como psíquicamente en el tiempo, sino que son cambiantes en la apreciación de los demás. Según el punto de vista de cada cual, un mismo objeto puede ser una cosa u otra completamente distinta. Bueno, entonces, ¿cuál es la verdad, la verdad definitiva? No la hay; o, si la hay, la hay en un plano suprafísico que, para nosotros, hoy por hoy, está fuera de nuestro alcance. De modo que esto acentúa el papel de búsqueda de la verdad. Y la palabra de Rosales de que sea una coincidencia consigo mismo está muy bien. Pero, claro, cuando nos ponemos a coincidir con nosotros mismos, también nos encontramos con un ser que se nos escapa constantemente. Porque no somos... a nuestra propia apreciación, no somos ahora lo que éramos hace dos minutos.

–Comentaba usted que Cervantes escribía en un mundo peligroso. ¿Escribe usted también en un mundo peligroso?
Creo que sí. Todos los escritores escribimos en un mundo peligroso y cada cual torea ese peligro de la mejor manera que puede, y alguna vez ese toro te pilla, claro, pero sí. Y todo ser humano actúa en un mundo peligroso. Y esos peligros, en determinados casos concretos, se acentúan, se concretan en alarmas muy determinadas. En el Siglo de Oro

esa alarma determinada se llamaba ascendencia conversa, Inquisición, etc., y era muy peligroso...

-¿Y ahora?

Ahora no tenemos Inquisición, ni nos importa nada la ascendencia conversa, por lo menos a la inmensa mayoría, pero, de forma -si se quiere- más sinuosa o más indirecta, las coerciones y las agresiones que el escritor puede recibir de la sociedad, son a menudo muy alarmantes también, o muy negativas, hasta el extremo de poder llegar a anularlo. De modo que una cierta sensación de inestabilidad y de riesgo ante una sociedad o ante unos sectores sociales que podrían incluso llegar a anularte..., eso creo que es una vivencia que el escritor no pierde, por lo menos la mayor parte de los escritores. Hay escritores de otro tipo, quizá muy acomodaticios y muy ligeros, o sólo festivos, a los cuales la sociedad a menudo también termina por anular, pero por otras razones, de otra manera. Pero la mayor parte de los escritores que quieren poner en su obra lo que podríamos llamar la responsabilidad humana, creo que están en una pugna con su sociedad que, aunque pueda derivar en situaciones más o menos armónicas, de hecho es una pugna y, por lo tanto, representa un riesgo.

-¿Ve usted el *Quijote* como una tragedia? Algunos prefieren olvidarse de la vuelta de la cordura y muerte de don Quijote porque es muy difícil justificarlas si se considera a don Quijote un idealista incomprendido.

Ése es un tema debatido. También Unamuno dijo algo sobre eso. No es fácil inclinarse a la aceptación o no aceptación de la vuelta de la cordura a don Quijote cuando se va a morir. Ahora, el hecho en sí yo no creo que sea negativo. Ahí, paradójicamente, lo que se puede discutir es la forma justamente en que Cervantes lo describe, las palabras concretas que pone en boca de don Quijote. Por eso alguien -no recuerdo quién- llegó a decir que era una astucia, una argucia de Cervantes. Es decir, terminar el libro haciendo volver don Quijote a la cordura para que la sociedad ante la cual estaba no se encalabrinase demasiado y dijera: Bueno. Este hombre reconoce que esto fue un disparate y que hay que salir del disparate. Bueno. Es posible que haya algo de eso, porque todas las cosas son muy complejas siempre, y muy contradictorias consigo mismas. Pero, aunque haya algo de eso, la vuelta de la cordura a don Quijote no parece que sea forzosamente un error, como algunos se lo han achacado. No parece que sea un error. Como digo, las palabras concretas con las que lo expresa el propio don Quijote se podrían analizar y discutir, pero eso bien se puede atribuir al lenguaje de la época, por decirlo así. El hecho en sí, es decir, que en el umbral de la muerte don Quijote recobre la razón, a mí me parece bueno. Y me parece bueno, no como una forma de desautorizar todo aquello que él imaginó y en lo que él creyó, que es lo que superficialmente la lectura del *Quijote* puede aportar. No. Es porque, sin desautorizar todo lo que anteriormente él creyó y siguió, como está realmente muriéndose, cabe perfectamente, según hoy afirman muchos enterados científicos, etc.,... cabe perfectamente que, cuando es realmente la muerte la que está en ti, aunque todavía alientes, tu cerebro, tu mente, ingrese en una situación nueva y superior a todo lo que te ha mantenido a lo largo de la vida en tus opciones y en tus limitaciones. No sé si me explico bien, pero "Yo fui loco y ahora soy cuerdo", dice más o menos. "Yo fui don Quijote y ahora soy Alonso Quijano". Bueno. Todo eso es una manera -si se quiere traducir al lenguaje vulgar, limitado, para que lo entiendan los que leen- de algo que, formulado en palabras más cercanas a nuestros conocimientos y a nuestra sensibilidad actuales, podría ser algo así como, en medio de un silencio meditativo: "Yo, don Quijote, yo me engañé en casi todo. Ahora empiezo a ver claro y me muero." Con lo cual, no sería, o no significaría, una desautorización concreta de la chifladura en la que estuvo. No. Sería una puesta en cuestión, y en su limitación, de todo lo que nos arrastra en la vida, a cualquiera, sea o no loco. Y que puede, tal vez desde un plano superior de conciencia, empezar a ver lo pequeño y limitado que fue todo. Pero, claro, ese plano superior de conciencia, muy rara vez se puede tener en la vida; y, en cambio, según dicen, es más asequible en la muerte, o muy cerca de la muerte.

-¿Hay esperanza en el *Quijote*?

Lo veo un poco como en casi todo. Es. decir, la tragedia desesperanzada tiene esperanza; pues el *Quijote* desesperanzado tiene esperanza.

-Cervantes deleitó e inquietó, y usted dice que le pasa lo mismo. Está claro que deleita. ¿Por qué dice usted que también inquieta?

Sí. ¿Por qué no? Desde el momento en que uno intenta hacer una obra que no solamente sea gustosa para el lector o el espectador sino además problemática e inquietadora, por enfocar en ella problemas que nos atañen a muchos o a todos, y que muchas veces tienen una carga sombría. Por todo ello entiendo que mi teatro, hablando en general, ha podido ser y seguir siendo un teatro inquietante para aquél que tenga - y Dios se la conserve- capacidad de inquietarse, claro.

-¿Me puede hablar un poco de su última obra?

Música *cercana* se estrenó primero en Bilbao, en agosto. Después se estrenó en San Sebastián, y algunos días después se estrenó en Madrid, donde sigue en cartel. En Bilbao tuvo un éxito enorme de público. La crítica fue mediocre. Esto me suele ocurrir desde hace muchos años, casi desde que empecé. En San Sebastián pasó tres cuartos de lo mismo: muy buen éxito de público también, no tanto como en Bilbao, pero bien. Y la crítica también mediocre. Luego ya vinimos a Madrid, y la obra empezó muy bien, con muy buen éxito de público; con dos críticas muy favorables, y una no mala, todas las demás insolentes, impertinentes y ofensivas. Pese a lo cual, la obra sigue en cartel, no entre las primeras recaudaciones de la ciudad, pero tampoco entre las últimas. Es decir, llevando una vida bastante positiva desde un punto de vista práctico. Va a continuar. La vamos a tener tres o cuatro meses más en Madrid. Luego saldrá a provincias. De modo que, en conjunto, la experiencia ha sido buena.

-¿Se va a publicar pronto?

Sí, vamos, depende de la editorial, que siempre se duerme. Pero está contratada. Por supuesto, a medida que van pasando los años, uno va notando que las voces discrepantes, siempre existentes, aumentan. Y que el comentario o la opinión crítica -en la crítica propiamente dicha, pero también en el comentario de la calle- es un comentario en el cual podríamos decir que se me está tratando de arrinconar, crecientemente. Lo que pasa es que yo no me dejo. Pero quizá un día podrán conmigo. ¡Quién sabe! No es tan difícil. Torres más altas han caído. No es tan difícil. Esto es un defecto de inseguridad, del que hablábamos antes. Uno no está nunca seguro, porque llegan a decir atrocidades, ¿eh? Y, como uno no deja de tener su pequeña vanidad, y uno piensa que una obra puede ser mejor o peor que otras, o que la anterior... Depende. Pero que, habiendo acreditado una suficiente calidad dramática en el conjunto de la labor, no parece razonable pensar que haya fallos estrepitosos. Puede haber decaimiento relativo: que no es tan buena como la otra, pero a lo mejor ésta es mejor que la anterior. En fin, esto cambia por las opiniones. Ahora, que un autor, del cual en los casos más felices se ha dicho que ha escrito obras maestras, y en los casos menos felices se ha dicho que todo su teatro en general era de calidad y era muy estimable... que, de pronto, no sólo en ésta sino en obras anteriores, haya voces que digan que es horrendamente malo, eso uno sinceramente no se lo termina de creer. Es decir, uno puede pensar: bueno; una obra puede ser peor que otra, pero algún nivel de calidad y de estimación no puedo haber perdido hasta ese extremo. Pues sí. Las desautorizaciones, los reproches, a medida que pasa el tiempo, se hacen más insolentes. Y seguramente esto es un fenómeno natural, aunque no sea grato. Es el fenómeno generacional. Es el fenómeno de que el tiempo pasa y que, lamentablemente, un autor de setenta y tres años está estorbando. Y esto se traduce en improperios, incluso de jóvenes autores que lo dicen en letra impresa; o bien en improperios de críticos, muchas veces no tan jóvenes, o acaso tan viejos como yo. Pero, claro, el crítico siempre quiere estar en una supuesta juventud inmarchitable. Y en esa lidia estamos.

En rigor, todas mis obras lo padecieron, incluso las más afortunadas desde el punto de vista crítico. No les faltó a ninguna de ellas una, o dos o tres voces discordantes que dijeron que eran malísimas. Pero, a medida que pasan los años, los que van diciendo que son malísimas frente a los que dicen que son muy buenas van creciendo. Esto no impide tampoco que, de vez en cuando, le caiga a uno encima un premio... estas consolaciones. Ahora en noviembre hubo un Congreso en Málaga dedicado a mi obra, un congreso universitario que quedó muy bien, que resultó muy agradable, y con ponencias muy interesantes y muy valiosas. Pasan esas cosas de vez en cuando, le dedican a uno un libro sobre su obra,... Ésta es la otra cara. Si no, estábamos perdidos.

Bibliography

Primary sources

CERVANTES

Don Quijote de la Mancha, ed. by J.J. Allen (Madrid: Cátedra, 1989)

Novelas Ejemplares, ed. by Juan Bautista Avalle-Arce (Madrid: Castalia, 1982)

ANTONIO BUERO VALLEJO

Aventura en lo gris (Madrid: Magisterio Español, 1974)

Caimán (Madrid: Espasa-Calpe, 1981)

Casi un cuento de hadas (Madrid: Narcea, 1983)

Diálogo secreto (Madrid: Espasa-Calpe, 1985)

El concierto de San Ovidio (Madrid: Espasa-Calpe, 1986)

El sueño de la razón (Madrid: Espasa-Calpe, 1988)

El terror inmóvil (Murcia: Secretariado de Publicaciones de la Universidad, 1979)

El tragaluz (Madrid: Espasa-Calpe, 1988)

En la ardiente oscuridad (Madrid: Espasa-Calpe, 1988)

Historia de una escalera (Madrid: Espasa-Calpe, 1989)

Hoy es fiesta (Madrid: Magisterio Español, 1974)

Irene o el tesoro, in *Teatro* (Buenos Aires: Losada, 1962)

Jueces en la noche (Madrid: Espasa-Calpe, 1981)

La detonación (Madrid: Espasa-Calpe, 1979)

La doble historia del Doctor Valmy (Madrid: Espasa-Calpe, 1984)

La Fundación (Madrid: Espasa-Calpe, 1986)

La señal que se espera (Madrid: Escelier, 1966)

La tejedora de sueños (Madrid: Cátedra, 1988)

Las cartas boca abajo (Madrid: Espasa-Calpe, 1981)

Las Meninas (Madrid: Espasa-Calpe, 1989)

Las palabras en la arena (Madrid: Espasa-Calpe, 1979)

Lázaro en el Laberinto (Madrid: Espasa-Calpe, 1987)

Llegada de los dioses (Madrid: Cátedra, 1988)

Madrugada (Madrid: Alfil, 1960)

Mito (Madrid: Espasa-Calpe, 1984)

Música cercana (Madrid: Espasa-Calpe, 1990)

Un soñador para un pueblo (Madrid: Espasa-Calpe, 1988)

'Brillante', *Diario 16* (8 marzo 1987)

'Comentario' to *En la ardiente oscuridad* (Madrid: Alfil, 1954)

'Comentario' to *Hoy es fiesta* (Madrid: Escelier, 1957)

'Del Quijotismo al "mito" de los platillos volantes', *Primer Acto*, 100-101 (noviembre-diciembre 1964)

'El teatro de Buero Vallejo visto por Buero Vallejo', in *Teatro* (Madrid: Taurus, 1980)

'Galatea', *ABC* (6 julio 1991)

'Texto autocrítico leído por Antonio Buero Vallejo dentro del ciclo "Literatura viva"', Fundación Juan March, in *Teatro Español Actual* (Madrid: Cátedra, 1977), 69-81

Tres maestros ante el público (Madrid: Alianza, 1973)

Critical studies

CERVANTES

Aguilera, Ricardo, *Intención y silencio en el Quijote* (Madrid: Ayuso, 1972)

Allen, John J., 'Don Quixote and the origins of the novel', in *Cervantes and the Renaissance*, ed. by Michael McGaha (Easton: Juan de la Cuesta, 1980)

_____, *Don Quixote: Hero or Fool? A Study in Narrative Technique*, University of Florida Monographs, Humanities no.29 (Gainesville: University of Florida Press, 1969)

_____, 'El duradero encanto del Quijote', *Ínsula*, 538 (octubre 1991)

Amezúa y Mayo, Agustín G. de, *Cervantes, creador de la novela corta española* (Madrid: Consejo Superior de Investigaciones Ciertíficas, 1982)

Aranguren, J.L., *Estudios literarios* (Madrid: Gredos, 1976)

Avalle-Arce, J.B., *Nuevos deslindes cervantinos* (Esplugues de Llobregat: Ariel, 1975)

_____, and E.C. Riley, eds, *Suma Cervantina* (London: Tamesis Books Limited, 1973)

Bell, Aubrey F.G., 'Cervantes and the Renaissance', *Hispanic Review*, 2 (1934)

Chevallier, Maxime, 'Cervantes, Rousseau, Dostoievsky', *Ínsula*, 538 (octubre 1991)

Castro, Américo, *El pensamiento de Cervantes* (Barcelona: Ed. Noguer, 1972)

Close, A.J., 'Don Quixote's Love for Dulcinea: A Study in Cervantine Irony', *Bulletin of Hispanic Studies*, 50 (1973)

_____, *The Romantic Approach to Don Quixote* (Cambridge: Cambridge University Press, 1978)

_____, 'Don Quixote and Unamuno's Philosophy of Art', in *Studies in Modern Spanish Literature and Art*, ed. by Nigel Glendenning (London: Tamesis Books Limited, 1972)

Fernández de Avellaneda, Alonso, *El ingenioso hidalgo don Quijote de la Mancha* (Madrid: Castalia, 1972)

Flores, R.M., *Sancho Panza through 375 Years* (Newark: Juan de la Cuesta Hispanic Monographs, 1982)

Forcione, Alban K., *Cervantes and the Humanist Vision: A Study of Four Exemplary Novels* (Princeton: Princeton University Press, 1982)

Garciasol, Ramón de, *Claves de España: Cervantes y el Quijote* (Madrid: Espasa-Calpe, 1969)

Giménez Caballero, Ernesto, *Don Quijote ante el mundo (Y ante mí)* (San Juan de Puerto Rico: Inter American University Press, 1979)

Gonthier, Denys Armand, *El drama psicológico del Quijote* (Madrid: Ediciones Studium, 1962)

Green, Otis H., 'El "ingenioso" hidalgo', *Hispanic Review*, 25 (1957)

Gutiérrez Noriega, 'La contribución de Miguel de Cervantes a la psiquiatría', *Cuadernos Americanos* (mayo-junio 1944), 82-92.

Madariaga, Salvador de, *Don Quixote. An Introductory Essay in Psychology* (London: Oxford University Press, 1961)

Mancing, Howard, *The Chivalric World of Don Quijote* (University of Missoury Press, 1982)

Martínez Ruiz, José, *La ruta de don Quijote*, ed. by H. Ramsden (Manchester: University Press, 1966)

Morales Oliver, Luis, *La heroicidad del Quijote en Cervantes* (Madrid: Fundación Universitaria Española, 1974)

Nabokov, Vladimir, *Lectures on Don Quixote*, ed. by Fredson Bowers (London: Butler & Tanner Limited, 1983)

Olmeda, Mauro, *El ingenio de Cervantes y la locura de don Quijote* (Madrid: Ayuso, 1973)

Ortega y Gasset, José, *Meditaciones del Quijote* (Buenos Aires: Espasa-Calpe Argentina, 1942)

_____, *Meditaciones del Quijote e Ideas sobre la novela* (Madrid: Revista de Occidente, 1960)

Parker, Alexander, 'Concepto de la verdad en el Quijote', *Actas de la Asamblea Cervantina de la Lengua Española* (Madrid: 1948)

Rey, Arsenio, 'Don Quijote, paladín de la justicia militante', in *Cervantes. Su obra y su mundo* (Madrid: EDI-6, 1981)

Riley, E.C., *Cervantes's Theory of the Novel* (London: Oxford University Press, 1962)

_____, *Don Quixote* (London: Allen & Unwin, 1986)

Rosales, Luis, *Cervantes y la libertad* (Madrid: Instituto de Cooperación Iberoamericana, 1985)

Rielo, Fernando, *Teoría del Quijote. Su mística hispánica* (Madrid: Studia Humanitatis, 1982)

Siciliano, Ernest A., 'Virtue in the Quijote', in *Cervantes. Su obra y su mundo.*

Sobré, J.M., 'Don Quijote, the Hero Upside-Down', *Hispanic Review*, 44 (1976)

Spitzer, Leo, 'On the significance of Don Quijote', *Modern Language Notes*, 77 (1962)

Togeby, Knud, *La estructura del Quijote*, edited and translated by Antonio Rodríguez Almodóvar (Sevilla: Secretariado de Publicaciones de la Universidad, 1991)

262

Unamuno, Miguel de, *Vida de don Quijote y Sancho* (Buenos Aires: Espasa-Calpe Argentina, 1946)

Weiger, John G., *The Substance of Cervantes* (Cambridge: Cambridge University Press, 1985)

Whibley, ed., *The Collected Essays of W.P. Ker* (New York: Russel & Russel, 1968)

ANTONIO BUERO VALLEJO

Antonio Buero Vallejo. Premio Miguel de Cervantes 1986 (Madrid: Biblioteca Nacional, 1987)

Alvar, Manuel, 'Presencia del mito: *La tejedora de sueños*', *Bulletin Hispanique*, LXXVIII (1976)

Benítez Claros, Rafael, 'Buero Vallejo y la condición humana', *Nuestro Tiempo*, no.107 (mayo 1963)

Borel, Jean Paul, 'Buero Vallejo: teatro y política', *Revista de Occidente*, no.17 (agosto 1964)

Cortina, José Ramón, *El arte dramático de Antonio Buero Vallejo* (Madrid: Gredos, 1969)

Díaz Castañón, Carmen, 'De la Residencia a la Fundación', *Nueva Conciencia*, no.9 (1974)

Dixon, Victor, 'The "immersion-effect" in the plays of Antonio Buero Vallejo', in *Themes in Drama 2: Drama and Mimesis*, ed. by James Redmond (Cambridge: Cambridge University Press, 1980)

_____, 'Los efectos de inmersión en el teatro de Antonio Buero Vallejo: una puesta al día', *Anthropos*, no.79 (diciembre, 1987)

_____, 'Pero todo partió de allí...: *El concierto de San Ovidio* a través del prisma de su epílogo', lecture given in Teatro Español.

Doménech, Ricardo, *El teatro de Buero Vallejo* (Madrid: Gredos, 1973)

_____, 'A propósito de *El tragaluz*', *Cuadernos para el Diálogo*, no.51 (diciembre 1967)

Dowd, Catherine Elizabeth, *Realismo trascendente en cuatro tragedias sociales de Antonio Buero Vallejo*, Estudios de Hispanófila, no.29 (University of North Carolina, 1974)

Fernández Santos, Ángel, 'Una entrevista con Buero Vallejo sobre *El tragaluz*', *Primer Acto*, no.40 (1967)

Fraile, Medardo, 'Charla con A. Buero Vallejo', *Cuadernos de Agora*, 79-82 (Madrid, 1963)

Gagen, Derek, '"Veo mejor desde que he cegado". Blindness as a dramatic symbol in Buero Vallejo', *Modern Language Review*, 81, 3-4 (1986)

González-Cobos Dávila, Carmen, *Antonio Buero Vallejo: el hombre y su obra* (Salamanca: Ediciones de la Universidad, 1979)

Halsey, Martha, T., *Antonio Buero Vallejo* (New York: Twayne Publishers, Inc., 1973)

———————————, 'The Dreamer in the Tragic Theater of Buero Vallejo', *Revista de Estudios Hispánicos*, no.2 (November 1968)

———————————, 'Buero's *Mito*. A contemporary vision of Don Quijote', *Revista de Estudios Hispánicos*, no.6 (May 1972)

Iglesias Feijoo, Luis, *La trayectoria dramática de Antonio Buero Vallejo* (Santiago de Compostela: Universidad, 1982)

Johnston, David, *Buero Vallejo. El concierto de San Ovidio*, Critical Guides to Spanish Texts (London: Grant and Cutler Ltd, 1990)

———————————, Doctoral thesis: "The influence of Miguel de Unamuno on the work of Antonio Buero Vallejo" (The Queen's University, Belfast, October 1982)

———————————, 'Entrevista a Buero Vallejo', *Ínsula*, 516 (diciembre 1989)

Kronik, John W., 'Buero Vallejo y su sueño de la razón', *El Urogallo*, no.5-6 (octubre-diciembre 1970)

Laín Entralgo, Pedro, 'La vida humana en el teatro de Buero Vallejo', in *Antonio Buero Vallejo* (Madrid: Biblioteca Nacional, abril-junio 1987)

264

O'Connor, Patricia, 'Confrontación y supervivencia en *El tragaluz*', *Anthropos*, no.79 (diciembre 1987)

Paco, Mariano de, ed. *Estudios sobre Buero Vallejo*, Los Trabajos de la Cátedra de Teatro (Murcia: Universidad, 1984)

Pajón Mecloy, Enrique, *Buero Vallejo y el antihéroe* (Madrid: Breogan, 1986)

_____, '¿Ciegos o símbolos?', *Sirio*, no.2 (abril 1962)

Pajón, Enrique, *El teatro de A. Buero Vallejo: marginalidad e infinito* (Madrid: Fundamentos, 1991)

Pennington, Eric, 'Buero Vallejo's *Diálogo secreto*: the masks of mortals', *Hispanófila*, 103 (septiembre 1991)

Pérez Minik, 'Buero Vallejo o la restauración de la máscara', in *Teatro Contemporáneo* (Madrid: Guadarrama, 1961)

Puente Samaniego, Pilar de la, Antonio Buero Vallejo. *Proceso a la historia de España* (Salamanca: Ediciones de la Universidad, 1988)

Ruggeri Marchetti, Magda, *Il teatro di Antonio Buero Vallejo o il processo verso la verità* (Roma: Bulzoni Editore, 1981)

_____, 'La mujer en el teatro de Antonio Buero Vallejo', *Anthropos*, no.79 (diciembre 1987)

Ruiz Ramón, Francisco, *Historia del teatro español. Siglo XX* (Madrid: Alianza, 1971)

Verdú de Gregorio, José, *La luz y la oscuridad en el teatro de Buero Vallejo* (Esplugues de Llobrebat: Ariel, 1977)

Ynduráin, Domingo, 'El teatro y la realidad', *Ínsula*, 493 (diciembre 1987)

Other works referred to in the text

Aeschylus, *The Oresteian Trilogy* (Harmondsworth: Penguin Books Ltd, 1972)

Aldridge, A. Owen, ed., *Comparative Literature. Matter and Method* (Urbana: University of Illinois Press, 1969)

Alter, Robert, *Fielding and the Nature of the Novel* (Cambridge, Mass.: Harvard University Press, 1968)

Bainton, Roland H., *Erasmus of Christendom* (London: Collins, 1970)

Berkowitz, H. Chonon, *Pérez Galdós, Spanish Liberal Crusader* (Madison: University of Wisconsin Press, 1948)

Boyers, Robert and Robert Orrill, eds, *Laing and Anti-Psychiatry* (Harmondsworth: Penguin Books Ltd, 1971)

Calderón de la Barca, Pedro, *Obras completas* (Madrid: Aguilar, 1959)

Campbell, Joseph, *The Power of Myth* (New York: Doubleday, 1988)

Cobb, Carl W., *Antonio Machado* (New York: Twayne Publishers, Inc., 1971)

Digeon, Aurelien, *The Novels of Fielding* (New York: Russel & Russel, 1962)

Dostoyevsky, Fyodor, *The Idiot* (London: J.M. Dent & Sons Ltd; New York: E.P. Dutton & Co., 1914)

Edwards, Gwynne, *Dramatists in Perspective* (Cardiff: University of Wales Press, 1985)

Eliot, T.S., *The Cocktail Party* (London: Faber & Faber Ltd, 1950)

Erasmus, *The Praise of Folly*, in *The Essential Erasmus*, ed. by John P. Dolan (New York: The New American Library, 1964)

Fielding, Henry, *The Adventures of Joseph Andrews* (London: Routledge, 1857)

Foucault, Michel, *Madness and Civilization. A History of Insanity in the Age of Reason*, translated by Richard Howard (New York: Random House, April 1973)

Freud, Sigmund, *The Standard Edition of the Complete Psychological Works of Sigmund Freud*, translated and edited by James Strachery (London: The Hogarth Press and the Institute of Psycho-analysis, 1971)

Friedenberb, Edgar Z., *Laing* (London: Fontana/Collins, 1973)

García Lorca, Federico, *La casa de Bernarda Alba*, ed. by H. Ramsden (Manchester: University Press, 1983)

Huarte de San Juan, Juan, *Examen de ingenios para las ciencias* (Madrid: Editora Nacional, 1977)

James, William, *The Will to Believe*, in *Ten Great Works of Philosophy*, ed. by Robert Paul Wolff (New York: The New American Library, 1969)

Johnson, Maurice, *Fielding's Art and Fiction* (Philadelphia: University of Pennsylvania Press, 1965)

Jung, C.G., *The Collected Works* (London: Routledge & Kegan Paul, Ltd, 1966)

Kaufmann, 'The Inevitability of Alienation', in Richard Schacht, *Alienation* (London: George Allen & Unwin Ltd, 1970)

Laing, R.D., *The Divided Self* (London: Tavistock Publications, 1969)

Machado, Antonio, *Campos de Castilla* (Barcelona: Ed. Laia, 1982)

Martínez Ruiz, José, *Visión de España* (Buenos Aires: Espasa-Calpe Argentina, 1948)

Meseguer, Pedro, S.J., *The Secret of Dreams*, translated by Paul Burns (London: Burns & Oates, 1960)

Pérez Galdós, Benito, *El caballero encantado*, ed. by Julio Rodríguez-Puértolas (Madrid: Cátedra, 1977)

Righter, William, *Myth and Literature* (London and Boston: Routledge & Kegan Paul Ltd, 1975)

Shakespeare, William, *King Lear*, ed. by Kenneth Muir (London and New York: Routledge, 1989)

Wells, H.G., *Christina Alberta's Father* (London: The Hogarth Press, 1985)

_____, *The Country of the Blind* (London: New Horizon, 1979)

Index

Aeschylus 24
Agamemnon 24
Aguilera, Ricardo 168
Alcalde de Zalamea, El 244
Allen, John J. 95, 179
Alvar, Manuel 12
Aranguren, J.L. 136
Avalle-Arce, J.B. 15, 136, 169
Avellaneda (See Fernández)
Aventura en lo gris 74-6, 150, 173, 178, 217
Azorín (José Martínez Ruiz) 7, 68, 131, 249

Bainton, Roland H. 39
Bell, Aubrey F.G. 194
Borel, Jean Paul 194

Caimán 7, 51-2, 155, 240
Calderón de la Barca, Pedro 244
Campbell, Joseph 4
Cartas boca abajo, Las 187
Casa de Bernarda Alba, La 24
Casi un cuento de hadas 32, 143-4, 184
Castro, Américo 2, 190, 239
Celoso extremeño, El 169
Cervantes, creador de la novela corta española 55
Chevallier, Maxime 57
Christina Alberta's Father 28-9, 244
Close, Anthony 16, 163
Cobb, Carl W. 90

Cocktail Party, The 44
Concierto de San Ovidio, El 7, 69-74, 109-111, 147, 182, 189, 213
Cortina, José Ramón 9
Country of the Blind, The 244

Detonación, La 6, 86-7, 121-4, 176
Diálogo secreto 32-6, 224-6
Díaz Castañón, Carmen 160
Divided Self, The 19
Dixon, Victor 91, 160
Doble historia del Doctor Valmy, La 36-7, 87, 174, 217, 241
Doménech, Ricardo 6, 91, 146, 170, 208
Dostoyevsky, Fyodor 25
Dowd, Catherine E. 145

Eliot, T.S. 44
En la ardiente oscuridad 6, 99-102, 140-3, 202
Erasmus 20
Examen de ingenios para las ciencias 18

Fernández de Avellaneda, Alonso 200
Fielding, Henry 163
Flores, R.M. 114
Foucault, Michel 21
Forcione, Alban K. 23
Freud, Sigmund 89

268

Fundación, La 49-51, 85-6, 118-121, 153, 240, 243

Gagen, Derek 93
Garciasol, Ramón de 40, 61, 196, 238
Generation 1898 7, 68
González de Amezúa y Mayo, Agustín 55
González-Cobos Dávila, Carmen 59, 133, 159, 195, 196
Gran inspirador de Cervantes...., Un 17
Green, Otis H. 18
Gutiérrez Noriega, Carlos 18

Halsey, Martha 7, 45, 90, 131, 133, 161, 195, 233
Historia de una escalera, 187
Horace 20
Hoy es fiesta 6, 124-7, 144-6, 179, 248
Huarte de San Juan, Juan 17

Idiot, The 25-6
Iglesias Feijoo, Luis 49, 91, 195, 215
Ingenio de Cervantes y la locura de Don Quijote, El 17
Ionesco, Eugene 43, 88
Irene o el tesoro 6, 42-3, 65, 209, 247

Johnston, David 9, 58, 61, 149, 160, 236
Joseph Andrews 163
Jueces en la noche 6, 42, 177, 220-4
Jung, Carl 135

Kaufmann, Walter 98
King Lear 24
Kronik, John W. 93, 118, 238

Laing, R.D. 19
Licenciado Vidriera, El 22, 169
Llegada de los dioses 41, 82-5, 176

Lázaro en el Laberinto 87, 127-8, 183, 226-7

Macbeth 24
Machado, Antonio 90
Madariaga, Salvador de 16, 114, 138
Madrugada 6, 102-4, 171, 208
Meninas, Las 50, 105-8, 147
Meditaciones del Quijote 66, 135
Mito 4, 48-9, 77-80, 112-4, 151, 188, 247
Morales Oliver, Luis 241
Moyers, Bill 4
Mr Blestworthy on Rampole Island 244
Música cercana 227, 241, 254-5

O'Connor, Patricia 111
Olmeda, Mauro 17, 169
Ortega y Gasset, José 66, 135, 196

Paco, Mariano de 127
Pajón Mecloy, Enrique 59, 133, 160
Paul, St 21
Pennington, Eric 233
Pérez Galdós, Benito 7
Plato 15
Praise of Folly, The 20
Puente Samaniego, Pilar de la 67, 91, 131, 241

Rielo, Fernando 15
Riley, E.C. 136, 237
Roa Bastos, Augusto 187
Rosales, Luis 165, 171, 238, 251
Ruggeri Marchetti, Magda 12, 77, 132, 161, 177, 238
Ruiz Ramón, Francisco 172
Ruta de don Quijote, La 68, 249

Salillas, Rafael 17
Schacht, Richard 98
Siciliano, Ernest A. 168
Soñador para un pueblo, Un 66-9, 104-5, 146, 212, 239

Suárez, Carlos 135
Sueño de la razón, El 39-40, 81-
 2, 114-8, 189

Tejedora de sueños, La 63-4,
 207
Terror inmóvil, El 31
Teoría del Quijote 15
Togeby, Knud 136
Torre, Esteban 18
Tragaluz, El 6, 28, 30, 47, 82,
 111-2, 150, 174, 218-220,
 243

Unamuno, Miguel de 7, 61, 68,
 98, 16, 163

Vida de don Quijote y Sancho
 68, 163
Vida es sueño, La 244

Wells, H.G. 4, 28, 244

DDP